3.75

# The Politics of Population

William Petersen, professor of sociology at the University of California at Berkeley, received his B.A. and Ph.D. from Columbia University in sociology, and studied graduate economics at the New School for Social Research. He is the author of *Planned Migration: The Social Determinants of the Dutch-Canadian Movement; University Adult Education: A Guide to Policy* (with Renee Petersen); *Population* (a textbook); and, most recently, *The Changing Population of Nevada* (with Lionel Lewis). He has also edited *American Social Patterns* (Anchor 86), *Social Controversy* (with David Matza), and *The Realities of World Communism*.

# THE POLITICS
# OF POPULATION

William Petersen

GLOUCESTER, MASS.

PETER SMITH

1970

*The Politics of Population* was originally published by
Doubleday & Co., Inc., in 1964.

Anchor Books edition: 1965

# CONTENTS

# INTRODUCTION

Apart from one or two published here for the first time, the essays in this volume were originally printed in various professional journals and general magazines over the past ten years. Such a collection is likely to suffer from two faults, lack of cohesion and repetition. While perhaps neither fault has been avoided completely, some account of how they have been minimized may be in order.

Apart from the unity that the essays derive from the over-all subject of population, they are all one also in that each relates to social policy in some way. Defined negatively, these criteria have induced me to omit not only my articles on nondemographic subjects but also my one or two papers in formal demography. The analysis of social policy is sometimes on the surface: I argue for a new one in a particular area, such as American immigration law. In other papers I attempt to delineate the inherent limitations of planning with respect to such demographic processes as international migration or urbanization. Population theories are analyzed so as to emphasize their policy implications, or (as in the paper on Keynes) to show how the value commitments of theorists have on occasion influenced their ostensible scientific objectivity.

A greater coherence may also have been realized, as well as a marked reduction in repetition, by the considerable editing to which I have subjected almost all of the essays. Under the pressure of competing commitments, whose effect may be reinforced by his own egotism, the author of such a collection as this finds it easy to convince himself that the readers would be disappointed if he changed a word of his deathless prose. Valiantly resisting such blandishments, I have reworked all of the papers except the two so marked and brought them up-to-date in terms of both their statistics and —what has often been more difficult—my own thinking. A barely visible thread ties the revised essays together through that repetition still remaining; for sometimes an idea sketched out in one paragraph is developed more fully later in the book, at a place usually indicated by a cross-reference.

There is, however, one almost total break in continuity. The volume is divided into two roughly equal parts, half on topics related to population growth and family planning, the other half to migration and the acculturation of ethnic minorities. While these are subjects with enormous bibliographies, I hope the reader will agree that I have something new and important to offer. Even so trite a topic as Malthusian theory, which too often is discussed partially and inaccurately, I have deemed to be worthy of a full and correct presentation. My particular interest in the Netherlands and in the Soviet Union is represented in a number of essays, and I trust that these will serve their purpose of reinforcing general points by making them in the context of one specific, not too familiar social setting. Five or six papers are mainly about the United States, the country of greatest concern to both myself and, presumably, most readers of the book.

The determinants and consequences of population change —this is a subject that excites a response in any twentieth-century mind. Many of those who have read again and again of the "population explosion" or the "baby boom" must want to get under such catch-phrases to the more fundamental issues that they reflect. I hope that this deeper interest will be nourished by these writings.

*William Petersen*

*Berkeley, June 15, 1963*

# ACKNOWLEDGMENTS

The largest part of "59 Million Babies" is printed here for the first time, and I am happy to acknowledge the detailed and useful criticisms of Judith Blake Davis. One section was originally published in *Encounter*, September, 1955. "First Impressions of Dutch Society" appeared first in *Encounter*, December, 1954.

Three articles were published originally in *Population Review* (Madras): "Marx versus Malthus" (July, 1957), "Malthusian Theory" (July, 1961), and "The Concept of Urbanization Planning" (July, 1962). The last paper is part of a larger study sponsored by International Population and Urban Research, University of California, Berkeley.

"Keynes' Theories of Population" was first published in *Population Studies*, March, 1955. A large section was deleted and the balance edited.

A shorter version of "Soviet Family Policy" was first published in *Problems of Communism*, September–October, 1956.

"Family Subsidies in the Netherlands," first published in *Marriage and Family Living*, August, 1955, has been brought up to date.

"A General Typology of Migration" was first published in *American Sociological Review*, June, 1958. "The Demographic Transition in the Netherlands," which was published in the June, 1960, issue of that journal, was based on research in Holland as a National Science Foundation Senior Post-doctoral Fellow. Both papers are somewhat altered from the original versions.

Two articles first appeared in *Commentary:* "The 'Scientific' Basis of Our Immigration Policy" (July, 1955), "Acculturation and Group Prejudice" (November, 1956, and October, 1958). The copyright is held by the American Jewish Committee, and the articles appear here with permission.

"Religious Statistics in the United States" appeared first in *Journal for the Scientific Study of Religion*, Spring, 1962.

"Internal Migration and Economic Development," first published in the *Annals of the American Academy of Political and Social Science*, March, 1958, has been brought up to date.

"Planned Migration" is a summary of the main thesis of a book of that title, published by the University of California Press in 1955. It was distributed mainly through such non-commercial channels as library exchanges. The reviews were flatteringly good, and I have always been sorry that so few in addition to the reviewers ever saw the book. I have used this occasion, therefore, to offer its principal ideas to a larger number of readers.

"The Population of Europe" was prepared as a broadcast, one of a series edited by Ronald Freedman for the Voice of America. It is published here for the first time, by permission of the U. S. Information Agency.

"The Socialist Position on Birth Control" is printed here for the first time.

During a portion of the time that I was writing these articles I was also working on a textbook, *Population* (Macmillan, 1961), and there is also some overlap with that book. In particular, large sections of the most general theoretical papers, that on Malthusian theory and that on migration typology, were used in the textbook. But even these were altered in that quite different context, and most of the articles in this volume have no counterpart in the other.

# PART I

# Population Growth
# and
# Family Planning

# 59 MILLION BABIES

During the first fifteen years after the war, from 1946 through 1960, a total of 59,362,000 babies were born in the United States.[1] This figure is about double the 1960 population of both New York and California, the two most populous states. It is roughly the population of Indonesia or of both East and West Germany. It is one and a half times the population of France, twice that of the Philippines or Turkey, more than three and a half times that of Canada.

If one uses what has become the standard appellation of this phenomenon, the "baby boom," it is well to put the term in quotation marks—unless one accepts the implication that a rise in fertility of these dimensions and duration can appropriately be described in the framework of a cycle. The downward swing that "boom" suggests may be around the next corner, as the recent slight decline in the crude birth rate suggests; or it may not. At the very least, one must grant that the issue has become problematic.

The postwar rise in fertility and its persistence at a high level were totally unexpected. In 1933, a group of social scientists who had been assembled at the order of President Hoover offered a composite work, *Recent Social Trends in the United States,* to the depression-ridden American public. In retrospect, perhaps the most remarkable contribution to this appraisal of American society was the forecast of the

[1] A few of these died, but so few that to ignore this small proportion will not affect the argument. In 1946, of every thousand babies born only 33.8 died during their first year; and even this low infant mortality rate fell by about a quarter over the next fifteen years. Indeed, if there were no deaths at all up to age forty, the increased growth in population would be much less than it has been from the actual rise in fertility. Barring catastrophes on the scale of all-out wars, by far the most important cause of death today is old age and its associated disabilities.

country's future population growth.[2] In 1940, the Bureau of
the Census found that its actual count of the population of
the United States, before it was corrected for underenumeration, was less accurate than the estimate these demographers
had made almost a decade earlier! But the same projection
that had predicted the 1940 population with such uncanny
accuracy set 134 to 142 million as the most probable range in
1950 (compared with the actual count of 150.7 million),
and 134 to 158 million in 1980 (compared with the 1960
population of almost 180 million). In 1946, the Bureau of
the Census forecast an increase of 4.6 million over the next
five years; the actual growth was *double* that. These instances[3] exemplify what has become a familiar complaint:
demographers, who among all social scientists seemed to have
the best data and the most reliable methods, turned out to be
the most fallible.

That they were fallible is certainly so, but the comparison
is hardly just. The notion that the family was being transformed from an institution to "companionship," to quote the
title of a very widely used college text,[4] was prevalent in
the 1930s; and even after the rise in fertility was well under
way it took years before commentators revised their analyses.
In 1939, in what became a very famous address, the president
of the American Economic Association predicted that the
population of the United States would increase by about five
to six million over the following decade;[5] the actual increase
was almost *four* times that. In 1946, Talcott Parsons, whom
many regard as the country's foremost sociological theorist,

[2] Natural Resources Committee, *The Problems of a Changing
Population* (Washington: U. S. Government Printing Office,
1938).

[3] For some other examples, see Harold F. Dorn, "Pitfalls in
Population Forecasts and Projections," *Journal of the American
Statistical Association*, 45:251 (September, 1950), 311–344.

[4] Ernest W. Burgess and Harvey J. Locke, *The Family: From
Institution to Companionship* (New York: American Book Co.,
1945). In this 800-page book on "the family," what the authors
term "birth folkways" is covered on pages 491–501.

[5] Alvin H. Hansen, "Economic Progress and Declining Population Growth," *American Economic Review*, Vol. 29, No. 1, Part 1
(March, 1939), pp. 1–15.

explained the decline in fertility in the most general terms. The growing girl, he wrote, discovers that "she must compete for masculine favor and cannot stand on her own feet," and this discovery cannot but be a source of insecurity and hence aggression. The aggression, in turn, "underlies the widespread ambivalence among women toward the role of motherhood, which is a primary factor in the declining birth rate."[6] In 1950, a full five years after the upturn in the birth rate, a more famous sociologist, David Riesman, based his whole analysis of the American "character structure" on a presumed "incipient decline" in the country's population.[7] It would be possible to add to these prominent examples a full array of economists, sociologists, journalists, and others, virtually all of whom held that Oswald Spengler's "decline of the West" was being enacted in literal fact.

## Why the Rise in Fertility?

By now we have a fairly good idea of the reasons for the "baby boom"—at least in the sense of *how* it happened. We can distinguish indisputably temporary factors from those that may indicate—or, in some cases, do indicate—a genuine reversal of the prior downward trend.

Part of our greater knowledge is based on improved measures of fertility. In the 1930s, the measure most gener-

[6] Talcott Parsons, "Certain Primary Sources and Patterns of Aggression in the Social Structure of the Western World," reprinted in *Essays in Sociological Theory, Pure and Applied* (Glencoe, Ill.: Free Press, 1949), pp. 251–274.

[7] David Riesman *et al., The Lonely Crowd: A Study in the Changing American Character* (New Haven: Yale University Press, 1950). An abridged edition published three years later (Doubleday-Anchor, 1953) still retained the same fallacious demography as the fundamental structure. In 1960, Riesman recalled that ten years earlier critics had pointed out the faults in the theory of the demographic transition, but that "the nice analogy between the three stages posited by such demographers as Notestein and our own hypothetical stages proved too tempting to resist." Riesman, *"The Lonely Crowd: A Reconsideration in 1960,"* in Seymour Martin Lipset and Leo Lowenthal, eds., *Culture and Social Character: The Work of David Riesman Reviewed* (New York: Free Press of Glencoe, 1961), pp. 419–458.

ally used was the net reproduction rate, or the ratio of female births in two successive generations, assuming no change in the age-specific birth and death rates. The net reproduction rate, thus, does *not* show whether the population is increasing or decreasing, but only whether it would decline if these demographic rates of any one year were to be permanently fixed. In short, the rate was a kind of population forecast, half-disguised as a fertility measure. Unfortunately, this distinction was often forgotten, sometimes even by professional demographers;[8] and in that case the tool was less helpful than misleading. That the average net reproduction rate of the United States during the 1930s, for example, was 0.98 (or 2 percent below the replacement level) does not mean that the population declined during that decade, or even that it would decline later. It meant, in part, that women were spacing their children so that fewer were born during the depression years.

If we want to know how fertility changes from one generation to the next, we must use a measure that includes the whole of each generation. This is the so-called completed family size, or the average number of children born from puberty to menopause. Among women who married and had at least one child, the completed family fell from an estimated eight children in 1800 to barely more than three 140 years later, or by almost one child per generation. Note that the decline got under way when the United States was a relatively empty country, when it was still overwhelmingly rural, when the very term *birth control* had not been coined and contraception was almost entirely by coitus interruptus. The decline began, that is to say, when almost all the factors later cited as its causes were still in the future.

The advantages of the completed family size in analyzing

[8] Dr. Charles, for instance, commented on the forecast implied in the net reproduction rate as follows: "In parts of Europe and America the population has already ceased to be capable of maintaining its numbers. It cannot be too clearly emphasized that this statement is not a prediction of future events . . . but a description of what is actually happening at the moment." Enid Charles, *The Menace of Under-Population: A Biological Study of the Decline of Population Growth* (London: Watts, 1936), p. 104.

a long-term trend are obvious, but one cannot use it to measure the current fertility among women who may still bear more children. Here the greatest technical advance is in what is called cohort analysis. A cohort comprises all those who are born (or are passing through some other stage, such as marriage) at the same time, and who are analyzed as a unit through their lifetime. A birth cohort, thus, is not only a particular age-group but also one that has experienced the same social history, and it thus combines the effects of physiological with social-economic determinants of family size.

Thus, for instance, one reason for the postwar rise in fertility was that women who had not married during the depression—or, if married, had not had children—started their families late in life, giving birth to their first child when they were in their middle thirties or even early forties. Of course, no substantial, continuing rise in fertility could be based on these middle-aged cohorts, but it was also true that at least some of the very small families of the 1930s on which the forecasts were based had not been completed. The very low prewar birth rates, in a sense, were being corrected; social analysts were being told that some married couples had not refused to have children, as they usually supposed, but only postponed having them.

As is usually the case immediately after any war, when the soldiers returned home there was a spurt in marriages, followed shortly by an especially large number of first births. The highest birth rate, thus, was in 1947. When persons who ordinarily would have married over three or four years all married and began their families during the one year of demobilization, this bunching of births suggested a marked rise in family size; but this suggestion was at least partly false. Once again, there were two sides to this coin.

The secular decline in fertility had resulted in part from the fact that a substantial minority (almost one-tenth of the women aged 20 to 44 before World War I) never married. But over the past several generations the percentage single among those aged 14 years and over has declined remarkably:

|  | Males | Females |
|------|-------|---------|
| 1890 | 43.6  | 34.1    |
| 1940 | 34.8  | 27.6    |
| 1950 | 26.2  | 19.6    |
| 1960 | 25.3  | 19.0    |

The postwar rise in marriages meant that there would be fewer spinsters, in part because young people are marrying earlier in life. In the portion of the population for which this information is available, in 1960 the median age at marriage was only 22.8 years for the groom, 20.3 years for the bride. Most males married at age 21, most females at age 18.[9]

Of the women who married, moreover, almost one-fifth of those whose fecund period coincided with the interwar years had had no children at all.[10] By the postwar pattern, the early age at marriage is typically followed by early child-bearing; the fertility of young women is greater not only than that during the depression, but even than that before World War I.[11] The median age of the mother at the birth of the first child is only 21.6 years; of the second, 24 years; of the third, 27 years; of the fourth, 28.8 years. Thus, with the current schedule of family formation, couples who have four children produce them all before the mother is 30, or while she has more than 15 years of potential reproduction still ahead of her.

Married women who reached the end of their fecund period (that is, were aged 45 to 49 years) in 1955 had an average of only 2.44 children. Most of these had been born

[9] For convenient summaries, see "Spotlight on Marriage," *Population Bulletin*, June, 1961; "Trends in Marriages, Births, and Population," U. S. Department of Health, Education, and Welfare, *Indicators*, March, 1963. The figures on the percentage married are from U. S. Bureau of the Census, *Statistical Abstract of the United States, 1962* (Washington: U. S. Government Printing Office, 1962), Table 32.

[10] Wilson H. Grabill, Clyde V. Kiser, and Pascal K. Whelpton, *The Fertility of American Women* (New York: Wiley, 1958), Table 16.

[11] For example, for women aged 20 to 24, the cumulative birth rates in 1955 were higher than those in 1910 for every order of births up to the sixth child. *Ibid.*, Table 114.

some two decades earlier, during the low point in American fertility. We do not know, of course, what the completed fertility will be of women still young enough to bear more children. But the average size of family desired, according to data from a nationwide survey, is 3.2 children,[12] and this in itself suggests that fertility will continue to be relatively high. One must remember, moreover, that while virtually all fecund couples eventually use some contraceptive means, this is often not the most efficient one, so that in many cases the actual number of births will be greater than the average planned family.

Among all these factors, we can distinguish some whose effect was obviously temporary, in particular the first births to middle-aged women and the piling up of marriages in the first year or two after the soldiers were demobilized. Other trends have inherent limits, and one can speculate about how much farther they will go. Will the age at marriage fall from its present figure, which by historical (though not physiological) standards is already very low? Will the percentage married rise above its present high level? Will the rather close spacing of planned pregnancies be compressed even more? Will the use of effective contraceptives spread more widely among the American population? Each of these questions is both difficult and important.

The most fundamental issue, however, is whether the planned family of slightly more than three children is a temporary aberration or a relatively permanent fixture. Why do the average parents want to have three children, and will this desire be dissipated in a new change in family living?

### The New American Family

Among the changes in "the American way of life" that might help stabilize a middle-sized family, the following seem to be important.

1. There was first, and most obviously, the transformation from the depression decade to the postwar economic boom.

[12] Ronald Freedman, Pascal K. Whelpton, and Arthur A. Campbell, *Family Planning, Sterility, and Population Growth* (New York: McGraw-Hill, 1959), Table 10–4.

The buoyancy of the American economy took the advocates of full employment by surprise: Henry Wallace's slogan of "Sixty Million Jobs" soon became as anachronistic as its author. The postwar economy has not, of course, lacked its difficulties and negative features—the hard core of unemployables, the industries or areas left behind by advancing technology, the periodic years with sharp rises in temporary unemployment. Most disturbing was the fact that unemployment gradually rose even from one boom period to the next, so that by 1959–60, years that fell between two recessions, unemployment averaged more than 5 percent. These troubles will not coalesce, I believe, into another great depression like that of the 1930s, less because of the advance in means of control than because of the greater will to use those that exist. Now that unemployment is seen as controllable, a president, or even a governor, who fails to control it thereby commits political suicide. From the Employment Act of 1946 to the Area Redevelopment Act of 1962, social legislation has shaped the market economy to new ends.

But even if the worst should come to pass and the United States should go through another major depression, the effect of this on the birth rate could not be predicted with assurance. While it is true that, to some degree, parents choose between having a child and alternative ways of spending money, a parent's role cannot be adequately expressed in the simplistic calculations of Economic Man. The depression of the 1930s helped reduce the birth rate, but partly because it came as the culmination of other forces. The fact that the wealthiest couples typically had the smallest families, and men on work-relief the largest, should warn us against a narrowly economic interpretation of fertility trends.

To the degree that fertility and economic conditions are associated, the causal relation may be in the opposite direction. Thus, from 1960 on, an increasing proportion of the unemployed is likely to be the very large numbers born from 1945 on, who try to find new jobs in greater numbers than they become available. More fundamentally, the principal danger in an economy at the American level of technology is less a lack of goods than one of investment opportunities. By a curious paradox, the larger American family, though it entails a monetary sacrifice on the part of the individual parents, tends to balance this out in social terms; for the millions of additions to the population each year establish a demand for new homes, factories, and other capital equipment. It is also true that the increasing numbers engender disequilibria and use up natural resources at an accelerating rate, but these are social problems less likely than unemployment to affect the attitude of each potential parent toward the size of his family.

2. The most significant increases in fertility have been among those social groups that had previously shown the greatest decline—urban as against rural, professional or managerial as against farm or unskilled workers, college-educated as against elementary school only, and so on. It has often been remarked that the American working class has hardly any ideological independence: every worker is a businessman *manqué*. There is enough truth in this aphorism to have warranted the recurrent observation that the example of the small middle-class family was an important influence in reducing the fertility of other social classes. Today, however, the middle class sets a different example. The fertility of the classes with the largest families is still declining, and that of the classes with the smallest prewar families has risen, so that these two are now both approaching a national norm of something like a three-child family. The momentum of the trend is no longer downward, but towards stabilization.

3. The new look in family size has some of the irrationality of any change in style, but it has also been motivated by the deepest aspirations of the American middle class. With a certain exaggeration, the United States can be termed the country of upward mobility. The behavior patterns of the typical American, to the extent that such a person exists, can probably be best defined in terms of the hopes and expectations excited by the American "unalienable right" to pursue happiness. In the past, middle-class parents regarded it as their duty to offer the maximum advantages to a very small number of children; and this value was certainly an important reason for the spread of the small-family system. Today, however, the psychologists' dictum that the single child is more likely to be "neurotic" has been spread through

women's magazines to become a commonplace of middle-class lore. Whether this is true or not is beside the point; the theory, even if spurious, has been widely enough accepted to affect present attitudes and behavior. If one has children at all, one must—for their sake—have at least two, and preferably at least three. The fact that the new trend in family size has been based on a reinterpretation of the parents' duty, rather than on an attempt to reject it, indicates a greater likelihood of permanence.

4. The small family of the recent past was, one might say, built into the small city apartment, which made an additional child an expensive and bothersome undertaking. Postwar building has been principally of a new type, which lacks even the words to describe it. The old census classification of "rural nonfarm" is clearly inappropriate, as is also the more usual term of "suburban," with its still remaining connotations of the upper-class cocktail set. Whatever one calls it, the New Suburb is setting the pattern of American life; the three- or four-bedroom homes are designed for children. About four-fifths of the population growth between 1950 and 1960 took place in the country's 180 metropolitan areas. But while almost half of the central cities actually lost people and the rest grew only slightly, the metropolitan rings—the suburbs—increased by almost half.

One typical suburb of the 1920s was the upper-class dormitory of a large city—Long Island or Westchester for New York, the North Shore for Chicago, and so on. Clustered as close as possible to these were middle-class settlements, usually named something as genteel as "Garden Park Manor." Today, suburban living is less restricted to the wealthy or the would-be wealthy. The miles on miles of identical mass-produced dwellings hold families of the lower-middle and working classes even when they are new;[13] and

[13] This fact, which has hardly been recognized by social analysts, has certainly not percolated down to journalistic commentaries. For outstanding exceptions to the ordinary picture of suburban life, see Bennett M. Berger, *Working-Class Suburb: A Study of Auto Workers in Suburbia* (Berkeley: University of California Press, 1960); S. D. Clark, "The Society of Suburbia," in William Petersen and David Matza, eds., *Social Controversy* (Belmont, Calif.: Wadsworth, 1963), pp. 304–315.

after they age a bit, they will become the lower-class
tenements of tomorrow.

What is the character of the family in these surroundings?
Of all the country's homes, the percentage occupied by
owners increased from 43.6 in 1940 to 55.0 in 1950 to
61.9 in 1960. In the New Suburb, hardly anyone rents a
house; and home ownership has always been correlated with
large families. In the New Suburb, the home is apparently
becoming the focus of a more meaningful family life. One
cannot so easily speak of the family's loss of function. If
the wife works, as she often does, it is not ordinarily in
order to establish a career independent of her role as wife and
mother, but in order to round out the family income by
supplementing her husband's salary or wage. If the man is
usually away at work during the day, he spends evenings and
weekends with his family; the do-it-yourself craze that has
spread through American suburbia is a mode of classifying
the continuous extension and decoration of one's home as
"fun." When details of this kind are added up, the sum is a
milieu in which a childless couple feels out of place.

5. These arguments that a middle-sized family has become a relatively fixed norm of the American way of life are,
as they must be, speculative. But the 59 million births
constitute a fact, and a fact that will soon become of great
relevance to the country's birth rate. The babies born in 1945
will reach age 20 in 1965, and even before that date, the
large cohorts produced in the postwar years will themselves
have begun to contribute to higher marriage rates. Even if
the average number of children per family were to go down,
the total reproduction by the larger number of parents will
probably at least remain constant. And if the pattern of three
or more children persists, as it is likely to if these arguments
are at all well based, then the combined effect of the age
structure and the middle-sized families will be a fairly rapid
cumulative population increase.

## Population Policy

Because of the sustained rise in fertility, reinforced by
the continuing decline in mortality and a slight increase in

immigration, the population of the United States jumped from something over 150 million in 1950 to not quite 180 million ten years later. Is this unprecedented intercensal growth a good thing, on balance, for the American economy, for American society? There is no simple answer to this question.[14] As we have intimated, population growth in a developed country both uses up natural resources and stimulates business activity, so that even the narrowly economic effects of an increase in numbers cannot be specified. Many of the country's social problems, however, are related more or less directly to this increase in numbers of people: the over-rapid expansion of metropolitan areas, with the attendant aggravation of urban congestion; the severe overcrowding of schools, filled to bursting with "boom babies," and possibly the consequent deterioration of educational standards; more debatably, the rise in juvenile delinquency as cohorts born in the middle 1940s move into the labor market and find—particularly at low levels of skill—too few jobs for their increasing numbers; the developing shortages of water, of recreational areas, even of space to park a car.

Whether the increase in numbers has been too great, or too rapid, depends of course on how much one values the costs paid to accommodate this growing population. Should an affluent society afford more than subsistence, and if so, what precisely? If one holds with the conservationists that the United States should maintain and extend its national parks and wildlife reservations, then by this criterion the optimum population density for sizable areas of the country is, and will remain, zero. If one believes that ideally an urban resident ought to have easy access to the real countryside, and not merely a park or a "greenbelt," then the merging of contiguous cities into vast, virtually unbroken areas of densely settled humanity is to be deplored. Such social goals as these are on a different scale from easing the Malthusian pressure in underdeveloped countries, but are they therefore less significant?

One could debate whether on balance the increase to date has been beneficial, or the contrary, with respect to such

[14] The point is discussed at greater length below, pp. 68–70.

goals; but this issue is, precisely, debatable. One is on firmer ground to contend less—not that the United States is over-populated, but that its population growth has been, and probably will remain, so great that the disadvantages con-sequent from it will become increasingly evident. Rational men need not agree that action is necessary at the moment in order to consider what action would be appropriate at some probable future date; and the day is near when most economists, sociologists, city and regional planners, and even statesmen will agree that some relief from increasing numbers should be sought. A policy to increase mortality is unthinkable. A further restriction of immigration would entail many political costs, and in any case would be of little significance: in recent years immigrants have made up only about a tenth of the annual population increase. The control of population growth means, in effect, the social control of fertility.

Whenever the suggestion has been made that the state should initiate a policy with respect to fertility, someone always counters with the objection that reproduction is an individual concern, a matter for the two parents alone to decide. It is remarkable how typically we overlook the degree of beneficent concern the modern state evinces in the family, reproduction, children. Fathers are exempted, in proportion to their begetting, from taxation and usually also from military service. In some firms and government agencies, employees are paid more for the same work if they are also parents, and when there is a layoff have greater tenure. From the Children's Bureau in Washington to the municipal clinic, social agencies help the mother perform her tasks. Primary and secondary schooling is free, as well as college in most states. In a hundred different ways, of which these are only some of the most significant, society intervenes to lift some of the burdens of family life from the parents' shoulders.

Indeed, it would be a queer world if this were not the case. The family, the institution where the next generation is born and reared, is manifestly not merely an individual matter; the dilemma arises precisely because some degree of social control of this personal relationship is both legitimate and necessary. The questions of what kind of intervention, and how much, cannot be disposed of by making a civil-liberties issue out of family life. If we agree that the decision whether or not to have another child is properly made by the potential parents, setting the framework of that decision—the costs and benefits of childbearing, the alternatives to parenthood, the means of implementing these alternatives—is in some degree the legitimate province of the state.

Public policy affecting fertility is concentrated on three purposes—to protect the family against various disturbing influences, to help rear and educate the children, and to give special assistance to indigent parents. One might quarrel with one or another mode of carrying out these goals, but the goals themselves are beyond dispute. Thus, to force women to mend their morals by denying them relief benefits for their illegitimate children, a practice advocated in a number of jurisdictions in the United States, is poor policy on two grounds: it is questionable whether it will achieve its alleged purpose of cutting down the incidence of illegitimate births; and the state, by thus aggravating the stigmata of poverty and bastardy, is likely to add to the number of those permanently alienated from lawful society. In short, the reduction of fertility should be implemented, if this is possible, without disturbing such fundamental government functions as the protection of the family and social welfare. Not only is it feasible to separate these effects, but in some cases the same policy would both reduce fertility and reinforce the family; and in the following list of criteria for reform, these are considered first.

1. *No child should be born unless it is wanted by its parents.* Given the limits set by human fallibility, this dictum will never be realized in full; but a much better record would be possible, with presumably a considerable improvement in family life, if social agencies assisted in achieving this goal. An adequate program would include tax-supported research to improve our knowledge of conception and means of controlling it; wide dissemination, preferably through public agencies, of accurate information on the relative efficacy of present methods of birth control; free contraceptive clinics in

poor neighborhoods, where those who want birth control but cannot afford it could be helped; legal abortion and steriliza-tion; no legal inhibition by which the moral code of a portion of the population is imposed on the whole of it.

The actuality is farther from this goal than most middle-class persons may realize. In the nineteenth century the laws of both the nation and various of the states prohibited the dis-semination of contraceptive information and devices, and in many jurisdictions—including the United States government—these laws still remain on the books, eroded by adverse court decisions but still a more or less significant deterrent.[15] The Connecticut statute is unique in that it prohibits not only the sale but even the use of contraceptives. All attempts to modify the law have failed; the U. S. Supreme Court refused to rule on it on the rather surprising ground that many persons in the state habitually violate the statute. The Massachusetts law is also in force and an important impediment to birth control. In other states the transition to a more liberal code has been started but not completed. For example, Mississippi both prohibits contraceptives and offers advice on birth control through the state's own health services; Nebraska for-bids the sale of contraceptives and sets quality standards for those sold. The frequent consequence of such legal anomalies is that middle-class married women, with sufficient education and money to use the law to their own ends, get contracep-tives, "and the poor get children."[16]

Unmarried persons constitute a second class that is subject to frequent discrimination. When antibiotics made it possible to effect rapid and complete cures of venereal disease, some of the country's moral leaders expressed concern about the effect of this medical advance on sexual behavior. Similarly, today many seem to believe it necessary to control extramar-ital sexual relations by the threat of illegitimate children, or

[15] For brief summaries of the relevant laws and their interpreta-tions, see Norman St. John-Stevas, *Life, Death and the Law* (Bloomington: Indiana University Press, 1961), pp. 60 ff.; Fowler V. Harper and Jerome H. Skolnick, *Problems of the Family* (New York: Bobbs-Merrill, 1962), pp. 170 ff.
[16] See the excellent study with this title by Lee Rainwater (Chicago: Quadrangle, 1960).

of marriages undertaken only in order to avoid having them. Even for one who condemns premarital sexual relations, this cure is worse than the disease. For example, in New York State the law prohibits the dissemination of contraceptive information and devices, but according to the courts' ruling on the restriction, it does not apply to a physician who "in good faith gives such help or advice to a *married* person to cure or prevent disease," which is interpreted to include pregnancy.

The laws concerning abortion, while not uniform from state to state, are even more restrictive.[17] Most states permit an abortion that is necessary to save the life of the mother, but even this basic therapeutic purpose is not consistently defined and interpreted. In no state is it legal to abort a fetus probably deformed by such a disease as German measles or such a drug as thalidomide,[18] not to say one to be born to a raped girl, a mental defective, a mother of eight children, a woman who will die of cancer before her baby is one year old. Not even Nevada, whose economy is largely based on legal gambling and facile divorce, flouts this national façade of respectability. Yet it is a façade. Most of the therapeutic abortions performed in reputable hospitals are not wholly within the law; and hundreds of thousands of otherwise law-abiding women—precise figures are of course not available—have subjected themselves to illegal operations, which are unduly expensive and frequently performed under conditions that endanger their health and future fecundity.

In the twenty-eight states with a law concerning sterilization, it is prescribed for persons with certain stipulated hereditary defects.[19] Voluntary sterilization is not sanctioned even when the woman's life would be endangered by a pregnancy, and certainly not as a means of family limitation; but the evidence suggests that these laws, like those pro-

[17] See Fowler V. Harper, "Abortion Laws in the United States," in Mary S. Calderone, ed., *Abortion in the United States* (New York: Hoeber-Harper, 1958), Appendix A.

[18] For one physician's cogent comments on the notorious case of Sherri Finkbine, see Robert E. Hall, "Thalidomide and Our Abortion Laws," *Columbia University Forum*, 6:1 (Winter, 1963), 10–13.

[19] St. John-Stevas, *op. cit.*, pp. 165 ff.

scribing contraceptive abortion, are often disobeyed. According to information from the national sample of married white women already cited, almost one in ten reported that either she or her husband had been sterilized—often presumably to effect contraception rather than to safeguard health.[20]

2. *Persons should be discouraged from entering into a marriage not likely to develop into a stable family.* Given our vast ignorance of how a "stable family" should be interpreted, the implementation of this dictum ought to be modest. Yet the evidence available does suggest that some checks on the official approbation of virtually all marriages would be appropriate.

Common sense suggests that hasty marriages often produce undesirable families, and divorce statistics confirm the supposition. According to the annual compilations, one-fifth to one-third of divorces are handed down within less than five years of the marriage; and if one subtracts the honeymoon euphoria from one end of this period and the legal delays from the other, such marriages cannot have lasted more than a year or two. In many societies an interval is institutionalized between a formal declaration of intent to marry and the ceremony, a period during which the commitment to remain together is gradually strengthened. The posting of banns to mark a betrothal has disappeared from our law, and even the custom of formal engagement seems to be less prevalent than a generation ago. Some sort of legal substitute would seem to be desirable. About half of the states require no waiting period at all; in the other jurisdictions it ranges between one and five days. One of six to twelve months would be more useful in eliminating overhasty marriages, but such a law could be evaded—as are the much milder restrictions today—by marrying in another state. Only if the right to marry, like in legal principle the right to divorce, were restricted to the residents of a state could such a reform acquire much meaning.

One effect of a legally imposed waiting period would be to counteract the trend we have noted toward marrying at an earlier age. The decline in the age at marriage is especially remarkable in that it has accompanied a gradual rise in the

[20] Freedman, Whelpton, and Campbell, *op. cit.*, pp. 26–31.

proportion attending college, and thus in the average time needed to prepare for one's life career. Sons of the middle class, when they made up most of the college population, used to have a regular progression prescribed for them: earn a degree, find a job and get established in it, marry, then—and not before—have children. This postponement of family formation until his late twenties or early thirties was the price a young man paid to start in a good position. The notion underlying the system was that marriage and parenthood are serious matters, not to be undertaken until a person is socially as well as physiologically mature. Adolescents are by definition in a period of transition from childhood to adulthood, and that two of them wedded together will typically develop along the same path, and thus remain a compatible couple, is on the face of it unlikely. Marriage counselors, who disagree on most of the prerequisites to a happy marriage, tend to unite in opposing one at early ages.[21]

A common-law marriage is considered legal if the partners have reached puberty, defined as 14 years for the male and 12 for the female.[22] In the various states the statutory minimum ages for marriage with the consent of the parents range from this common-law principle up to 18 for males and 16 for females. Without parental consent, the usual minimum —though with some variation—is 21 for males and 18 for females. In about half the states persons under age may marry if the female is pregnant or for other stipulated reasons. How effective any of these laws is, however, is open to question, for as with a prescribed waiting period, the age limitation set in any one state can easily be avoided.

In short, to place effective impediments to marriages deemed inappropriate is all but impossible so long as each state has the right both to set its own laws and to apply those

[21] A contrary opinion, however, is given in Thomas P. Monahan, "Does Age at Marriage Matter in Divorce?" *Social Forces,* 32:1 (October, 1953), 81–87. The author holds that forced marriages and other types not likely to be successful are concentrated in the younger ages, and that the relation between age per se and the higher divorce rate may be spurious.

[22] See Women's Bureau, *The Legal Status of Women in the United States of America,* Bulletin 157 (Washington: U. S. Government Printing Office, 1956), pp. 60–62.

laws to visitors from other states. The only thing that can be done short of a revolutionary change in family law is to withhold some of the actual encouragements to early and hasty marriages—such as sponsored dating in elementary and high schools, tax-supported housing for married students and their families, draft deferments to young fathers, and so on.

3. *The public interest demands that bad marriages be dissolved.* As with the law on contraceptives, so also with that on divorce: the more or less absolute ban of an earlier age has been partly chopped away, leaving behind an illogical barrier that makes a tawdry farce of the whole procedure. Virtually all divorces are in fact sought jointly by the two marriage partners; only one divorce action in seven is contested at all, and that litigation is generally not over whether the decree should be granted but over the disposition of the property or the children. Yet the laws of every state demand a court action in which the spouses are formally opposed; the almost universal collusion is a criminal act. Even Nevada requires the opposition between plaintiff and defendant, though the complaint is usually "extreme mental cruelty," or, in effect, incompatibility. In such a state as New York, where adultery is both the only ground for divorce and also a crime, thousands of persons—cooperating with reputable lawyers and the courts of law—fake evidence to have themselves recorded as adulterers.

Any divorce obtained, in short, is gotten in spite of the public effort to prevent it; the courts have no concept of a good divorce. On the face of it this is a stand that can be supported only by prejudice and doctored figures. It is usual, for example, to compare the development of children of divorced and undivorced parents; the relevant contrast, of course, is between families that get a divorce and those that, in spite of the same kind of disorganization, do not. Consider a child who has a habitual drunkard as a father, and who once a week watches him beat up its mother and go to sleep on the kitchen floor; a priori, would such a child be worse off living only with its divorced mother? And if such an extreme case suggests that *some* divorces are good, by what criteria does one draw the line?

The legitimate interest of the state in the family pertains

mainly to ensuring the adequate welfare of minor children. If a childless couple both want a divorce, they should be able to get it with only enough of a deterrent to test the seriousness of their intent—say, a fee based on their joint income plus a year's waiting period. No public end is served if the judge persuades them to start a family and, in effect, to use the child to reconcile their differences. Whether a divorce between a couple with minor children is in the public interest is a more complex question, which would take a whole essay to examine adequately. Suffice to repeat that it *is* a question, and that the concept of a good divorce needs defining.

4. *The father of a child should be held responsible for its support.* A legal marriage, even if it ends in a formal divorce, includes the proviso that the father must support his children. In theory, the same is true of consensual unions and of marriages brought to a de facto termination by the husband's desertion, but actually in such cases parental responsibilities are more often evaded.

In the procreative system of the lower classes, and particularly of lower-class Negroes, the women carry the main financial and moral burden of rearing the children. The advantages of this way of life have often been pointed out. The man lives "healthily" and "naturally," following the dictates of D. H. Lawrence and his present-day imitators. The mother of illegitimate children "does not lose status," and the children themselves are free from "warping social condemnation."[23] The disadvantages are no less apparent. A quasi-family in which the mother must be both breadwinner and principal guardian of the children lacks the normal two-adult team cooperating to rear them. It is not an efficient socializing instrument; the effects of growing up in a slum neighborhood are aggravated by the absence of a father.

And society must pay out of tax funds the subsistence the

[23] Charles S. Johnson, *Shadows of the Plantation* (Chicago: University of Chicago Press, 1934), p. 49. Cf. E. Franklin Frazier, *The Negro Family in the United States* (Chicago: University of Chicago Press, 1939), passim. For a different interpretation of the Negro family in the Caribbean area, see Judith Blake, *Family Structure in Jamaica: The Social Context of Reproduction* (New York: Free Press of Glencoe, 1961).

father refuses to furnish. In a number of state legislatures, bills have been offered excluding illegitimate children from social-welfare benefits, but these manifestly irresponsible proposals either were not enacted or, if passed, were vetoed or declared unconstitutional.[24] On the other hand, the various efforts to force runaway fathers to support their children have not been very successful.[25] Until recently crossing a state line was sufficient to put a man out of reach, for extradition was too cumbersome and expensive to be feasible. Now, finally, all of the states have entered reciprocal agreements by which a court order stipulating support can be executed throughout the nation; but the new system is still inadequately administered. In terms of optimum social policy, how much should the public authorities spend in tracking down delinquent fathers and forcing them to support their families? If the amount so spent is greater than that saved by reducing the welfare benefits to the mother, society is still the gainer; for if males know that they will be held responsible for their random sexuality, one can reasonably suppose that more of them will take care not to produce illegitimate offspring or other unwanted children.

5. *Females doing equivalent work should receive the same pay and other perquisites as males.* The restriction of respectable women's work to household and farm duties, which was general up to about 1914, has broken down in most occupations. But as a matter of routine, apart from a few exceptional individuals, females are still placed in positions subordinate to males of no greater experience and ability. Many gifted women, thus, who otherwise might have developed a career and made a substantial contribution to society are induced to join their sisters in adding to the birth rate. The same vicious circle applies as with Negroes or other minorities suffering from discrimination. While still in school,

[24] Social Security Administration, *Illegitimacy and Its Impact on the Aid to Dependent Children Program* (Washington: U. S. Government Printing Office, 1960), pp. 52–54.

[25] Maurine McKeany, *The Absent Father and Public Policy in the Program of Aid to Dependent Children* (Berkeley: University of California Press, 1960); Thomas P. Monahan, "Family Fugitives," *Marriage and Family Living*, 20:2 (May, 1958), 146–151.

girls become aware that they will hardly be able to compete for the highest jobs, and therefore typically set their sights lower; they aspire to a life's work less demanding, less remunerative, and less useful than the best they are capable of.

The realization of this five-point program, to repeat, would neither undermine the family nor impair social welfare. Nor would the state be called upon to impose a lower fertility on any couple against its will. And what little we know about the determinants of family formation suggests that this program would work.

## Summary

In the fifteen years following the end of World War II, more than 59 million babies were born in the United States. Over the same period the population increased by about 40 million. In a country with the size and wealth of the United States, even so rapid a growth does not exert a Malthusian pressure; but that does not mean that no social costs are incurred. These costs, already heavy, will become greater if the population increase continues at a comparable rate, and everything indicates that marriage and a three-child family have become a universal and relatively permanent element of American life. Merely to wait until a presumed downturn in the birth rate eases the population pressure would be socially irresponsible. One should consider now what social forces could be mobilized to cut down the rate of population growth—that is, to reduce the average size of the family.

One avenue toward this goal would be to help prevent the reproduction of unwanted children. By definition, they bring no satisfaction to their parents, and society suffers in part because they help swell an already swollen society, in part because unwanted children are in many cases less likely to be adequately reared. If the full range of birth-control measures, including legal abortion and sterilization, were made available to both well-to-do and poor, to both married and unmarried, one could reasonably anticipate a considerable drop in illegitimate births, in the size of poor families, and in the over-all birth rate.

It must be noted, however, that even the average desired family size of 3.2 children, combined with the almost universal marriage and the very low mortality, would also result in a rapid increase in population, especially now that the large cohorts born after 1945 will be reaching the present age of marriage and parenthood. Social policy in that case must be to manipulate the desire for children, and to do so without undermining the family or disrupting legitimate social-welfare benefits. Several broad principles seem to be advisable: to impede hasty or early marriages; to facilitate divorces, particularly of childless couples; to provide alternative satisfactions to marriage, for example to adolescents and to women; to impose on males more financial responsibility for their sometimes reckless procreation; in general, to put a public emphasis on fewer children who would receive better care.

# MALTHUSIAN THEORY: A COMMENTARY AND CRITIQUE

After some decades of relative eclipse, Malthus' name has again become the standard opening to almost every analysis of population trends. As during his lifetime so still today, his views are typically distorted and misjudged, both by supporters and detractors, in both popular and scholarly presentations. It is unfortunately still appropriate to restate his theory, to put it against its intellectual and political background, and to relate it to the present day—and to do this without repeating the recurrent myths and errors.

Thomas Robert Malthus was born in 1766, one of eight children of a country gentleman. He was educated privately and at Jesus College, Cambridge, where he read English and French literature and ancient history, and won prizes in Latin and English declamation. At the age of 22 he took orders and for a period became a curate. His main interest, however, lay in political economy. In 1804, the year of his marriage, he was appointed professor of history and political economy in the newly founded East India College in Hertford. This was the first professorship in the latter discipline established in Britain, and he filled the post with distinction until his death in 1834.[1]

Malthus was one of the founders of nineteenth-century economics. He was a good personal friend of David Ricardo, and their detailed discussions of many points of social policy and economic analysis have been preserved in a voluminous

[1] John Maynard Keynes has written a delightful biographical sketch of Malthus, included in his *Essays in Biography* (New York: Harcourt Brace, 1951). For a more detailed account, see James Bonar, *Malthus and His Work* (New York: Macmillan, 1933). G. F. McCleary, *The Malthusian Population Theory* (London: Faber & Faber, 1953) is an excellent analysis of Malthus' work, with a few chapters devoted to the man and his life.

correspondence. Ricardo incorporated Malthus' principle of population virtually intact into economic theory and, indeed, carried it even farther than the author himself. In one important respect Malthus stood outside the main line of development of classical theory. In the 1930s, when Keynes started a new trend in economics by emphasizing effective demand, he based this concept in part on insights of Malthus that had been neglected for more than a century.

Malthus' most important work, however, the one for which he is most honored and maligned, is his *Essay on the Principle of Population*. It was published anonymously in 1798, when the author was 32 years old. This first edition was written with an aggressive confidence, a dashing style that passed over exceptions, anomalies, minor points, and swept on to the main conclusion with youthful confidence. It brought the author immediate fame and notoriety, but if he had been content to let his work rest with this version, his name would not be known today to every literate person. Malthus spent a good portion of the rest of his life collecting data on the relation between population and environment in various cultures, bringing his theory in accord with these facts and adjusting it to criticism. Since most countries of the Western world were just beginning to compile reliable demographic statistics, this empirical orientation required an extraordinary effort. The second edition of the *Essay*, published after five years of travel and study, was four times as long as the first. The style was much soberer; "I was willing," Malthus wrote in the preface, "to sacrifice all pretensions to merit of composition to the chance of making an impression on a larger class of readers." There were seven editions of the *Essay*, the last of which was published posthumously in 1872.

## Background to the Theory

As his critics have often pointed out, Malthus' ideas were not wholly original with him. According to the author of the *Essay* himself, before he wrote the first edition he had read the works of only four writers on population—David Hume, Adam Smith, Robert Wallace, and Richard Price; and of these only Wallace is really relevant to Malthus' specific theory. For Hume and Smith, population was a relatively subordinate subject, and Price was convinced that England's depopulation was proceeding apace. But in his later study, Malthus found a much longer list of men who had anticipated him. As Bonar pointed out, the *Essay* was original in the same sense that Adam Smith's *Wealth of Nations* was: "In both cases the author got most of his phrases, and even many of his thoughts, from his predecessors; but he treated them as his predecessors were unable to do; he saw them in their connection, perspective, and wide bearings."[2] By putting these ideas that other men had expressed into a larger framework and examining in detail the interrelation of population growth and economic and political development, Malthus did more than any of his predecessors or all of them together. He wrote a book that, whether as guide or as target, all have had to recognize as the beginning of modern population theory. And while in certain respects the *Essay* was derivative, in more important ways it opposed two strong schools of thought, mercantilism and revolutionary utopianism.

Mercantilism is, as Heckscher put it, "a phase in the history of economic policy,"[3] a transition between the medieval and the modern periods. The universalist elements of the Middle Ages, the Church and the Empire, had lost their ability to hold society together, and their place was taken by highly centralized national states. There was a close interaction of political and economic institutions. Very often state officials planned, initiated, developed, and regulated economic enterprises;[4] and the trading companies they formed had powers so broad that within their territories they were equivalent to sovereign states.[5] According to a prime tenet of mercantilist

[2] Bonar, *op. cit.*, pp. 32–33.

[3] Eli F. Heckscher, *Mercantilism* (London: Allen & Unwin, 1935), Vol. 1, p. 19.

[4] When the French East India Company was about to be formed, for example, Colbert had Louis XIV write a letter to various financiers "to the effect that he did not doubt their willingness to take so favorable an opportunity of placing themselves at the service of God, himself, and the community by subscribing shares" (*ibid.*, Vol. 1, p. 346).

[5] "The companies had the right to administer newly discovered or appropriated territories, set up law-courts there, make local

theory, any nation could benefit only at the cost of others. The main end of both political and economic policy was to prepare for war, which came frequently. A wise state produced goods cheaply—that is to say, with the lowest feasible wages—and exported them in exchange for the maximum amount of gold.

And just as it hoarded bullion, so also the state hoarded people, and for the same reason, to increase its economic, political, and military power. During this period, "an almost fanatical desire to increase population prevailed in all countries."[6] France under Colbert in particular attempted to stimulate fertility and to proscribe emigration.[7] The asylum that Huguenots and Jews found in England and Holland was not merely a reflection of the greater tolerance in these Protestant countries, but also of a competition for foreign workers, particularly skilled craftsmen. The main emphasis in mercantilist demography, however, was on quantity, not quality. "As far as the mass of the working population was concerned, they were counted rather than weighed."[8] Their function was to produce for the greater power of the state, and to this end no child was too young to begin working.

Whereas from the beginning of the nineteenth century onwards, after tentative beginnings, stronger and stronger measures were taken to limit child labor by law, under mercantilism the power of the state was exerted in precisely the opposite direction. . . . In a decree of 1668 affecting the lacemaking industry in Auxerre, . . . [Colbert] commanded . . . that all the inhabitants of the town should send their children into this industry

laws, grant titles, build fortresses, mobilize troops, wage war and conclude peace with non-Christian princes and nations, ruthlessly crush whatever threatened their privileges and arrest and deport anybody trading in their territory without permission, in certain cases even the right to have coinage struck for local currency. . . . [Disobedience was described] as an offence against 'God and company'" (*ibid.*, Vol. 1, p. 451).

[6] *Ibid.*, Vol. 2, p. 158.

[7] See D. V. Glass, *Population Policies and Movements in Europe* (Oxford: Clarendon, 1940), pp. 92 ff.

[8] Heckscher, *op. cit.*, Vol. 2, p. 44.

at the age of six, on pain of a penalty of 30 sous per child.[9]

Wages should be at subsistence but never higher. A worker, in the words of Sir William Petty, should be able only to "live, labor, and generate," and "if you double wages, then he works but half so much as he could, or otherwise would."[10]

In spite of the axiom that a large population is good and a larger one better, mercantilist writers continually noted the "overcrowding" evidenced by a high incidence of vagrancy and crime. Anxious about both the insufficiency of people and their unemployment, they never reconciled these two positions. "At the most they believed that *other* countries must, for this reason, be careful about increases in their population."[11] The way to solve overcrowding in the mercantilist framework was to ship the surplus to colonies, where they could aggrandize the state's power in another quarter of the globe. And here the same cycle was started again, with renewed efforts to increase the overseas populations as rapidly as possible. Whole boatloads of women, usually corraled from houses of correction but sometimes also young country girls, were sent to the French colonies, where soldiers who refused to marry them were punished. In the innumerable letters back and forth, these females were quite clearly seen simply as breeders. "In the same breath mention is made of shiploads of women, mares, and sheep, the methods of propagating human beings and cattle being regarded as roughly on the same plane."[12]

During the eighteenth century, a new conception of humanity gradually evolved, particularly in the writings of French political philosophers. With respect to demographic theory and policy, however, there was neither a definite line of development nor a clean break with mercantilism.[13]

[9] *Ibid.*, Vol. 2, p. 155.

[10] Quoted in Eduard Heimann, *History of Economic Doctrines: An Introduction to Economic Theory* (New York: Oxford University Press, 1945), p. 36.

[11] Heckscher, *op. cit.*, Vol. 2, p. 163.

[12] *Ibid.*, Vol. 2, p. 300.

[13] The following discussion is based on Anita Fage, "La révolution française et la population," *Population*, 8:2 (April–June, 1953), 311–338.

Barnave was exceptional in his view that growth in numbers does not always benefit society. For Mirabeau, or for Brissot de Warville, a large population was symptomatic of a nation's happiness, but the state should foster it only indirectly by increasing the people's well-being. Saint-Just, later one of the instigators of the Jacobin terror, adhered most closely to mercantilist ideas. In his view, misery could never be the effect of overpopulation, but only of social institutions. One can depend on nature "never to have more children than teats," but to keep the balance in the other direction nature needs the state's assistance. Saint-Just's ideas on marriage law, inspired by Rousseau, were "surprisingly harsh" in Fage's estimation. Not only should marriage be encouraged by state loans, but a couple still childless after seven years ought to be forcibly separated.

The Revolutionary Assembly, like the earlier philosophers, was in the main pronatalist. As defined in the new constitution itself, "No one can be a good citizen who is not a good son, a good father, a good brother, a good husband."[14] Membership in the Conseil des Anciens was constitutionally restricted to married persons. A national celebration to honor Husbands and Wives provoked a deluge of sentimental panegyrics. The principal instrument used by the republican government to stimulate population growth was the same as Colbert's, differential taxation; single persons 30 years old and over paid 25 percent more taxes. A campaign against celibates was reflected both in legislation and in crackpot ideas of fanatics —for example, that all celibates be required to wear clothing of a specific color, so that they might not escape the just ridicule of the people; or the petition to the Convention that celibacy be made a capital offense.[15]

The population policy under Napoleon represented a compromise. Pronatalist decrees continued; in 1813, though the need for soldiers was great, married men were exempted from military service. Under the Civil Code, marriage remained a civil contract and divorce, though possible, was difficult. The

[14] Quoted in Marcel Reinhard, "La révolution française et le problème de la population," *Population,* 1:3 (July–September, 1946), 419–427.

[15] Fage, *op. cit.;* Glass, *op. cit.,* p. 146.

authority of the father was strengthened, both over his children and over his wife. As under the Republic, primogeniture was supplanted by a law requiring each owner of property to divide the bulk of it equally among all his children; and at one time some analysts believed that this clause had effected a decline in French fertility, particularly among the peasants, for whom a numerous progeny would mean a rapid subdivision of the farm into uneconomic plots. Actually, however, even before the Revolution equal division of property had been the usual practice except among the nobility, so that the decline in family size cannot be ascribed to the law, and certainly not to its purpose.[16]

In the context of a discussion of Malthus, two revolutionary ideologues are especially relevant, Condorcet and Godwin. The first edition of Malthus' *Essay*, as its very title indicated, was intended to reply to "the speculations of Mr. Godwin, M. Condorcet, and other writers."

Marie-Jean-Antoine-Nicolas Caritat, Marquis de Condorcet, was an ardent revolutionary, a prominent member of the moderate Girondin faction. In 1793, after the more radical Jacobins gained full control, Condorcet was tried in absentia and sentenced to death. He remained in Paris, hiding in a students' boarding house, and over the next six months, while the tumbrils were rolling by almost under his windows, he wrote his famous *Esquisse d'un tableau historique des progrès de l'esprit humain*, a history of human progress from its earliest beginnings to its imminent culmination in human perfection. According to Condorcet, all inequalities of wealth, of education, of opportunity, of sex, would soon disappear. Animosities between nations and races would be no more. All persons would speak the same language. The earth would be bountiful without stint. All diseases would be conquered, and if man did not become immortal, the span of his life would have no assignable upper limit. The question of whether production would always suffice to satisfy the people's wants could not be answered, for the problem would not have to be faced for ages to come, by

[16] J. G. C. Blacker, "Social Ambitions of the Bourgeoisie in 18th-Century France, and Their Relation to Family Limitation," *Population Studies*, 11:1 (July, 1957), 46–63.

which time man would have acquired new types of now still unimagined knowledge. In the rational age to come, men would recognize their obligation to those not yet born and to the general well-being both of their society and of all humanity, and "not to the puerile idea of filling the earth with useless and unhappy beings." At that time, a limit could be set to the population other than by premature death of a portion of those born. "Thus we find in Condorcet the entire genesis of the Malthusian population law, but in France these ideas remained unnoticed."[17]

In the same year in which Condorcet went into hiding, a book published across the channel, William Godwin's *Enquiry Concerning Political Justice*, looked forward to the early establishment of another perfect society, in which a half hour's work a day would amply supply the wants of all.

> There will be no war, no crimes, no administration of justice, as it is called, and no government. Besides this, there will be neither disease, anguish, melancholy, nor resentment. Every man will seek, with ineffable ardor, the good of all.[18]

Malthus has often been characterized as a reactionary for his rejection of these effusions of Condorcet and Godwin, but in that case there are few indeed who do not deserve the epithet.

### The Principle of Population

"In an inquiry concerning the improvement of society," Malthus begins the final edition of the *Essay*, the natural procedure is to investigate past impediments to "the progress of mankind towards happiness" and the probability that these would be totally or partially removed in the future.[19] He does not pretend to be able to discuss so large a subject in its entirety, but "one great cause" is "the constant tendency

[17] Fage, *op. cit.* See also McCleary, *op. cit.*, pp. 86–88.
[18] Quoted in *ibid.*, p. 17.
[19] This quotation and the following all come from T. R. Malthus, *An Essay on the Principle of Population* (7th ed.; London: Reeves and Turner, 1872), Book 1, Chaps. 1 and 2.

in all animated life to increase beyond the nourishment prepared for it."

Population, "when unchecked," doubles once every generation. Among plants and "irrational animals," the potential increase is actual, and its "superabundant effects are repressed afterwards by want of room or nourishment." The matter is "more complicated" in the human species, for man, a rational being, can consider the effects of his potential fertility and curb his natural instinct. With man, there are two types of control of population growth, which Malthus terms the preventive and positive checks. "In no state that we have yet known, has the power of population been left to exert itself with perfect freedom."

The principal preventive check is "moral restraint," or the postponement of marriage with no extramarital sexual gratification. Other types of preventive checks he terms "vice," namely, "promiscuous intercourse, unnatural passions, violations of the marriage bed, and improper arts to conceal the consequences of irregular connections"—or, in modern terminology, promiscuity, homosexuality, and birth control applied either within or outside marriage.

Positive checks include "wars, excesses, and many others which it would be in our power to avoid"; but in a country already fairly densely populated (Malthus used Great Britain as an example, and specifically excluded the America of his day), lack of food is the decisive factor. If the average produce from the land were doubled over one generation, or about 25 years, this would be "a greater increase than could with reason be expected." A second doubling in the following 25 years "would be contrary to all our knowledge of the properties of land." That is to say, the "tendency" or "power" of every species, including the human one, is to increase at a geometric rate, while under the most favorable circumstances usually to be found, its subsistence increases at an arithmetic rate. Thus, "the human species would increase as the numbers, 1, 2, 4, 8, 16, 32, 64, 128, 256; and the subsistence as 1, 2, 3, 4, 5, 6, 7, 8, 9. In two centuries the population would be to the means of subsistence as 256 to 9; in three centuries as 4,096 to 13, and in two thousand years the difference would be almost incalculable." Lack of food, then, is the principal ultimate check to population growth, but "never the immediate check, except in cases of actual famine."

Apart from migration, the population growth of any area depends on the preventive and positive checks taken together —or, in modern terminology, on practices affecting fertility and those affecting mortality. Moreover—

> The preventive and the positive checks must vary inversely to each other; that is, in countries either naturally unhealthy, or subject to a great mortality, from whatever cause it may arise, the preventive check will prevail very little. In those countries, on the contrary, which are naturally healthy, and where the preventive check is found to prevail with considerable force, the positive check will prevail very little, or the mortality be very small.

Or, as we would say today, fertility and mortality, apart from transitional periods, are generally either both high or both low.

Population tends to oscillate around the number possible with the means of subsistence available. If a country with a population of 11 million, say, has food adequate for this number, then in most cases the population would increase sooner than the subsistence, which eventually would have to be divided among perhaps 11.5 million. Because of the consequent distress among the poor, more would put off getting married (the high negative correlation between the price of wheat and the marriage rate that Malthus noted has been repeatedly confirmed in subsequent studies). With a fall in the wage rate, farmers would be encouraged to hire more hands to "turn up fresh soil and to manure and improve more completely what is already in tillage," until the food supply was again on a par with the population—and the cycle began again. In primitive societies, where there is no market system, the same kind of oscillation takes place more directly. "When population has increased nearly to the utmost limits of the food, all the preventive and the positive checks will naturally operate with increased force . . . till the population is sunk below the level of the food; and then the return to comparative plenty will again produce an increase, and, after a certain period, its further progress will again be checked by the same causes."

The tension between population and subsistence, which Malthus saw as the major cause of misery and vice, could also have a beneficial effect. A man who postpones marriage until he is able to take care of his family is driven by his sexual urge to work hard. Malthus was therefore opposed to contraceptives, for their use permits sexual gratification free, as it were, and does not generate the same drive to work as would either a chaste postponement of marriage or children to care for. If a misunderstanding of Malthus' meaning was possible in the early editions, this should have been removed by a very specific denunciation of birth control that he made in the appendix to the 1817 edition, answering one James Grahame:

> I should always particularly reprobate any artificial and unnatural modes of checking population, both on account of their immorality and their tendency to remove a necessary stimulus to industry. If it were possible for each married couple to limit by a wish the number of their children, there is certainly reason to fear that the indolence of the human race would be very greatly increased, and that neither the population of individual countries nor of the whole earth would ever reach its natural and proper extent. But the restraints which I have recommended are quite of a different character. They are not only pointed out by reason and sanctioned by religion, but tend in the most marked manner to stimulate industry.[20]

A considerable difference in average family size was already discernible among social classes in Malthus' day, and the lower fertility of the upper classes was effected, at least in large part, by the postponement of marriage that he considered desirable. If prudence is practiced among the upper classes, "the obvious mode" of extending this practice to the lower classes is "to infuse into them a portion of that knowledge and foresight which so much facilitates the attainment of this object in the educated part of the community."[21] The

[20] *Ibid.*, p. 512.
[21] *Ibid.*, p. 437.

way to do this, Malthus continued, would be to set up a universal educational system, as had been proposed by Adam Smith. Educating the mass would afford everyone the possibility of improving his situation, and this was, in Malthus' view, a strong counterforce to the principle of population. "The desire of bettering our condition, and the fear of making it worse, has been constantly in action and has been constantly directing people into the right road."[22]

Once the people have been educated to regard prudential restraint as both feasible and good, this mode of checking the growth of population can be spread through society by raising the standard of living. This argument, which is merely suggested in the last chapters of the *Essay*, Malthus developed more fully in his *Principles of Political Economy*.[23] The lowest level to which wages can fall, in his theory as in the classical school generally, is the cost of bringing another generation of laborers into the world at a subsistence level. Malthus believed, however, that wages can be raised from this minimum by an increase in "the amount of those necessaries and conveniences without which [the workers] would not consent to keep up their numbers to the required point." In spite of this clear statement, Malthus has often been associated with a contrary theory, if not actually designated as the advocate of the vice and misery he discussed.[24]

## Criticism and Analysis

It is standard that important books are more often cited than read, but in the whole development of the social disciplines, there has probably never been anyone attacked and defended with so little regard for what he had written as Malthus. The errors and misrepresentations have been so general and so persistent that an analysis of his theory

[22] *Ibid.*, p. 477.

[23] 2nd ed.; New York: Kelley, 1951. See also Joseph J. Spengler, "Malthus' Total Population Theory: A Restatement and Reappraisal," *Canadian Journal of Economics and Political Science*, 11:1 (February, 1945), 83–110; 11:2 (May, 1945), 234–264.

[24] McCleary cites a passage to this effect from an introductory text "emanating from a famous American seat of learning, Dartmouth College," and published in 1941 (*op. cit.*, p. 96).

cannot be considered complete until some attention has been paid them. Accounts in responsible works are sometimes mistaken even on matters of simple, easily ascertainable facts—where Malthus was educated, what his profession was,[25] how many editions there were of the *Essay*,[26] whether or not he was married,[27] and so on. Those most interested in Malthus, whether to praise or to damn him, have often started out with a misconception so fundamental that it enveloped the whole man. The "Malthusian" (later "neo-Malthusian") Leagues sometimes took several generations to discover that the person whose name they used had been opposed in principle to the birth control they advocated. And the opponents of Malthus have often propagated the myth that he was a reactionary, that "the *Essay on Population* chimed with a growing tendency to repress—discussion, association, political organization were becoming less free, as the wars became more exacting and more intense."[28] A widely used text denounces Malthus as "an apologist for feudalism on a capitalist and utilitarian basis"—feudalism in England of 1800! Malthus, we are told, was "probably thinking in terms of a permanent social structure having the qualities of the transitional phase of the eighteenth century."[29]

These arguments, one might say, have a certain relevance to the highly simplified version of Malthus' theory that appeared in the first edition of the *Essay*, or that his avid supporters later bandied about in his name. Anyone in favor of absolute laissez-faire found in Malthus' principle of population, as later in Darwin's principle of natural selection, a doctrine that seemed to give his political views scientific backing. The main contemporary impact on social and political events was not made by the *Essay* or the *Origin of*

[25] *Ibid.*, pp. 94–95.

[26] We are told, for example, that there were five during his lifetime in H. L. Beales, "The Historical Context of the *Essay* on Population," in D. V. Glass, ed., *Introduction to Malthus* (New York: Wiley, 1953), pp. 1–24.

[27] See below, p. 78, n. 14.

[28] Beales, *op. cit.*

[29] Erich Roll, *A History of Economic Thought* (Rev. ed.; London: Faber & Faber, 1954), pp. 205, 211.

*Species*, but by vulgarized caricatures of these works, which generally had, it is true, a pernicious influence on British social policy. Malthus has been criticized for ignoring the many distortions of his theory that appeared during his lifetime; he might have answered that to refute all of them he would have had to devote full time to the task, and that in the prefaces to successive editions of the *Essay* he did try to correct the most important errors. Yet while subsequent generations have managed to distinguish Darwin from Social Darwinism,[30] Malthus is still usually pictured as a cartoon figure, Good or Evil incarnate, depending on one's politics.

Malthus was no revolutionary. His sensibilities were revolted by the Terror in Paris, and his solid English empiricism by such utopian extravagances as that man can become immortal by establishing a new form of government. But neither was he a reactionary. He is vilified for having denounced the Speenhamland system,[31] but he is less well known as the advocate of free universal education, free medical care for the poor, state assistance to emigrants, and even direct relief to casual laborers or families with more than six children; or as the opponent of child labor in factories, and of free trade when it benefited the traders but not the public.[32] More fundamentally, these policy recommendations derived from Malthus' underlying principles. That his sympathies lay with the well-to-do classes is true, but these sympathies were weakened by the fact that they were divided between the gentry and the urban middle class. Brought up the son of a country gentleman, he ended his life as a staunch Whig. Appreciative of certain elements of country life ("feudalism"), he was for parliamentary reforms that would shift the political power to the cities.

[30] Even Jacques Barzun, who has written what is undoubtedly the least sympathetic recent account of Darwin, distinguishes "The Newton of Biology" from "The Uses of Darwinism"; see *Darwin, Marx, Wagner: Critique of a Heritage* (New York: Doubleday-Anchor, 1958), Chaps. 4–5.

[31] A modern liberal view of the Speenhamland system thoroughly in accord with Malthus' is given in Karl Polanyi, *The Great Transformation* (New York: Rinehart, 1944). See below, pp. 77–78.

[32] Cf. Bonar, *op. cit.,* p. 343, where citations are given to the passages in Malthus' work expressing these opinions.

When he termed "most" men lazy, who would "sink to the level of brutes" if permitted to remain idle, he certainly had some basis for this judgment among the declassed peasants of his day. The key to his social philosophy is not his unflattering appraisal of the illiterate mass, but his conviction that their state was not ingrained, that social classes are *not*, as Edmund Burke later wrote, "as it were, different species of animals." Following the example of Adam Smith in *The Wealth of Nations*, Malthus proclaimed the right of each individual to seek happiness rather than serve the state, and to do this by following his own conscience rather than traditional usages. A full break with mercantilism—and with its paternalistic obverse, represented in Speenhamland—was a necessary prerequisite to the development of modern democracy. However, unlike some proponents of laissez-faire liberalism, who demanded of each man only that he seek his own interest, Malthus did not see the upper classes as automatically right by reason of their social position. If they failed to assist the lower classes in becoming self-reliant, they were thereby censurable.

To reject the frequent errors and misrepresentations in discussions of Malthus' work does not mean that we must accept it as gospel. He is still worth reading today because he forcefully posed a few very important questions, but his answers to them are inadequate by today's standards. These deficiencies derive in large part from three contradictions in his work that were never wholly resolved.

1. *Moralist vs. Scientist.* To this day, social theorists find it difficult to separate an analysis of what *is* from what, in their opinion, *ought* to be. The theory of the population optimum is a good modern example of this recurrent dilemma. Malthus wrote at a time when such subjects as population were ordinarily discussed in the context of "moral philosophy"; he himself, as mentioned above, was England's first professor of political economy. The pages of his books, reflecting this transition from a moralist to a scientific frame of reference, are sprinkled with allusions to "the Creator" and what He would prefer. The present-day reader, even a pious one, finds such stylistic mannerisms inappropriate to a work in social science.

Sometimes the competition between the two analytical systems comes to the surface. Consider the proposition that "vice" leads to "misery." This might be the topic of a sermon, and Malthus the moralist would be pleased with the formulation. Malthus the scientist could hardly be. The main impetus to rapid population growth and thus, in his system, to misery, came from early marriage. While he strongly advocated "moral restraint," he never quite designated the failure to exercise it—getting married—as "vice." And on the other hand, as he pointed out in an interesting footnote, some vice —for example, extramarital intercourse—may "have added to the happiness of both parties and have injured no one."

> These individual actions, therefore, cannot come under the head of misery. But they are still evidently vicious, because an action is so denominated which violates an express precept, founded upon its general tendency to produce misery, whatever may be its individual effect; and no person can doubt the general tendency of an illicit intercourse between the sexes to injure the happiness of society.[33]

Or, as a sociologist would put it today, no society can be viable if it lacks so fundamental an institution as the family, which, to persist, must be protected by a principle of legitimacy and moral injunctions against extramarital relations. In the *Essay*, a hint of such a functional analysis is sometimes vaguely perceptible, intertwined with "moral philosophy."

Or, as another example, compare his opposition to birth control with that in Catholic dogma. When contraceptives are denounced as "unnatural," there is no way of translating this moral judgment into scientific language. Malthus disapproved of them "both on account of their immorality and their tendency to remove a necessary stimulus to industry," and of the two reasons he stressed the second. Birth control was what some modern sociologists would term "dysfunctional." Malthus was wrong on this point, of course: man's ambition can be excited by many stimulants other than his sexuality. But the interesting point is that he was not

[33] Malthus, *Essay*, p. 9.

satisfied with labeling birth control as "immoral"; he tried to state his opposition also in an empirical context, in which he *could* be proved wrong.

Although he was for a period a curate of the Church of England, whom Marx and others referred to as "Parson Malthus," many clergymen found his interpretation of Providence not to their liking, and one went so far as to charge the author of the *Essay* with atheism.[34] The population theory appropriate to a "parson," they felt, was something along the lines of Luther's adage, *"Gott macht Kinder, der wird sie auch ernähren"*—God makes children, and He will also nourish them. The principle of population, on the contrary, brought man fully into nature, one species among others. As Darwin himself remarked, his casual reading of the *Essay*, "for amusement," furnished the first clue out of which the theory of evolution developed. Thus, in the dispute between evolutionists and traditionalist theologians, a momentous struggle that set the tone of intellectual life during the whole second half of the nineteenth century, the role of Malthus was not that of a theologian but rather a forerunner to scientific biology.

2. *Biological Determinist vs. Sociologist.* Sometimes Malthus' emphasis on the fact that man is an animal, with sexual passions and the need for food, has been taken as the sum of his theory, so that he is attacked (or defended) as a biological determinist. This is a reasonable interpretation of the first edition of the *Essay*, on which critics have usually concentrated as the easier target. Malthus' lifelong effort to improve the first statement of his theory has failed to impress many analysts, who note the later editions only to point out the inconsistencies.[35]

[34] Cf. Bonar, *op. cit.*, p. 365.

[35] Bowen tells us, for example, that "the clear alternative" to Malthus' biological theory is "the hypothesis that economic as well as social conditions affect the growth and size of populations, and that sexual passions operate only within the restrictions or stimuli imposed by these conditions." And yet two pages earlier the reader was informed that Malthus had "emphasized the dependence of the actual level of population upon the laws, institutions and habits of each society." Ian Bowen, *Population* (London: Nisbet, 1954), pp. 109, 111.

Malthus' emphasis on man's biological nature, which today often sounds like an insistence on the obvious, was not so pointless in his day. Many then believed that the fecundity of the human species was being reduced by its new urban setting or by food it was then eating. Sadler, for instance, was not the first to contend that "the fecundity of human beings under similar circumstances varies inversely as their numbers on a given space";[36] or Doubleday, that abundant food destroys the physiological ability to reproduce, so that "in a nation highly and generally affluent and luxurious, population will [necessarily] decrease and decay."[37] And according to Godwin, if sexual intercourse were stripped of "all its attendant circumstances, . . . it would be generally despised."[38] Against such adversaries, it was relevant to stress man's physiological drives and needs.

In Malthus' final statement of his population theory (that is, the last edition of the *Essay* together with portions of the *Principles*), some remnants of the initial framework remain in an occasional turn of phrase. But basically he was less of a biological determinist than many other nineteenth-century economists. For most members of this school, the problem to be analyzed was production, and consumption was viewed rather mechanically in terms of a reified Economic Man. For Malthus the standard of living was not a biological factor, but a cultural one. It is worth recalling the debt Keynes acknowledged to Malthus on this point:

The idea that we can safely neglect the aggregate demand function is fundamental to Ricardian economics, which underlie what we have been taught for more than a century. Malthus, indeed, had vehemently opposed Ricardo's doctrine that it was impossible for effective demand to be deficient; but . . . Ricardo conquered England as completely as the Holy Inquisition conquered Spain. . . . [Malthus was one of] the brave

[36] Michael Thomas Sadler, *Ireland, Its Evils and Their Remedies* (London: Murray, 1829), p. xxviii.

[37] Thomas Doubleday, *The True Law of Population Shewn To Be Connected with the Food of the People* (London: Simpkin, Marshall, 1842), p. 7.

[38] Godwin, *Political Justice,* quoted in Malthus, *Essay,* p. 392.

army of heretics, . . . who, following their intuitions,
have preferred to see the truth obscurely and imperfectly rather than to maintain error, reached indeed
with clearness and consistency and by easy logic, but
on hypotheses inappropriate to the facts.[39]

3. *Deductive vs. Inductive System.*[40] The principle of
population, as enunciated in the first edition of the *Essay,*
was wholly deductive. It started with axioms and then proceeded with conclusions inferred from them. Subsequent
editions, as we have seen, were based also on a mass of
empirical data, gathered to check and support the original
thesis. In its final statement, Malthus' theory is not clearly
either deductive or inductive, but a sometimes confusing
mixture of the two.

An indication of this confusion is the ambiguity of a
number of key words. In the phrase, "the ultimate check to
population appears to be a want of food," what is the meaning of "ultimate"? Sometimes it seems to mean "in the long
run" (if the potential population increase is realized, then
ultimately the lack of food will become the most important
check), but Malthus emphasized that the potential had never
been fully realized, and if moral restraint became general,
the population need never press on the means of subsistence.
Sometimes "ultimate" seems to mean "fundamental, underlying all other checks" (for both vice and moral restraint
were often the consequence of hunger, or of the fear of it);
yet Malthus also emphasized that the standard of living
could rise above the subsistence level, so that hunger would
be completely irrelevant to actual population trends—as
indeed it has become in the countries of the West since his
day.

A more important symptom of the confusion between
Malthus' deductive and inductive systems is the ambiguity

[39] John Maynard Keynes, *The General Theory of Employment,
Interest, and Money* (New York: Harcourt Brace, 1935), pp. 32,
371. Cf. below, pp. 60–63.
[40] See Kingsley Davis, "Malthus and the Theory of Population,"
in Paul F. Lazarsfeld and Morris Rosenberg, *The Language of
Social Research: A Reader in the Methodology of Social Research*
(Glencoe, Ill.: Free Press, 1955), pp. 540–553.

of the word "tendency."[41] In the sentence—apart from "extreme cases, . . . population always increases where the means of subsistence increase"—the tendency seems to be a summary of empirical data. In other contexts, however, the "tendency" of population to increase up to the means of subsistence means its "power . . . when unchecked."

If we try to resolve these confusions, expressing Malthus' ideas in present-day terms, he seems to be making these assertions:

Man's physiological ability to reproduce is great enough to permit any population to double each generation (true). Actual fertility has never been so high as fecundity (probably true). In most cases, however, the checks on population growth imposed by reduced fertility were less important than those effected by heavy mortality (generally true of Malthus' day and of prior periods, though the postponement of marriage had also been a significant factor). The most important reason for late marriage and for high death rates was usually an actual or threatened shortage of food (the postponement of marriage had been enforced by institutionalized regulations; and at least in Europe, disease was more significant than hunger as the cause of early death).

In short, though Malthus' population theory suffers from inconsistencies and ambiguities, his principle of population has been one element in almost every subsequent theory, and many of the later reformulations were no great improvement in either logical or empirical terms.

> Malthus' results were not all new and were not all true; but his work has the merit of being the first thorough application of the inductive method to social science. The chief workers therefore in the modern historical school of economics justly regard him as one of the founders of that school and his work as a solid possession for ever.[42]

[41] See the interesting exchange between Malthus and Nassau Senior, reprinted in McCleary, *op. cit.*, pp. 114–128.

[42] Alfred Marshall, *Principles of Economics*, quoted in McCleary, *op. cit.*, p. 50.

# JOHN MAYNARD KEYNES' THEORIES OF POPULATION AND THE CONCEPT OF "OPTIMUM"

Though Keynes never wrote a long, serious work on demography, his persistent interest in the subject was expressed in a number of articles and in portions of books on other topics. At the time they were written, these rather fugitive pieces had a considerable influence in shaping the development of population theory, so that it is more than Keynes' general importance as a theorist that makes them of interest today. Immediately after the First World War, Keynes had much to do with the revival of Malthusian thought; and in the 1930s the contrary, underpopulationist mood was often analyzed in terms of his *General Theory*. The contradiction between these two views, which Keynes himself passed over lightly, is still an important weakness of demographic theory. Policies with respect to immigration, family subsidies, and a dozen other specific matters are set, explicitly or implicitly, partly in terms of what is taken to be an optimum population; but this optimum ordinarily differs according to whether it is defined in a Malthusian frame of reference or what might be termed a Keynesian one.

## Keynes as a Malthusian

Malthus' principle of population, which had been incorporated into classical economic theory at the beginning of the nineteenth century, lost much of its axiomatic authority before the start of the twentieth; but it was not so much replaced by a better theory as displaced by empirical data. Malthus had underestimated the importance of the continued industrial development and of the spread of birth control; and these flaws were to become crucial. By 1900 the widespread criticism of Malthus in various countries began to develop into an almost general rejection of his thesis. In 1895 Cannan wrote what later became a very famous article predicting a long-term decline in British fertility.[1] Among others, Brentano did a statistical analysis of trends in several countries to show that since 1870 there had been a marked increase in prosperity combined, particularly among the well-to-do classes, with a decline in fertility.[2]

The March 1912 issue of the *Economic Journal*, the very first that Keynes edited, contained an article with a contrary emphasis. "The name of Robert Malthus," it began, "far from falling into oblivion in the course of time, is quoted with increasing frequency in latter-day discussions"; for though he was mistaken in certain respects, he raised fundamental problems.[3] Whether Keynes commissioned this article or took it over from the backlog of Professor Edgeworth, his predecessor, is not known; but in either case the fact that he printed it indicates that he may have begun to think along Malthusian lines even before 1914.

In *The Economic Consequences of the Peace*, Keynes introduced his criticism of the economic sanctions under the Versailles Treaty with a short chapter on "Europe before the War." Until 1870, he wrote, Europe had been substantially self-subsistent; and after this date, with the flow of goods from overseas, "the pressure of population on food became, for the first time in recorded history, definitely

[1] Edwin Cannan, "The Probability of a Cessation of the Growth of Population in England and Wales during the Next Century," *Economic Journal*, 5:20 (December, 1895), 505–515. In his projection there were fewer than 35.5 million persons in England and Wales in 1951, but this projected population was better balanced in its age structure than the actual one today.

[2] For an English summary and a reference to the longer German original, see Lujo Brentano, "The Doctrine of Malthus and the Increase of Population during the Last Decades," *Economic Journal*, 20:79 (September, 1910), 371–393. A similar study, more in sympathy with Malthus' views but reaching the same conclusions, was George G. Chisholm, "Malthus and Some Recent Census Returns," *Scottish Geographic Magazine*, 29:9 (September, 1913), 453–471.

[3] Gustav Cohn, "The Increase of Population in Germany," *Economic Journal*, 22:1 (March, 1912), 34–45.

reversed." However, this unprecedented progress may have ended at the turn of the century: "Up to 1900, a unit of labor applied to industry yielded year by year a purchasing power over an increasing quantity of food. It is possible that about the year 1900 this process began to be reversed." That the change did not become evident immediately was the consequence of, for example, the influx of new commodities from Africa. In short:

> Before the eighteenth century, mankind entertained no false hopes. To lay the illusions which grew popular at that age's latter end, Malthus disclosed a Devil. For half a century, all serious economic writers held that Devil in clear prospect. For the next half century he was chained up and out of sight. Now perhaps we have loosened him again.[4]

This passage became so familiar that a polemical article could be entitled "A Word for the Devil."

This analysis was immediately attacked, first of all by Beveridge in an answering article and in his rebuttal to Keynes' rejoinder.[5] Within the narrow limits of their discussion, Beveridge had the best of it. The index that Keynes used to show a major turning point at around 1900 revealed what might well have been only a short-term fluctuation; in any case, the series was defective and, when corrected, it showed no reversal at all. Keynes pointed out that his remarks on overpopulation were intended as no more than *obiter dicta*, and that "an author may have more to say in support of his general attitude than can be well expressed in a single page of a book on another topic."[6] Beveridge ad-

[4] J. M. Keynes, *The Economic Consequences of the Peace* (London: Macmillan, 1919), Chap. 2.

[5] W. H. Beveridge, "Population and Unemployment," *Economic Journal*, 33:132 (December, 1923), 447–475; J. M. Keynes, "Reply to William Beveridge," *ibid.*, 476–486; W. H. Beveridge, "Mr. Keynes's Evidence for Overpopulation," *Economica*, 4:10 (February, 1924), 1–20.

[6] In Harrod's biography of Keynes, the 30-page chapter devoted to *The Economic Consequences* deals with the question of overpopulation in precisely one sentence: "The precariousness of European prosperity was analyzed under three heads—the pressure

mitted the justice of this (rather generously, for at least the "single page" was an exaggeration), but added that the book had been read by some hundreds of thousands of persons who knew nothing of this issue and were misled by Keynes' analysis. He did not doubt that there was a Devil abroad, but the Devil was Keynes' careless statements.

In 1923, in a short article entitled "Is Britain Overpopulated?"[7] Keynes expressed his resentment of such epithets as "Malthusian moonshine" sprinkled through the polemics of Beveridge's supporters. While it is true that one cannot argue directly from unemployment to overpopulation, he wrote, the "prolongation and intensity" of the current unemployment in Britain made it necessary to seek causes in other than "transitory influences." Although the birth rate in Britain had fallen, there were still twice as many births as deaths. "Is not a country overpopulated when its standards are lower than they would be if its numbers were less?" The failure to answer this question precisely was the principal reason the Keynes-Beveridge exchange remained rather sterile. In spite of the status of the contenders, the issue was never clearly drawn.

> If we are thinking of overpopulation as a condition which cannot arise so long as there are conceivable ways in which more people can be employed so as to produce larger real incomes, then apparently Sir William was right, and there is no overpopulation in England or in Europe. . . . On the other hand, if we think of overpopulation as a condition in which there are too many people to be employed at good real wages under the conditions which actually exist and which

---

of population, entailing an abnormally large dependence on overseas supplies; the intense division of labor in Europe, which made the surrounding countries peculiarly dependent on German prosperity; and the insecurity of the psychological basis of capitalism." R. F. Harrod, *The Life of John Maynard Keynes* (London: Macmillan, 1951), p. 280.

[7] J. M. Keynes, "Is Britain Overpopulated?" *New Republic,* October 31, 1923, pp. 247–248. Cf. J. M. Keynes, "Population and Unemployment," *Nation and Athenaeum,* October 6, 1923, pp. 9–11, which was another version of essentially the same article.

appear likely to exist for some time to come, it would seem that Professor Keynes was fully justified in saying that England and Europe are overpopulated.[8]

Keynes' interest in Malthus' population theory was also expressed during this period in a number of incidental ways. He delivered a talk on Malthus to his Cambridge seminar.[9] He wrote a biographical sketch of "the first of the Cambridge economists,"[10] which attempted both to round out the human figure of Thomas Robert Malthus and to comment briefly on all of his works.

In 1922 Keynes edited a series of twelve issues of the *Manchester Guardian Commercial* on the theme of "Reconstruction in Europe," and in his short article introducing the section on population he repeated his *"obiter dicta"* in still more provocative terms. The article is illustrated by a photograph of "Malthus Island," a barren rock crowded with birds.

> The guillemots on these islands off the coast of Northumberland [the legend reads] sit shoulder to shoulder on their eggs, covering the entire superficies. If one more egg is laid another egg rolls off into the sea, [and] by this ingenious social custom the population can

[8] Warren S. Thompson, *Population Problems* (2nd ed.; New York: McGraw-Hill, 1934), p. 426. Cf. Hugh Dalton, "The Theory of Population," *Economica*, 8:22 (March, 1928), 28–50.

[9] Harrod writes concerning this: "He also dwelt on modern conditions; the Malthusian devil was evidently still with us. In the discussion Mr. Dennis Robertson produced some recent statistics; he was not so sure about the Malthusian devil. Indeed, he hinted that the modern danger might be the opposite one, a decline in numbers. Robertson seemed to know what he was talking about, and I had an uncomfortable feeling that it was he, and not my master, who was in the right on this occasion" (*op. cit.*, p. 328).

[10] This was published only in 1933: J. M. Keynes, *Essays in Biography* (New York: Harcourt, Brace, 1933), pp. 95–149. The study begins with a modest disclaimer: Keynes had used only readily available sources, and "added such other details as I have come across in miscellaneous reading which has been neither systematic nor exhaustive." Yet the first reference is to a monograph history of the Malthus family, of which 110 copies had been privately printed. See above, p. 27.

be maintained in a state of stability. . . . The most interesting question in the world (of those at least to which time will bring us an answer) is whether, after a short interval of recovery, material progress will be resumed, or whether on the other hand, the magnificent episode of the 19th century is over.[11]

Now it was "a question" whether the population pressure was the consequence of a long-term decline (as, three years earlier, the Keynes of *The Economic Consequences* had definitely stated it was) or the presumably more remediable effect of the war. The phrase "magnificent episode," a red flag to all firm believers in Western progress, became almost as much of a shibboleth as "the Devil."[12]

The text of *Population*, which Wright wrote under the editorial guidance of Keynes, can be taken as the fullest statement of the latter's views on population at this time. This "emanation from the seat of Devil-worship," as Robertson termed it,[13] began with a summary of Malthus' doctrine, largely in the words of the *Essay*, and then attempted to substitute for the "fallacious" arithmetical ratio the Law of Diminishing Returns as finally formulated by J. S. Mill, who "adhered firmly to the general teaching of Malthus and Ricardo, which he restated in a more complete and scientific form."[14] The argument of Malthus' *Essay*

[11] J. M. Keynes, "An Economist's View of Population," *Manchester Guardian Commercial*, August 17, 1922, pp. 340–341. The text of the article was largely reprinted in a more easily accessible form as the preface to one of the Cambridge Economic Handbooks—Harold Wright, *Population* (New York: Harcourt, Brace, 1923).

[12] Hayek has made the point that Keynes' "gift for phrasemaking," his "puckish delight in shocking his contemporaries," often led him to overstate his case. "Certainly such phrases as the 'humbug of finance,' 'the end of laissez-faire,' and 'in the long run we are all dead' must often have recoiled against their author when he was in a more conservative mood." F. A. Hayek, review of Harrod's biography, *Journal of Modern History*, 24:2 (June, 1952), 195–198.

[13] D. H. Robertson, "A Word for the Devil," *Economica*, 3:9 (November, 1923), 203–208.

[14] In a review of the book (entitled, with already a certain ennui, "Two More Books on Population"), Dalton remarked, "While the

is relevant to the present day, for while diminishing returns in production (for example, of cotton) are offset to some degree by the tendency to control fertility, they nonetheless result in population pressure (pp. 34 ff.). The section on the "Economic Advantages of a Growing Population" does not, as might be supposed, foreshadow Keynes' later theory, but rather discusses the increased efficiency resulting from mass production (pp. 67 ff.). The "way out" of the population problem is to increase production and restrict the birth rate (pp. 172–173).[15]

## The Malthusian Revival

There has been a certain tendency to dismiss this Malthusian phase as an unfortunate personal vagary of Keynes—in the words of Schumpeter, for example, "perhaps the least felicitous of all his efforts and indicative of an element of recklessness in his make-up which those who loved him best cannot entirely deny."[16] Similarly, in the view of Paul Samuelson, Keynes "unleashed with a flourish the Malthusian bogey of overpopulation at a time when England and the Western European world were undergoing a population revolution in the opposite direction."[17]

Whether Keynes was right or wrong, however, he was certainly not alone in his views. The battle of words between Cambridge and the London School was perhaps the most prominent feature of the Malthusian revival, but even in

---

'Law of Diminishing Returns' is treated as a grave menace perpetually overhanging the world, 'increasing returns' appear only as an occasional happy incident, without the title of 'Law' or even the dignity of capital letters" (*ibid.*, pp. 224–228).

[15] Three years later another Cambridge economist repeated Wright's general thesis in a shorter, more popular version: P. Sargant Florence, *Over-Population: Theory and Statistics* (London: Paul, Trench, Trubner, 1926).

[16] Joseph A. Schumpeter, "Keynes, the Economist," in Seymour E. Harris, ed., *The New Economics: Keynes's Influence on Theory and Public Policy* (New York: Knopf, 1947), p. 81, n. 10.

[17] Paul A. Samuelson, "The General Theory," *ibid.*, p. 154.

England it was not restricted to this. The international range of Malthusian works in this period can be symbolized by one on the population of England, written in French by the dean of Greek statisticians, and published in Italy: A. Andreades, *La population anglaise avant, pendant et après la grande guerre* (Ferrara, 1922). In Germany, a half dozen doctoral dissertations—always an accurate barometer of trends in university thought—were written in reappraisal of Malthus and his period.[18] Even France, the country whose fertility had declined first and farthest—where pronatalist sentiment was very much in evidence before 1914 and after, say, 1930—fell in with the Malthusian trend of the 1920s at least negatively. As Wolfe has noted: "Curiously, the French, who before the war were so prolific of popular and propagandistic publications on population, have since the war published relatively little."[19] At the World Population Conference of 1927, two out of the six sessions were devoted entirely to discussing the relation between population and resources, and the main speakers showed a very heavy preponderance of one or another version of Malthusianism.[20]

How widespread this revival became can be indicated by a chronological listing of some of the more important titles in various countries, with an occasional telling quotation:

[18] Jessie Marburg, *Die sozialökonomischen Grundlagen der englischen Armenpolitik im ersten Drittel des 19. Jahrhunderts* (Karlsruhe, 1912); Alice Guhrauer, *Beiträge zur Malthus-Literatur* (Erlangen, 1917); Alice Flatow, *Die Entwicklung und Wandlung der Malthus'eschen Ansichten in den sechs Auflagen seines Essays* (Frankfort, 1924); Ursula Schian, *Die englischen Optimisten in ihren Bevölkerungstheorien* (Giessen, 1926); Hilde Nebelung, *Die Malthus'sche Bevölkerungslehre: Versuch einer Interpretation* (Cologne, 1928); Fritz Baum, *Ueber den praktischen Malthusianismus, Neo-Malthusianismus und Sozialdarwinismus* (Leipzig, 1928).

[19] A. B. Wolfe, "The Population Problem since the World War: A Survey of Literature and Research," *Journal of Political Economy*, 36:5 (October, 1928), 529–559; 36:6 (December, 1928), 662–685; and 37:1 (February, 1929), 87–120, at p. 537. This very thorough survey documents the thesis that the postwar generation rediscovered Malthus.

[20] Margaret Sanger, ed., *Proceedings of the World Population Conference* (London, 1927).

Edward Isaacson, *The Malthusian Limit: Theory of a Possible Static Condition for the Human Race* (London, 1912). The following year, this was published in the United States under the title *The New Morality*.

Siegfried Budge, "Zum Malthus-Problem: Eine Antikritik," *Archiv für Sozialwissenschaft und Sozialpolitik*, 37 (1913), 930–941: The Malthusian law "operated in the past, operates in the present, and, according to our best estimate, will continue to operate in the future."

Warren S. Thompson, *Population: A Study of Malthusianism* (New York, 1915): "For the great majority of the people of the Western world, the pressure on the means of subsistence is the determining factor in the size of the family. . . . [If the rural-urban trend continues] population cannot continue to increase at its present rate without being more and more subjected to actual want of food" (pp. 156 ff.).

George H. Knibbs, "Mathematical Theory of Population," in Commonwealth of Australia, *Census 1911*, Vol. 1, Appendix A (1917).

Paul Mombert, *Die Gefahr einer Uebervölkerung für Deutschland* (Tübingen, 1919): "During the next years and decades [Germany's] most important and most urgent problem will be how much leeway our economy will offer with respect to food production and what consequences this will have on the size of the population and the standard of living."

Edward M. East, *Mankind at the Crossroads* (New York, 1923): "Manifestly, the only relief for the situation is to call a halt on population growth at a point . . . where there is no intense struggle for mere existence; and the only means of accomplishing this feat which recommends itself to the ethically inclined is conscious, deliberate control of fecundity. . . . Enhanced efficiency and prudent conservation of resources are means of bringing about increased happiness only if numbers remain constant" (p. 344).

G. Talbot Griffith, *Population Problems of the Age of Malthus* (Cambridge, 1926), one of two studies of this subject published in this year. The second, M. C. Buer, *Health, Wealth, and Population in the Early Days of the Industrial Revolution* (London, 1926).

A. B. Wolfe, "The Optimum Size of Population," in Louis I. Dublin, ed., *Population Problems in the United States and Canada* (New York, 1926), pp. 63–76: An essential part of the problem "is to get people to see they are confronted with a condition, not a theory. . . . The American farmer will not soon believe that overpopulation is imminent."

Edward Alsworth Ross, *Standing Room Only?* (New York, 1927): "Utilizing the life-saving means now available, a flourishing and enlightened modern population which welcomed large families might grow from its own loins at a rate which would double it in twenty years" (p. 11).

George H. Knibbs, *The Shadow of the World's Future: or the Earth's Population Possibilities and the Consequences of the Present Rate of Increase of the Earth's Inhabitants* (London, 1928): "For computers it may be of interest to note that an increase of even one percent leads to large numbers. . . . The . . . number of earths necessary to provide bodies, each of 100 lb. weight, for the population from a couple, increasing for ten thousand years continually at the rate of one percent per annum, would be no less than . . . 248,293,-000,000,000,000,000" (p. 49, n. 1).

When the second edition of Bonar's classic study of Malthus was published in 1924 (the first edition had appeared in 1885), the author remarked in the introduction that "there are signs that the twentieth century will give [Malthus] a fair hearing."[21] In 1926, developing this theme, Bonar pub-

[21] James Bonar, *Malthus and His Work* (New York: Macmillan, 1924).

lished a whimsical little essay in which Malthus' shade faces a present-day critic and puts him to rout.[22]

Although Keynes played an important part in developing this climate of opinion, it is too much to say that he "unleashed the Malthusian bogey" through a spirit of "recklessness." No one man was responsible for the large degree of international agreement that this superficial survey indicates.

Even the differences between Cambridge and the London School, when they were not exaggerated by polemical enthusiasm, were differences within a common Malthusian framework. Writing in *Economica*, the Journal of Exorcism, Robertson stated:

> Whether our standards were rising slightly or falling slightly between 1900 and 1910, there can be no doubt that they were miserably lower than we should have wished, and equally little doubt, surely, that they would have been higher if there had been fewer of us. To deny that in such circumstances we were suffering from the pressure of population seems to me to be trifling with words.[23]

Similarly, Cannan's critical review of Thompson's first book began with a flat, uncompromising endorsement of its fundamental thesis. He quoted a long passage to the effect that the economic prerequisites to the unprecedented expansion of the European peoples were disappearing, because, among other reasons, the improvement in transportation and agriculture probably could not be duplicated. "I should like to suggest," Cannan remarked, "that the next bishop who proposes to recommend unreasoning multiplication as a universal rule of human conduct should take this passage from Dr. Thompson's book as his text. The predictions which it contains may be premature, but they cannot be erroneous in any other sense."[24] Similarly, in remonstrating with

[22] James Bonar, "The Malthusiad: Fantasia Economica," *The Tables Turned* (London: King, 1926), pp. 52–61.

[23] Robertson, *op. cit.*

[24] Edwin Cannan, review of W. S. Thompson, *Population: A Study of Malthusianism, Economic Journal,* 26:102 (June, 1926), 218–222.

Wright for his failure to adopt the terminology of the optimum theory, Robbins pointed out that the two views could be adapted to each other: "Nothing in the optimum theory precludes insistence on the dangers of overpopulation." More fundamentally: "It is one of the great unsolved questions of our modern world whether, with our unprecedented degree of taxation, we *can* save enough to keep pace with the growth of population."[25] The contrast with the stagnation theory of the following decade could hardly be more marked.

If the term *neo-Malthusianism* had not already been appropriated by the advocates of birth control, it would be an apt designation of the school (whether that in England or its Continental analogue) that developed the concept of population optimum. Certainly, neither Malthus nor Cannan would have found this a happy link, but then Malthus was also a firm and principled opponent of birth control; in either sense, "neo-Malthusianism" denotes not a continuation of Malthus' ideas but their projection to a new level.

At best, Malthus' principle could be called no more than a first approximation: population tends to increase by a geometrical ratio and food by an arithmetical ratio; therefore, population tends to press against the means of subsistence. Like all other economists of his day, Malthus was describing the workings of a "natural law"; but he introduced a notion of policy when, in the second edition of the *Essay*, he added "moral restraint" to the "positive" (that is, nondeliberate) checks on population growth. Supposedly, this

[25] Lionel Robbins, "The Optimum Theory of Population," in T. E. Gregory and Hugh Dalton, eds., *London Essays in Economics in Honour of Edwin Cannan* (London: Routledge, 1927), pp. 103–134. This tendency to bring together into a unified theory the Malthusianism of Cambridge and the optimum population of the London School was, of course, greater outside these two opposed strongholds. For example, Mukerjee wrote, "It is obvious that human numbers tend to approach the equilibrium density and also that the optimum density is much smaller than the equilibrium density." Radhakamal Mukerjee, "Optimum and Over-Population," *Indian Journal of Economics*, 10:3 (January, 1930), 407–421. That is, he accepted fully the Malthusian doctrine as formulated in the 1920s, and expressed this view in the language of the London School, as Robbins wanted Wright to do.

line of thought might have continued in the direction of specifying the point at which the pressure of population on the means of subsistence becomes critical—that is, toward a first statement of population optimum. In what Robbins termed the "most penetrating and comprehensive" statement of the theory of optimum population, in Chapter 3 of *Wealth,* Cannan built the argument parallel to the development of his own thought on the subject, from *Elementary Political Economy* (1888) to the first edition of *Wealth* (1914). The chapter begins with a rejection of Malthus' "misleading mathematical jingles," and continues by amending the law of diminishing returns in agriculture to include both expanding and diminishing returns in both agriculture and the rest of the economy.[26] That is, the polemics against the specific crudities of Malthus' theory overlaid a general agreement with its fundament.

More generally, the dominance of Malthusian ideas in this period can be demonstrated by showing how they permeated certain of the works of other avowed opponents. Reuter, for example, termed the first edition of the *Essay* "a brief, ephemeral political tract." After its success "had somewhat unduly inflated the author's self-esteem," Malthus wrote his second edition, a "labored statistical and historical afterthought."[27] In spite of his low estimate of Malthus, however, Reuter accepted Malthusianism virtually in toto. The principal arguments he cited against it were that conservatives welcomed it as a weapon against social reform (but this use of the doctrine had nothing to do with its validity) and that it was a truism.[28] A population might

[26] Edwin Cannan, *Wealth: A Brief Explanation of the Causes of Economic Welfare* (3rd ed.; London: King, 1928).

[27] Edward B. Reuter, *Population Problems* (Philadelphia: Lippincott, 1923), pp. 62–63. It was on the basis of such judgments that the London School pronounced Reuter's work an "admirably objective book"—Dalton's review in *Economica,* 5:13 (March, 1925), 100–102.

[28] "It was perhaps always a matter of universal knowledge that the number of people is likely to increase in the presence of sufficient food to support increased numbers[!] . . . Little, if anything, more than a solemn statement of the obvious . . ." (Reuter, *op. cit.,* pp. 61, 69).

double in twenty-five years if it were not for the "checks to population increase" that make this rate impossible. In former times, population increase was checked by famines, "but the limitation of population by shortages of food, if less spectacular, is no less real" (pp. 115–125).

Similarly, in his *Population Problem*, Carr-Saunders combined a curt rejection of Malthus with an essentially Malthusian analysis. The central argument of the book is that the power of human reproductivity is "very great." "Nearly all discussions of questions of quantity [tend] to underestimate the power of increase." The results of this "huge" human fecundity are kept in check by war and disease and, since these are not generally sufficient, by conscious restrictions—delayed marriage, abstention from intercourse, abortion, infanticide, birth control. Not only European culture but *all* primitive cultures include customs whose primary function is to restrict population increase.[29]

By 1934, the hundredth anniversary of Malthus' death, the revival was over. In commemorative articles, Bonar retained all his lifelong enthusiasm for his master; but Keynes wrote, "Malthus' name has been immortalized by his *Principle of Population*, and the brilliant intuitions of his more far-reaching *Principle of Effective Demand* have been forgotten."[30] Another commemorative article combined the hope that "there should be no overpopulation" with one

[29] A. M. Carr-Saunders, *The Population Problem: A Study in Human Evolution* (Oxford: Clarendon, 1922), p. 291 and passim. A short book published three years later, essentially a popular summary of the earlier work, differed from it in that it resolved this contradiction by acknowledging Carr-Saunders' debt to the *Essay*, both symbolically, with a photograph of Malthus as the frontispiece, and more fundamentally. In spite of all the contributions that have been made to demographic theory since the *Essay*, "it is now admitted that, insofar as the essential features of his point of view are concerned, Malthus' view was correct." A. M. Carr-Saunders, *Population* (London: Oxford University Press, 1925), p. 23.

[30] James Bonar, C. R. Fay, and J. M. Keynes, "A Commemoration of Thomas Robert Malthus," *Economic Journal*, 45:2 (June, 1935), 221–234.

that the "increase of population should not be on too low a scale."[31]

## Keynes as an Underpopulationist

After the focus of Keynes' enthusiasm for Malthus shifted from the *Essay* to the *Principles of Political Economy*, from the principle of population to the principle of effective demand, various disciples and critics traced this momentous development in economic theory.[32] In 1929, when Lloyd George promised to reduce unemployment by expenditures on public works, Keynes discussed this pledge wholly within the classical framework. His *Treatise on Money*, published in 1930, was also in the classical tradition, but it contained one short "isolated insight," as Alan Sweezy has termed it: "The population [of Great Britain] will soon cease to grow. Our habits and our institutions keep us, in spite of all claims to the contrary, a thrifty people saving some 10 percent of our income. In such conditions one would anticipate with confidence that, if Great Britain were a closed system, the natural rate of interest would fall rapidly."[33]

In an essay also written in 1930, Keynes rejected the pessimism of his "magnificent episode" as "wildly mistaken":

> We are suffering just now from a bad attack of economic pessimism. It is common to hear people say that the epoch of enormous economic progress which characterized the 19th century is over; that the rapid improvement in the standard of life is now going to slow down—at any rate in Great Britain; that a decline

[31] Charles Balás, "Malthus and the Population Problems of Today," *Journal de la Société Hongroise de Statistique*, 13:4 (1935), 373–409.

[32] For one interesting analysis of Malthus' influence on this element of Keynesian theory, worked out by comparing passages on effective demand in the works of the two men, see James J. O'Leary, "Malthus and Keynes," *Journal of Political Economy*, 50:6 (December, 1942), 901–919.

[33] J. M. Keynes, *Treatise on Money*, p. 188; quoted by Alan Sweezy, "Declining Investment Opportunity," in Harris, *op. cit.*, p. 428.

in prosperity is more likely than an improvement in the decade which lies ahead of us. I believe this is a wildly mistaken interpretation of what is happening to us. We are suffering not from the rheumatics of old age but from the growing-pains of overrapid change.[34]

This curious call to optimism thus formed the bridge between his Malthusian pessimism of the 1920s and his underpopulationist pessimism of the 1930s.

The year 1933 seems to have been a crucial one in the development of Keynes' thought,[35] and in 1935 *The General Theory* appeared. According to classical theory, since every supply elicits its own demand, local crises are checked by the automatic adjustment between supply and demand; thus, a *general* economic crisis—a general fall of prices to below cost, general overproduction, general unemployment—is impossible by the very nature of the economic system. The automatic circuit posited by Say's Law, however, is completed according to Keynes' new theory only in the special case when planned savings and planned investments are equal; in all other cases, a portion of the potential purchasing power is siphoned off into idle savings, or "hoards." It is particularly in wealthy countries (that is, in countries with an "incipient decline" in population) that investment tends to be inadequate, for two reasons: because a smaller proportion of the national income is consumed and thus a larger proportion is left to be invested, and because the larger capital stock means that new investment opportunities are more difficult to find. Extended over time, as the stock of capital grows in any one country, the possibilities for new investment are less; or, in Keynes' terms, other things being equal, the marginal efficiency of capital is the lower, the greater the existing amount of capital.[36]

---

[34] Keynes, *Essays in Persuasion,* p. 358.
[35] Cf. Lawrence R. Klein, *The Keynesian Revolution* (New York: Macmillan, 1947), pp. 38–40.
[36] Keynes fully acknowledged his debt to Malthus with respect to effective demand, but he nowhere noted that this portion of his theory is highly reminiscent of Marx. According to Marx, because the value of any commodity is based on the human labor expended on it, as the ratio of capital to labor

Why should this long-term decline in the marginal efficiency of capital not have been operative during the nineteenth century? Because, Keynes wrote, "the growth of population and of invention, the opening-up of new lands, the state of confidence and the frequency of war over the average of (say) each decade seem to have been sufficient."[37] In the twentieth century, however, in countries with more or less adequate capital stocks and populations approaching a stationary level, the incentive to private investment has tended to disappear, and the state has had to take over some of the functions of the entrepreneur.[38]

Two years after the publication of *The General Theory*, in a lecture delivered to the Eugenics Society—thus specially prepared for a Malthusian audience—Keynes attempted to link this theory with his earlier views on population. In an era of declining population, he wrote, the demand for capital tends to be below what is expected, and the pessimistic atmosphere that may result may have "very disastrous" short-term effects. Over the period from 1860 to 1913, there had been an increase in capital by 2.7 times, required in roughly equal parts by the rising standard of living and the increasing population; but with a declining population it would be necessary to alter institutions so that a smaller percentage of income would be saved, and to reduce the rate of interest sufficiently to make entrepreneurial activity more attractive.

We have now learned that we have another devil at our elbow at least as fierce as the Malthusian—namely the devil of unemployment escaping through the breakdown of effective demand. . . . When devil P. of Population is chained up, we are free of one menace; but we

---

increases in any society, the value of its total social product tends to decrease and the rate of profit tends to fall to zero. Keynes repeated essentially the same theory in different terms, even to the point of tentatively reviving the generally discarded labor theory of value. *The General Theory of Employment, Interest, and Money* (New York: Harcourt, Brace, 1935), pp. 213–214. Cf. S. S. Alexander, "Mr. Keynes and Mr. Marx," *Review of Economic Studies*, 7:2 (February, 1940), 123–135.

[37] *The General Theory*, p. 307.

[38] *Ibid.*, pp. 220–221.

are more exposed to the other devil U. of Unemployed Resources than we were before.[39]

Thus, as he stated specifically, Keynes did *not* reject the essential argument of Malthus' principle of population, but rather opposed it to a contrary principle that must also be considered. Malthus' model was basically correct and still relevant, but too simple. A stationary population (when he analyzed the difficulties, it was usually—as in the title of the article—"a declining population") does facilitate a rise in the standard of living, but only on condition that the *possible* increase    consumption per head takes place. The interesting implications of this point, however, Keynes did not develop, either in this article or elsewhere.

As in *The Economic Consequences of the Peace,* so in *The General Theory,* Keynes' primary concern was with another problem; but, again, his few *"obiter dicta"* on the significance of population trends started a cycle of articles and books more specifically demographic in emphasis. These began with reviews of *The General Theory* itself. Population, Hicks wrote, is Keynes' "strongest card," and he continued—

It does become very evident, when one thinks of it, that the expectation of a continually expanding market, made possible by an increasing population, is a fine thing for keeping up the spirits of entrepreneurs. With increasing population, investment can go roaring ahead, even if invention is rather stupid; increasing population is therefore actually favorable to employment. It is actually easier to employ an expanding population than a contracting one, whatever arithmetic would suggest—at least this is so when expansion or contraction is expected, as we assume generally to be the case.

Consider the situation which is likely to arise when the population of this country [Great Britain] is declining, and the population of most of those countries with which she is in close trading connections are stationary or tending to decline. The time will come, so it already seems likely, when this tendency, and its probable future continuance, will not be the secret only of a few economists, but will be fully realized by the mass of the public. In these circumstances the incentive to construct houses, ships, factories, all sorts of capital equipment will be depressed by the anticipation that capital is wearing out and population dying off at convergent rates. Investment will proceed only with great difficulty, and employment will be low, in spite of the fact that population may have already declined in the past. . . . This population point is enough in itself to establish the high significance of Mr. Keynes' theory of long-period unemployment.[40]

The ramifications of this passage can be examined most conveniently in terms of Reddaway's *Economics of a Declining Population*, which in relation to Keynes is analogous to Wright's earlier *Population*.[41] Reddaway began with a summary of Enid Charles' "classic study" of British population trends.[42] According to her "more reasonable forecast," the

[40] J. R. Hicks, "Mr. Keynes's Theory of Employment," *Economic Journal*, 46:182 (June, 1936), 238–253.

[41] W. B. Reddaway, *The Economics of a Declining Population* (London: Allen & Unwin, 1939). True, the link of the earlier book to Keynes' Malthusian phase was more direct: Keynes was the editor of the series in which Wright's volume appeared, and he wrote a preface for this particular work. Moreover, Wright could have filled in Keynes' allusions to population theory even without his teacher's personal guidance, for they were in the Malthusian frame of reference. Reddaway had to combine a good deal of interpretation with his exposition, but in the main *The Economics of a Declining Population* can also be taken as Keynes' ideas on demography, developed and expounded by one of his students.

[42] Charles had projected the population of England and Wales on the basis of three postulates with respect to fertility and mortality: (a) that fertility and mortality would continue at the 1933 rate; (b) that fertility and mortality would continue to fall as they had in recent years; and (c) that fertility would rise to the 1931 level, or to about 10 percent higher than in 1933, while mortality would continue to fall. In a volume published three years later, the substance of the memorandum was republished but the estimate based on the third assumption—the one closest to the actual trend—was omitted altogether. Enid Charles, *The Effect of Present Trends in Fertility and Mortality upon the Future Population of England and Wales and upon Its Age Composition*

population of England and Wales would start to decline in 1939 and would be reduced to one-tenth its size over the next century. Reddaway's book was published in 1939, four years after the low point in British fertility, when the actual population was larger than the upper limit in Charles' forecast. The reasons that, even so, he accepted her argumentation are worth quoting as an example of why demographers held to this view so long:

> The recorded number of births has each year been in excess of the estimates, since these assumed no rise in fertility above the 1933 level. . . . However, we must not make too much of this discrepancy. . . . It is small [and] easily . . . shown to be a temporary phenomenon. The explanation is simply that the years in question had the benefit not only of the "normal" number of births, but also of the arrears accumulated during the depression. . . . The significant fact is that even with this temporary aid the fertility rate rose so little, and did not nearly reach the 1931 level (pp. 32–33).

Reddaway (and with him many other analysts) concluded that it was the making up of the "arrears" that had to be depreciated—because an increase in fertility so based was limited by the number of marriageable couples or childless families. However, if a rise in fertility can be controverted as a consequence of the sharp rise in the marriage rate, should it not follow that the very low fertility during the years that these marriages were being postponed should also be discounted for a long-term analysis? Moreover, the postponement of marriage and of the first child can reasonably be regarded as personally the most onerous of the relevant changes occasioned by the depression. Thus, when natality began to rise because of an increased marriage rate, this might have raised the question whether other causes of the

(London: Royal Economic Society, Memorandum No. 55, December, 1935); "The Effect of Present Trends in Fertility and Mortality upon the Future Population of Great Britain and upon Its Age Composition," in Lancelet Hogben, ed., *Political Arithmetic: A Symposium of Population Studies* (New York: Macmillan, 1938), pp. 73–105. Cf. above, p. 6.

low birth rate might not also soon be mitigated. That is to say, the distinction between the secular trend and its intensification by the depression could not be drawn merely by extrapolation of the predepression curve.

Having posited a "declining" population, Reddaway began his analysis of its economic significance with a discussion of unemployment, which he divided into frictional and cyclical. As in Keynes' system, "it is the rule, rather than the exception, for there to be an appreciable volume of general unemployment" (p. 89). Typically, a declining population results in a decline in capital outlays, but (in an important addendum to Keynes' thesis) this effect is mitigated by the fact that, for such important commodities as homes, the consuming unit is not the individual but the family. Since families are smaller, their number may continue to rise even after the number of persons has begun to decline. Thus, demand for new housing was an effective one even during the depression, for those with relatively fixed money incomes enjoyed a considerable rise in real income (pp. 101–106). Nevertheless, "unless special measures are taken to maintain it, the volume of capital outlay undertaken on behalf of private interests is likely to fall. Moreover, it will be of a more precarious nature than in the past, more sensitive to falls in the industrial barometer" (p. 110).

> The problem is essentially a "man-made" one, which human ingenuity should be capable of solving. Our difficulty is not to overcome the niggardliness of nature, but so to organize ourselves that we can make use of the (relative) abundance which should be available, but seems likely somehow to elude our grasp (p. 119).

The remedies he recommended are the usual ones of Keynesian theorists, beginning with public works and ending with various modes of distributing income more widely among those who will spend it rather than save it.

While Reddaway was of the opinion that "the economic importance of population change is often grossly exaggerated" (p. 233), others have developed the relation studied in his work into a theory that the economic progress of the modern era has been based largely on its unprecedented increase of population.

One is tempted to a "population interpretation" of modern capitalism. Professor Cannan sensed it. Professor J. R. Hicks now toys with it as he wonders in a footnote at the end of his *Value and Capital* whether the "whole industrial revolution of the last centuries has been nothing else but a vast secular boom, largely induced by the unparalleled rise in population." Professor Schumpeter has little to say about population, yet perhaps the "first Schumpeter," as Dr. Innis in his review of Schumpeter's recent *Business Cycles* has playfully christened the long cycle (1787–1929), was mainly conditioned by population growth; and it may prove to be the only "Schumpeter." Modern capitalist free enterprise may prove to have been a boom enterprise, and the modern trend to something like the old mercantilism may be a trend toward institutions appropriate to an era of stationary population.[43]

To this list must be added the name of Alvin Hansen, who of all American economists has stressed most the possible consequences of a cessation of population growth.[44]

## Malthusian versus Keynesian Optimum

One might suppose that precisely demographic analysis would be relatively unsusceptible to such wide fluctuations as have taken place during the past four decades; for the units ordinarily used, such as the generation or the nation, are large, and trends can often be most meaningfully analyzed over as long a span as a century. The population pressure of the 1920s (of which one of the main symptoms, according

[43] V. W. Bladen, "Population Problems and Policies," in Chester Martin, ed., *Canada in Peace and War: Eight Studies in National Trends Since 1914* (Canadian Institute of International Affairs; Toronto: Oxford University Press, 1941), pp. 86–119, at p. 101.

[44] See in particular Alvin H. Hansen, "Economic Progress and Declining Population Growth," *American Economic Review*, Vol. 29, No. 1, Part 1 (March, 1939), pp. 1–15. Cf. above, p. 4.

to Keynes and others, was mass unemployment) did not disappear in the 1930s, and the decline in fertility so evident in the 1930s had begun in most Western countries by 1875 or before. Today, the unforecast rise in the birth rate and the greater importance (in Western thought) of the "underdeveloped areas" have occasioned another Malthusian revival; but, again, the first *could* have been forecast, and the Malthusian pressure in China or India was always there to be seen, if one but looked. Typically, Keynes spoke of "the world" only metaphorically, so that when Beveridge challenged his argument, he restricted it again to Western Europe. The Malthusians of the 1920s, with a few honorable exceptions, were provincial, and the underpopulationists of the 1930s much more so. Today, what Ralph Linton termed "most of the world" has become too important to be ignored by anyone.

The cycle, that is to say, has been one in opinion—it might even be said, one in mood. While the shift was based on a change in real conditions, the violence of the shift was totally unrelated to the secular development continuing throughout the period. On the basis of everything that we know about social change, the observed trend in the birth rate should have been analyzed in terms of an assumed eventual reversal; instead, it was extrapolated to "standing room only," or "the depopulation of Britain." Even if there had been no prior indications of the postwar baby boom, it should have been considered a real possibility; and there were such indications.

One can suppose that, if Keynes had not died in 1946, his interest in demography would have been revived by the postwar developments. If he had tried to reconcile his Malthusian and his underpopulationist phases by attempting to define optimum population unambiguously, he would have had to begin by restricting the discussion once again to an economic framework. The very word "optimum" has been an invitation to broaden the concept by introducing such factors as "general welfare," military strength, mean longevity, international trade, and even popular mood.[45] However, even if a narrow

[45] Thus, according to a League of Nations committee, "overpopulation may be said to exist not so much in actual figures as in the consciousness of the country concerned," so that a country may be overpopulated compared with one neighbor and underpopulated

economic criterion (real income per head or an approximate equivalent) is retained, one definition of the optimum population is not thereby specified. It is true, as Keynes has put it, that "when devil P. of Population is chained up, we are more exposed to devil U. of Unemployed Resources"; it is true, that is to say, that if the population of a country is at its optimum point by one economic criterion, by another it may be too small—or, better, its rate of growth may be too low. Thus, within the economic framework, there are at least two optima, a Malthusian one and a Keynesian one. The first is the population that, in terms of present or prospective technology and institutions, affords the highest standard of living per head. The second is a population growing at the rate that, in terms of . . . etc. Though it is obvious that these are not the same concept, they are often treated as though they were. Thus, as one example out of many, Forsyth summed up the interwar period's argument against immigration to Australia in the cogent phrase, "the myth of open spaces": Australia's empty land was largely uninhabitable desert.[46] The postwar proponents of immigration have answered this in part within the same framework (by pointing to the potentialities of irrigation, for example), but principally in Keynesian terms: a rapidly growing population makes for a healthy economy.

The Malthusian optimum is concerned with *level* of population, the Keynesian with the rate of *growth* of population. The confusion between the two, moreover, is often compounded by the tendency of writers on this subject to extrapolate one, but only one, of the relevant factors. As Kingsley Davis has put it—

A startling fact about the controversy is that both sides agree rather well on what is *theoretically* possible. The

compared with another. Fergus Chalmers Wright, *Population and Peace: A Survey of International Opinion on Claims for Relief from Population Pressure* ("International Studies Conference, Peaceful Change"; Paris: International Institute of Intellectual Cooperation, League of Nations, 1939), p. 80.

[46] W. D. Forsyth, *The Myth of Open Spaces: Australian, British and World Trends of Population and Migration* (Melbourne: Melbourne University Press, 1942).

belief of the Mather side that science has the *capacity* to work miracles of food and industrial production is not seriously challenged by the other side. Indeed, who could challenge it? There is no way to determine any inherent limits to science. On the other hand, the Vogt-Osborn contention that population has the *capacity* to grow beyond the point of permanent or decent support is also admitted. Indeed, given enough time, any continued rate of population increase, no matter how small, would use up the entire earth's substance, and the current global rate would do it quickly.[47]

In addition to these two factors, population and resources-technology, there is a third, institutional structure, which again may or may not be extrapolated to some supposed future state. Thus, the issue between Keynes and Beveridge, as has been noted, was largely terminological; with the actual social conditions, Keynes considered Britain overpopulated, while for Beveridge—with optimum conditions—it was not. On the other hand, Reddaway (following Keynes' lead) contrasted the "man-made" problem of a social system that flourishes only with a growing population with the "niggardliness of nature" that impedes such growth.

The concept of optimum population can be clarified only when those who use it stop trying to weight the definition in order to support their particular views. In an ultimate sense, all of the relevant terms can be viewed as absolutes; in a practical sense, none of them is. Niggardly nature, population growth, and the capitalist economy are all subject to policy decisions; all must be treated as independent variables. The resultant range of ambiguity of the term "optimum population," however, is then rather wide. From the Malthusian and Keynesian frames of reference we get two optima. With either one of them, we may posit either the actual or an optimum technology, and this gives us four optima. With each of these

[47] Kingsley Davis, "The Controversial Future of the Underdeveloped Areas," in Paul K. Hatt, ed., *World Population and Future Resources* (New York: American Book Co., 1952), pp. 14–15.

four, again, we may posit either the actual or an optimum institutional structure, and this gives us eight optima.

Principled opponents of birth control, who tend to define the physiological maximum as the optimum rate of population growth, extrapolate the latest scientific advances to the underdeveloped areas of the world. That is, population growth is "natural" and the other factors must be adjusted to it. The century-long dispute between Malthusians and Marxists is based on a similar confusion, though here the emphasis is more on the institutional framework than on technology; and natives of colonies or of new countries with a colonial past also tend to ascribe their population pressure to the maladministration of the imperial power. If both the institutional framework and the technology are optimum, then—at least according to some theorists—the optimum population is infinitely large. In 1947, at the first session of the United Nations Population Commission, the Soviet delegate asserted "more or less the following":

> I would consider it barbaric for the Commission to contemplate a limitation of marriages or of legitimate births, and this for any country whatsoever, at any period whatsoever. With an adequate social organization it is possible to face any increase in population.[48]

The dilemma is not resolved by abandoning, as Myrdal has proposed, the concept of optimum population—"one of the most sterile ideas" ever developed in economics.[49] When Myrdal, as one member of a government population commission, recommended means of increasing Sweden's birth rate, he did so in the belief that the population of the country ought to be larger. Like all moderns, he is concerned with policy; that is, he has some vague, implicit notion of optimum population. With this name or another, the concept will remain, and also the task of clarifying it.

[48] Cited by Alfred Sauvy, *Théorie générale de la population* (Paris: Presses Universitaires de France, 1952), Vol. 1, p. 174.

[49] Gunnar Myrdal, *Population: A Problem for Democracy* (Cambridge: Harvard University Press, 1940), pp. 26–27.

# MARX VERSUS MALTHUS:
## THE SYMBOLS AND THE MEN

In a number of recent discussions of how to cope with population pressure in underdeveloped countries, Malthus and Marx have been taken as symbols of the two principal alternatives open to policy-makers. For example, Alfred Sauvy, the dean of French demographers, has used the opposition between these two figures to structure an analysis of the underdeveloped world.[1] At a more popular level, Raymond Aron wrote a stimulating article entitled "Asia—Between Malthus and Marx."[2] Communists have mounted an obsessive attack on "Malthusians," defined broadly enough to include a wide range of Western social commentators.[3] A compilation of Marx's works on Malthus, published in London and New York by the Communist press, was introduced with the following statement: "If the social struggles of the early nineteenth century were essentially summed up in the controversy between Malthus and Ricardo, those of our own time are perhaps not unfairly summed up in that between Malthusians and Marxists."[4]

Does this opposition between Marx and Malthus accurately represent the views of the two men? Presenting them as polar opposites began, of course, during Marx's own lifetime,[5] so

[1] "Les pays sous-développés: Marx ou Malthus?" *Théorie générale de la population* (Paris: Presses Universitaires de France, 1952), Vol. 1, Chap. 18.

[2] *Encounter*, August, 1954.

[3] See below, pp. 113–119.

[4] Ronald L. Meek, ed., *Marx and Engels on Malthus* (New York: International Publishers, 1955), p. 47.

[5] For analyses of some of the earlier works, see James Bonar, *Malthus and His Work* (New York: Macmillan, 1924), pp. 388 ff.; Samuel M. Levin, "Marx vs. Malthus," *Papers of the Michigan Academy of Arts and Letters*, 22 (Ann Arbor: University of Michigan Press, 1937), 243–258.

that the current mode has at least the support of a long tradition. But one must still question its validity. The common designation of Malthus as a "reactionary"—that is, the other pole from a Marxian "progressive"—ignores important parallels between the two men, not only in their economic analyses but even in their social philosophies. Specifically, when Marx's criticisms of Malthus' principle of population are examined, it becomes evident that neither Marx himself nor any Marxist has developed a population theory to replace the Malthusian one they rejected. The appealing simplicity of a Marx-Malthus axis as a framework for population analysis has been achieved by amalgamating divergent and even contradictory theories and policies into "Malthus" and into "Marx," so that once the two names have recalled to progressives their faith that social planning is superior to a laissez-faire system, "Malthusian" proponents of family-planning are attacked by "Marxians" who believe that the rational control of human fertility is iniquitous.

## Parallels between Malthus and Marx

That Malthus wrote his *Essay on the Principle of Population* in a political context is a commonplace. In its very title, as we have noted earlier, the first edition was directed against two of the more extravagant of the eighteenth-century perfectibilists—Condorcet, who foresaw not only the complete abolition of war and disease but the indefinite prolongation of human life, and Godwin, who looked forward to the wholly rational society where no one would work more than half an hour a day. In any case, the dispute would have probably been largely in political rather than scientific terms; for Malthus' "principle of population" was both a convenient rationalization for resolute defenders of the status quo and a block to the facile millennium of the Jacobins. "It is only to be expected that the early socialists would be hostile to the Malthusian theory. From Dr. Charles Hall . . . to Marx, there is a clear-cut repudiation. At bottom they have a different rating of humanity and human institutions, different social and political aims, and a different expectation of the future."[6]

The division along political lines was not, however, either necessary or complete. Even Cobbett, who later termed Malthus' population theory "infamous and really diabolical," a "mixture of madness and blasphemy," began by endorsing it —before it had been used in the debate over the poor law.[7] And on the other side, Nassau Senior, whom Marx attacked in language as strong as his usual epithets to characterize Malthus, was also among the first to challenge the *Essay*.

In any case, Marx might well have stood above the usual political division. He did not typically defend the views of the men he and Engels dubbed "utopians"; and the theory of such an economist as Ricardo, Malthus' good friend, he treated with respect. His total rejection of Malthus is remarkable, moreover, for on some fundamental issues the difference between these two was smaller than that between Marx and the classical school as a whole. This is particularly so on the key question of whether a general glut can develop in a capitalist economy. By the classical theory of the market, the very production of goods distributes the power to purchase them; and local disturbances, the consequence of having produced particular goods for which there is no demand, are adjusted automatically through a change in prices and so do not accumulate into an over-all disruption of the system. A general crisis, which for Marx was capitalism's inevitable end, was thus impossible. The only thinker in the main line of nineteenth-century economics who recognized the possibility of general underconsumption was Malthus.

"It is a most important error," Malthus wrote, "to couple the passion for expenditure and the passion for accumulation together, as if they were of the same nature." Manufacturers

---

[6] H. L. Beales, "The Historical Context of the Essay on Population," in D. V. Glass, ed., *Introduction to Malthus* (New York: Wiley, 1953), pp. 1–24. For further evidence that pre-Marxist socialists generally repudiated Malthus, see United Nations, *The Determinants and Consequences of Population Trends,* Population Study No. 17 (New York, 1955), pp. 32–33.

[7] See Herman Ausubel, "William Cobbett and Malthusianism," *Journal of the History of Ideas,* 13:2 (April, 1952), 250–256.

and merchants "produce very largely and consume sparingly," for their whole way of life induces them to live ascetically and to accumulate more capital. But if luxuries are manufactured and not consumed, then the workers who produce them will be thrown out of work and will be unable to buy even necessities; and the underconsumption will become general. To prevent this, "there must be a considerable class of persons who have both the will and the power to consume more material wealth than they produce, or the mercantile classes could not continue profitably to produce so much more than they consume." These unproductive consumers are the landlords and their servants of various types, and this seemingly parasitic class is thus seen to serve the function of keeping the economy in a healthy state. "A country such as our own, which has been rich and populous, would, with too parsimonious habits, infallibly become poor and comparatively unpeopled."[8]

How important underconsumption is in Marx's theory of capitalist crises is a matter of dispute even among Marxian economists,[9] but all agree that, while less important in his system than the long-run fall in the rate of profit, the tendency to produce more than could be consumed was also a significant factor in his view of capitalist development. For orthodox Ricardians, on the contrary, the continuous accumulation of capital was an unmixed good, leading only to a

[8] Malthus, *Principles of Political Economy* (2nd ed.; New York: Kelley, 1951), Book 2, Chap. 1, Sections 3, 9.

[9] Sweezy writes concerning this: "It could be maintained that Marx regarded underconsumption as one aspect, but on the whole not a very important aspect, of the crisis problem. This appears to be the opinion of Dobb, and there is no doubt much to back it up. Another view is possible, however, namely, that in these scattered passages [which Sweezy had analyzed in detail] Marx was giving advance notice of a line of reasoning which, if he had lived to complete his theoretical work, would have been of primary importance in the overall picture of the capitalist economy; . . . and, on the whole, it seems to me the more reasonable of the two alternatives." Paul M. Sweezy, *The Theory of Capitalist Development: Principles of Marxian Political Economy* (New York: Oxford University Press, 1942), p. 178. Cf. Maurice Dobb, *Political Economy and Capitalism* (London: Routledge, 1937), pp. 118–121; and *Studies in the Development of Capitalism* (London: Routledge, 1947), Chaps. 6–8.

higher standard of living for all. However, in the few places where he discussed Malthus' concept of effective demand, Marx gave him scant praise for having abrogated Say's Law. On the contrary, his economic theory was interpreted as a rationalization of his reactionary politics:

> Malthus represents the interest of the industrial bourgeoisie only to the extent that it is identical with the interest of the landlords, the aristocracy—that is to say, against the mass of the people, the proletariat. But when these interests diverge and are opposed to one another, then he puts himself on the side of the aristocracy against the bourgeoisie, as in his defense of the "unproductive worker."[10]

Malthus' defense of the unproductive consumer derived indeed from a fundamentally different appreciation of the role of the aristocracy in English society, but it derived also from a significant improvement—in Marx's view—on the classical theory of the market. For Marx, however, it was less important that Malthus had analyzed the working of the economy "correctly" than that he had drawn "reactionary" political conclusions from this analysis.[11]

The difference between Malthus and Marx is not that one accepted misery and vice as inevitable and the other railed against them; the difference lies in the means by which they believed misery might be overcome. According to Marx, the

[10] Marx, *Theorien über den Mehrwert* (3rd ed.; Stuttgart: Dietz, 1919), Vol. 2:1, pp. 306–307.

[11] Inevitably, a Marxist has gone beyond Marx and declared that since Malthus was right for the wrong reasons, he was not right. In his attack on Ricardo's theory, according to Erich Roll, Malthus insisted on "the possibility of economic dislocations for reasons inherent in the capitalist system." The "main purpose" of that attack, however, "was to defend the unproductive consumer. Historically, therefore, it was reactionary. Malthus . . . seems to have aspired to a sort of balance between Whig-aristocrat and primitive industrial-bourgeois elements at a time when a complete victory of the latter was already inevitable. For this reason, Ricardo's theory was clearly superior because it was appropriate to the direction of contemporary economic development." *A History of Economic Thought* (London: Faber and Faber, 1938), p. 203.

industrial workers would acquire from their common way of life an awareness of their common interest and, strong in this knowledge, would overthrow the capitalist system and establish a more or less unspecified substitute called "socialism." According to Malthus, on the contrary, society could be improved only by the development of individual responsibility, and he judged specific institutions according to whether or not they tended to foster such a sense of responsibility.

This was true in particular of his stand on the poor law, which excited more scurrilous comment than even his principle of population. The Speenhamland system, which assured a minimum family income to the poor irrespective of their earnings, had eventually obliterated the distinction between worker and pauper, and the ostensible protection of labor had become synonymous with its utter subordination. Malthus argued for the Poor Law of 1834, which by a surgical operation on sentimentality transferred to each worker the responsibility for his own welfare. It would be difficult to overstate the importance, whether actual or theoretical, of this shift. Family allowances like those paid under the Speenhamland system are not only a social-welfare measure but very often a good index of what Karl Mannheim has termed the "basic intention" of the state. There is hardly a better bolster to conservatism than to strengthen the family, for so long as the older generation is able to set the thought and behavior patterns of the younger generation, social change is likely to be slow. Socialist parties have usually opposed family subsidies or, at most, half-heartedly supported them; for such a policy, while it does distribute aid to the poor and is therefore good, also contradicts the fundamental trade-union tenet of equal pay for equal work.[12] Socialists have seldom noted, however, that the political effect of revoking the Speenhamland system was similarly ambiguous. The workers, told to depend on themselves, suffered for it; but this shift to a free labor market was a prerequisite to the later development of a self-conscious working class and the trade-union movement. Only when the traditionalist paternalism had been ended by

[12] Cf. below, pp. 154–158.

emphasizing the self-dependence of the common people could they indeed become self-reliant.[13]

Another important indication of Malthus' reactionary tendencies, according to Marx, was the fact that he was a curate of the Church of England, "Parson Malthus."[14] The point would be relevant if Marx had attempted to show that Malthus' ecclesiastical background introduced a consistent bias into his nontheological writings. Actually, as we noted earlier, many clergymen found his interpretation of Providence not to their liking. When Marx wrote that "an abstract law of population exists for plants and animals only,"[15] he unwittingly set the minimum level at which a Malthusian approach must be taken as valid. If much of Malthus is as unacceptable as the work of any pioneer, he remains worth studying just because of his emphasis on the fact that man *is* an animal, living in a finite world. According to Engels, offering his final tribute to his lifelong collaborator at the latter's graveside, Marx's prime virtue, similarly, had been that he stressed man's biological necessities as basic: "As Darwin discovered the law

[13] Compare the following passage from Karl Polanyi: "As long as a man had a status to hold on to, a pattern set by his kin or fellows, he could fight for it, and regain his soul. But in the case of the laborer this could happen only in one way: by his constituting himself the member of a new class. Unless he was able to make a living by his own labor, he was not a worker but a pauper. To reduce him artificially to such a condition was the supreme abomination of Speenhamland. This act of an ambiguous humanitarianism prevented laborers from constituting themselves an economic class and thus deprived them of the only means of staving off the fate to which they were doomed in the economic mill." *The Great Transformation* (New York: Rinehart, 1944), p. 99.

[14] Indeed, according to Marx, "most of the population-theory teachers are Protestant parsons . . . —Parson Wallace, Parson Townsend, Parson Malthus and his pupil, the arch-Parson Thomas Chalmers, to say nothing of the lesser reverend scribblers in this line." However, in contrast to other Protestant clergymen, who "generally contribute to the increase of population to a really unbecoming extent," Malthus "had taken the monastic vow of celibacy" (*Capital*, Chicago: Kerr, 1906, Vol. 1, pp. 675–676). That Marx did not know Malthus was a married man and the father of three children indicates that he knew rather little about the man whose character and motives he impugned.

[15] *Ibid.*, Vol. 1, p. 693.

of evolution in organic nature, so Marx discovered the law of evolution in human history: the simple fact, previously hidden under ideological growths, that human beings must first of all eat, drink, shelter and clothe themselves before they can turn their attention to politics, science, art and religion."[16]

If Malthus' social philosophy does not make him a reactionary, neither do his more specific policy recommendations. He is notorious for having opposed a poor law that had reduced free workers to pauperdom; but he is less well known for his support of the liberal measures listed in a previous chapter.[17] Malthus' main reaction to the French Revolution and especially to some of its perfectibilist ideologues was negative; and such a political sentiment, personified best in England by Burke, has ordinarily been used to define modern conservatism. On the other hand, in several respects Malthus was markedly unconservative. The answer to this contradiction, perhaps, is that for figures as complex as Malthus or Marx the usual one-dimensional continuum from Left to Right is not a useful analytical model. This point can be illustrated by making use of one of the richest and most stimulating efforts to define one end-point of this continuum, namely, Mannheim's essay on conservative thought in the early nineteenth century.[18] One important difference between progressives and conservatives, Mannheim writes, is the way they experience time: "the progressive experiences the present as the beginning of the future, while the conservative regards it simply as the latest point reached by the past." But the whole thrust of Malthus' arithmetical and geometrical progressions was to the future; and Marx, though he hypothesized the extrapolation of present trends to a future utopia, concentrated in his writing on connecting the capitalist system with its historical past. Or: "The conservatives replaced Reason with concepts such as History, Life, the Nation."

[16] Franz Mehring, *Karl Marx: The Story of His Life* (New York: Covici-Friede, 1935), p. 555.

[17] See above, pp. 39–40.

[18] Karl Mannheim, "Conservative Thought," *Essays on Sociology and Social Psychology* (New York: Oxford University Press, 1953), pp. 74–164.

Malthus, on the contrary, extended the legitimate use of reason to the family, that sanctum of traditionalist norms, while for Marx reason was indeed subsumed in an irrepressible History. Or: The conservative "starts from a concept of a whole which is not the mere sum of its parts. . . . The conservative thinks in terms of 'We' when the liberal thinks in terms of 'I.'" Marxist analysis is wholly in terms of social classes, wholes greater than the sum of the individuals that make them up; and Malthus, like all who participated in developing the theory of market relations, began his analysis with the individual consumer or individual parent.

These paradoxes could be continued, but the point has been made: political reality ordinarily has more than one dimension. This is true of the differences between Marx and Malthus and, a fortiori, of those between Marxists and Malthusians. In the radical-liberal heyday, "Left" meant toward increased personal freedom; and then it acquired an additional meaning—toward increased state control over the economy. It is now apparent, however, that these two goals do not always lie in the same direction. With respect to population control, on the contrary, the right of individual parents to decide on the size of their family, established during one of the momentous struggles of the liberal era, is now often challenged because of the state's obsessive desire for more manpower.

## Marx and Malthus on Population

In spite of these parallels between the two men, Marx rejected Malthus and his works, and did so in language strong even by his standards—"the contemptible Malthus," a "plagiarist," "a shameless sycophant of the ruling classes" who perpetrated a "sin against science," "this libel on the human race." The constant hyperbole suggests a polemical weakness: vituperation is no more a sign of strength with Marx than with any other social analyst. In order to preserve his faith in the inevitability of the socialist society, Marx found it necessary to discard Malthus' principle of population, for it undermined his entire system.

If Malthus' theory of population is correct, then I can *not* abolish this [iron law of wages] even if I abolish wage-labor a hundred times, because this law is not only paramount over the system of wage-labor but also over *every* social system. Stepping straight from this, the economists proved fifty years ago or more that Socialism cannot abolish poverty, which is based on nature, but only *communalize* it, distribute it equally over the whole surface of society![19]

Marx's main objection to the principle of population can be stated in a single sentence: "every special historic mode of production has its own special laws of population, historically valid within its limits alone."[20] With the proviso, already noted, that man is an animal and that at one level of analysis biological generalizations are therefore relevant, this is certainly a valid criticism. Indeed, the demographic-cycle hypothesis, one might say, is a specification of Malthusian theory in the sense that Marx suggested, since it divides the human species into three stages related to their "modes of production." Marx himself, however, had nothing to say of what governed the population growth of primitive, feudal, or socialist societies, and what he termed his law of population for capitalist society was markedly incomplete.

According to Marx's theory, the competition in a capitalist economy drives all entrepreneurs to increase their efficiency to the utmost by installing more and more machinery. "Accumulate, accumulate! This is Moses and the prophets!"[21] The growing stock of capital goods that results, by the very fact of its greater efficiency, tends to displace some of the workers that had been employed at a lower technological level. "The laboring population therefore produces, along with the accumulation of capital produced by it, the means by which [it] itself is made relatively superfluous, is turned into a relative surplus population; and it does this to an always

[19] Marx, *Critique of the Gotha Program* (New York: International Publishers, 1933), p. 40.
[20] Marx, *Capital,* Vol. 1, p. 693.
[21] *Ibid.,* p. 652.

increasing extent."[22] Moreover, the composition of the employed force steadily deteriorates; the capitalist "progressively replaces skilled laborers by less skilled, mature labor-power by immature, male by female, that of adults by that of younger persons or children."[23] No amelioration is possible under capitalism, for the capitalist mode of production depends on this "industrial reserve army" of the technologically unemployed; employers, if they are to remain in business, must respond promptly to the state of the market and cannot afford to adjust their production also to the supply of laborers.

This line of reasoning, a generalization from Ricardo's demonstration that mechanization *may* lead to unemployment, cannot be regarded as one of Marx's successful prophecies.[24] Since machines and labor are interchangeable to some degree, the increase in the stock of capital did mean that fewer workers were required to produce the same amount of goods. The general consequences of this greater efficiency, however, were the higher standard of life, the shorter work-week for the industrial labor force, and the development of tertiary services. And in presently underdeveloped countries, where the surplus agrarian population—what Marx termed the latent industrial reserve army—is often large, the consequent very low wage standard is ordinarily not the stimulus to capital accumulation it should be by Marx's analysis, but a serious impediment to it.

But even if Marx's main point is granted—that with increasing mechanization there is a long-term trend toward an ever larger number of unemployed—it still does not follow that this trend operates "independently of the limits of the

[22] *Ibid.*, p. 692.

[23] *Ibid.*, p. 697.

[24] As Professor Meek remarks in an article in *Science and Society,* "Marx's basic 'law of population' (like a number of his other laws) will have to be worked out more fully and adapted to the new conditions before it can be safely employed in the analysis of the present situation." Ronald L. Meek, "Malthus—Yesterday and Today," *Science and Society,* 18:1 (Winter, 1954), 21–51. The reason given for this judgment, however, is not that Marx lacked total prescience but that conditions have changed: "capitalism is now in its imperialist stage of development."

actual increase of population."[25] Marx's theory of the industrial reserve army pertains not to population as such but to the labor force; and while the two are related, they are not identical. Given the state of the market, the proportion of the labor force able to find work depends—as one of the important variables—on the number of new workers seeking jobs.[26] According to Marx, if wages rise because of a relative shortage of labor, the rate of capitalization will increase and the labor surplus will thus be re-established.[27] But Marx's analysis began, it will be recalled, with the thesis that every capitalist is driven to accumulate at the highest possible rate under all conditions; and it was illogical—to put it no stronger —to develop the argument with an assertion that under certain conditions the rate of mechanization will be accelerated.

[25] Marx, *Capital*, Vol. 1, p. 693.

[26] As Marx points out in a different context, "the demand for laborers may exceed the supply and, therefore, wages may rise" (*ibid.*, p. 672); and one of his examples of this process is the fifteenth century, after the extraordinary mortality of the Black Death had reduced the population, and thus the labor force, by a considerable proportion.

[27] "A limitation of the increase in the working population, through diminishing the supply of labor and hence through raising its price, would only accelerate the use of machinery and the transformation of circulating [capital; that is, labor] into fixed capital and in this fashion would create an artificial surplus population." Marx, *Theorien über den Mehrwert*, Vol. 2:2, p. 373; cited in Sweezy, *op. cit.*, p. 223. Sweezy comments: "From this it is but a short step to the conclusion that any slowing down in the rate of population growth not only has the paradoxical effect of creating unemployment but also strengthens the tendency to underconsumption." This may be a short step, but it takes one outside a Marxian framework. The large increase in population did help, as Sweezy points out, to keep the nineteenth-century capitalist world in a healthy state, but only because the increasing "immiseration" of the masses, which Marx had postulated as the necessary consequence of the inevitable fall in the rate of profit, was nowhere to be observed.

Cf. Malthus: "Almost universally, the actual wealth of all the states with which we are acquainted is very far short of their powers of production; and among these states, the slowest progress in wealth is often made where the stimulus arising from population alone is the greatest. . . . Population alone cannot create an effective demand for wealth." *Principles*, Book 2, Chap. 1, Section 2.

If Marx freed Ricardo's theory of the effect of capital growth on employment from a "fatal dependence on the Malthusian population dogma," as Sweezy declares,[28] this "great accomplishment" was at the cost of taking the essence of Malthusianism for granted. In the 1930s, demographers generally forecast that the population of the West would soon decline, but for Marx this was not even a hypothetical contingency. In this respect, his usual historical perspective failed him: he took the rapid population increase typical of the nineteenth century as the norm and built his system around it—and without even so imperfect a theory as Malthus' principle to account for this increase. If the population were to decline at the same rate as machines displaced workers, then there would be no industrial reserve army, no "immiseration," no Marxist model altogether. Such an extreme example illustrates strikingly how completely dependent Marx's system is on the unanalyzed variable of population growth, and this dependence exists to one degree or another, no matter what the rate of growth.

As with their general theories so with their analyses of population movements, there are many parallels between Marx's system and what Spengler has termed Malthus' total population theory,[29] which was developed in both the *Essay* and the *Principles*. The effect of the economic system on employment and thus on population growth, the problem with which Marx was mainly concerned, Malthus analyzed at length only in the *Principles;* and many of Marx's criticisms of the *Essay*, in any case rather casual, are still less cogent when applied to the argument of both works together.

In Malthus' system, the psychological base of any human society consists in the opposed drives of man's natural sloth and the passion between the sexes, the first inducive to stagnation and the second to progress. (Marx's reply to this, as we have noted, was to deny the relevance of such psychological universals to a social analysis at any level

[28] Sweezy, *op. cit.*, p. 89.
[29] See Joseph J. Spengler, "Malthus' Total Population Theory: A Restatement and Reappraisal," *Canadian Journal of Economics and Political Science,* 2:1 (February, 1945), 83–110; 2:2 (May, 1945), 234–264.

whatever.) The balance between the two drives in any specific society, Malthus continues, is set by its institutions. While the "struggle for existence" is viewed in the first instance as that of man against nature, the character of this struggle and its probable success depend on the social order. (Here the divergence from Marx is no longer absolute.) That is to say, according to Malthus, the growth of a population depends not only on the resources available to it (in a biological-geographical context) but also on the effective demand for labor (in an economic-cultural context). "An increase of population, when an additional quantity of labor is not required, will soon be checked by want of employment and the scanty support of those employed."[30] These two determinants, moreover, need not operate in the same direction. For example, a population can be too great with respect to job openings and yet smaller than the available resources make possible; Marx's industrial reserve army is thus a special case in Malthus' broader analysis. On the other hand, if the effective demand for labor remains greater than the supply, the consequent growth of population will be brought to an end ultimately by the limit of the resources available (exploited with whatever technical efficiency a particular society may have) and, short of this ultimate point, by its consumption standards—a cultural rather than an economic factor. The lowest point at which real family income can be stabilized, as with Marx, is the minimum cost of producing another generation. According to Marx, there was a long-term tendency for wages to fall to this level; but with Malthus this minimum could be raised by an increase in "the amount of those necessaries and conveniences, without which [the workers] would not consent to keep up their numbers to the required point." When Gunnar Myrdal wrote that the conscious limitation of family size is a powerful lever with which to force governments to enact social legislation, he was expressing a point of view whose germ is to be found in Malthus.

This point is important enough to deserve some amplification, and this can be given it in a passage from Sidney

[30] *Principles*, Book 1, Chap. 1, Section 2.

and Beatrice Webb, who had a juster appreciation of Malthus' social philosophy than probably any other socialist. They wrote—

> No argument could be founded on the "principle of population" against Trade Union efforts to improve the conditions of sanitation and safety, or to protect the Normal Day. And the economists quickly found reason to doubt whether there was any greater cogency in the argument with regard to wages. . . . From the Malthusian point of view, the presumption was, as regards the artisans and factory operatives, always in favor of a rise in wages. For (as Malthus had written in the *Principles*) "in the vast majority of instances, before a rise of wages can be counteracted by the increased number of laborers it may be supposed to be the means of bringing into the market, time is afforded for the formation of . . . new and improved tastes and habits. . . . After the laborers have once acquired these tastes, population will advance in a slower ratio, as compared with capital, than formerly." . . . The ordinary middle-class view that the "principle of population" rendered nugatory all attempts to raise wages, otherwise than in the slow course of generations, was, in fact, based on sheer ignorance, not only of the facts of working-class life, but even of the opinions of the very economists from whom it was supposed to be derived.[31]

Thus the person the Webbs designated, somewhat inappropriately, as "the fanatical Malthusian" was mistaken in his fear of "the devastating torrent of children," mistaken because Malthus had been correct in his theory that a rising standard of living would tend to reduce the birth rate.

For Marx, the overthrow of the system was both inevitable and the prerequisite to all social betterment; and the solution of the population problem would be so automatic under socialist institutions that he did not find it useful even to sketch in how this would be achieved. For Malthus, as we have

[31] Sidney and Beatrice Webb, *Industrial Democracy* (London: Longmans, Green, 1919), pp. 632–635.

noted, social betterment was defined as the increase in individual responsibility[32] or, specifically with respect to population, in the wider practice of moral restraint. While such social changes as the extension of free education to the poor would foster this sense of responsibility, and were thus defined as good, the moral differentiation already existing in any society made a gradual improvement possible for some.

> It is not required . . . to pursue a general good which we may not distinctly comprehend, or the effect of which may be weakened by distance and diffusion. The happiness of the whole is to be the result of the happiness of individuals, and to begin with the first of them. No cooperation is required. Every step tells. He who performs his duty faithfully will reap the full fruits of it, whatever may be the number of others who fail.[33]

Compared with a view of the future that declared the perfect society to be inescapable, Malthus' admonitions are more than a bit astringent, particularly since "few of my readers can be less sanguine than I am in their expectations of any sudden and great change in the general conduct of men on this subject."[34] That the course of action he advocated was not wholly fanciful is suggested by the one example of Ireland, where the dramatic stimulus of the famine and the strict

[32] This criterion was applied even to social changes as thoroughgoing as the French Revolution: "The effect of the revolution in France has been to make every person depend more on himself and less upon others. The laboring classes are therefore becoming more industrious, more saving and more prudent in marriage than formerly; and it is quite certain that without these effects the revolution would have done nothing for them." Malthus, *An Essay on the Principle of Population* (7th ed.; London: Reeves and Turner, 1872), p. 320.

[33] *Ibid.*, p. 404.

[34] *Ibid.*, p. 403. He adds: "The chief reason . . . I allowed myself to suppose the universal prevalence of this virtue [of moral restraint] was that I might endeavor to remove any imputation on the goodness of the Deity, by showing that the evils arising from the principle of population were exactly of the same nature as the generality of other evils which excite fewer complaints, that they were increased by human ignorance and indolence, and diminished by human knowledge and virtue."

regulation of morals by the Catholic Church have resulted in the control of population growth by institutionalized late marriage.

More generally, neither Malthus nor Marx can be regarded as having forecast the future of the Western world with great accuracy. Dogmatists of either school find it difficult to cope with the fact that the marked rise in the working-class living standard was within the capitalist system, on the one hand, and was concomitant with an unprecedented increase in the population, on the other. If we include in Marx's foresight the improvements within the capitalist system effected by the rise of trade unions and the consequent change in power relations, and in Malthus' the reduction in average family size by contraceptives rather than by postponement of marriage— common extensions of their views that do violence to the essential ideas of the two men—then both can be said to have been partly correct.

In summary, both Malthus and Marx welcomed the new capitalist era,[35] but both with important reservations. Neither saw the market as a perfect instrument for translating the self-interest of individuals into the optimum social policy, and they both, though to different degrees, therefore rejected the laissez-faire norms of liberal industrialism. Neither was a sen-

---

[35] Marx, however, in more glowing terms than Malthus. Consider this passage from *The Communist Manifesto:* "The bourgeoisie has played a most revolutionary role in history. . . . It has been the first to show what man's activity can bring about. It has accomplished wonders far surpassing Egyptian pyramids, Roman aqueducts, and Gothic cathedrals; it has conducted expeditions that put in the shade all former migrations of nations and crusades. . . . The bourgeoisie has through its exploitation of the world market given a cosmopolitan [not yet a pejorative term] character to production and consumption in every country. . . . The bourgeoisie, by the rapid improvement of all instruments of production, by the immensely facilitated means of communication, draws all nations, even the most barbarian, into civilization. . . . The bourgeoisie . . . has created enormous cities, has . . . rescued a considerable part of the population from the idiocy of rural life. . . . The bourgeoisie, during its rule of scarce one hundred years, has created more massive and more colossal productive forces than have all preceding generations together." Marx and Engels, *The Communist Manifesto* (New York: International Publishers, 1948), pp. 11–14.

timentalist: when they thought it necessary, Malthus was willing to advocate the abrogation of a bad poor law and Marx to call for revolution. Both offered these programs in a rational effort to establish similar humanitarian values. As against Economic Man, both stressed to some degree the whole man, Malthus in part by seeking to preserve a portion of preindustrial tradition and in part by espousing certain fundamental reforms, Marx by seeking to establish a new society with an industrial-agrarian balance. Marx's concept of democracy, while it laid a basis for present theories of social control by planning boards, also had a community of socially responsible persons as its fundament. The working class would lead the world to a better state because workers, unlike peasants, had been disciplined by their style of life; of the undisciplined, irresponsible mass, the "Lumpenproletariat," Marx had the same horror and the same fear as Malthus.

# NOTES ON THE SOCIALIST POSITION
# ON BIRTH CONTROL

To my knowledge, Marx never commented on the birth-control movement so active in England during the last years of his life, particularly from the Bradlaugh-Besant trial (1876) to his death (1883). The Marxist views of the good society, as expressed in such classic documents as *The Communist Manifesto* and Engels' *Origin of the Family,* included as a main feature the emancipation of the woman from household drudgery; but whether she should also be emancipated from bearing many children was not made explicit. In a letter to Kautsky, Engels spoke of the "abstract possibility" that the number of persons in a communist society might have to be limited by conscious control, but he declined to discuss the matter further.[1] By such a comment, Engels avoided having to discuss in any detail either the economic significance of population growth or the moral system of the socialist society he was advocating.

This abstention on the part of Marx and Engels was not reflected, however, in the socialist parties of the Western world. Since both contradicted the conventional values of pre-1914 middle-class society, neo-Malthusianism and socialism have sometimes appealed to the same rebellious spirits, so that a number of individuals (Annie Besant, for instance) wrote pamphlets in support of both. However, the usual relation between the movements, all but invariable for or-

[1] "It is for the people in the communist society themselves," Engels wrote, "to decide whether, when, and how this is to be done, and what means they wish to employ for the purpose. I do not feel called upon to make proposals or to give them advice about it. These people, in any case, will surely not be any less intelligent than we are." Letter of Engels to Kautsky, February 1, 1881; cited in Ronald L. Meek, ed., *Marx and Engels on Malthus* (New York: International Publishers, 1955), p. 47.

ganizations rather than individuals, was antagonistic. Socialist opposition to planned parenthood—in contrast to the widely debated Catholic opposition—is all but forgotten; and it is worth reviewing it in some detail.

*Germany.* Antagonism was especially strong in the German party, the direct inheritor of the Marxist tradition and the largest and most influential unit of the Second International. According to a very thorough survey by Lewinsohn, German socialists were opposed to neo-Malthusianism "almost without exception,"[2] and even so extreme a statement had some warrant. Party leaders like the elder Liebknecht, Lassalle, and Bebel, together with dozens of lesser figures, repeated Marx's attack on Malthus and applied his arguments also against the neo-Malthusians. The most widely distributed version of the party's view was Bebel's *Woman,* which can be taken as the main example of German Social Democratic orthodoxy.

Only in a capitalist society, Bebel wrote, does population tend to grow faster than the food available to it. "Socialism is better able to preserve the equilibrium between population and means of subsistence than any other form of community," for under socialism man will for the first time "consciously direct his entire development in accordance with natural laws." That family size differed among the social classes of capitalist societies was not due, in his view, to the differential use of contraceptives. Rather, the poorest classes concentrated on sex as their sole diversion, and the fecundity of middle-class persons was reduced by their rich diet.

There can be no doubt that the reproductive power of the male and the capacity for fructification of the female

[2] Richard Lewinsohn, "Die Stellung der deutschen Sozialdemokratie zur Bevölkerungsfrage," *Schmollers Jahrbuch,* 46 (1922), 813–859 (191–237). See also Erich Unshelm, *Geburtenbeschränkung und Sozialismus: Versuch einer Dogmengeschichte der sozialistischen Bevölkerungslehre* (Leipzig: Kabitzsch, 1924); Heinrich Soetbeer, *Die Stellung der Sozialisten zur Malthus'schen Bevölkerungslehre* (Berlin: Puttkammer and Mühlbrecht, 1886). Many of the same arguments are repeated in a sharply critical Nazi appraisal of Malthus: Johannes Oestreich, *Die Stellung des Nationalsozialismus zur Bevölkerungslehre von Thomas Robert Malthus und seinen Anhängern: Eine nationalsozialistische Studie* (Würzburg: Triltsch, 1936).

are modified by the nature of the food habitually consumed; and it is therefore not impossible that the increase
of the population may depend materially on the kind of
nourishment eaten. If this were once ascertained with
certainty, the number of the inhabitants might be more
or less exclusively regulated by the manner of eating.

In any case, the problem of population control was not an
urgent one, for the world had "a superabundance of land
capable of cultivation, awaiting the labor of fresh hundreds of
millions."[3] Rosa Luxemburg, similarly, dismissed the future
increase of population as of no economic importance.[4]

Karl Kautsky's first book on the subject, *The Influence of
Population Increase on Social Progress* (1880), is interesting
for its unusual attempt to find a compromise between Marx
and Malthus. In the view of the young Kautsky, Malthus was
wrong in his main thesis, that population *always* tends to
increase faster than the supply of food on which it must subsist. But he was right in his assertion that every improvement
in the state of the lower classes is accompanied by an increase in their numbers, an increase that has no automatic
check to its indefinite continuation.[5] While improved production methods could postpone the danger of overpopulation,
they could not remove it altogether; "in the first case overpopulation will develop after three or four years, in the second
case after three or four decades." The great practical question
consists in finding a means of reducing the number of births.
Infanticide and abortion are not immoral per se, but rather
because man now has a better means of limiting births, contraception, which is "the least of the evils among which we
must choose."

The question can no longer be *whether* birth control
should be used, but only *when* it should be used, and

[3] August Bebel, *Woman in the Past, Present, and Future* (San
Francisco: Benham, 1897), pp. 160 ff.

[4] *The Accumulation of Capital* (New Haven: Yale University
Press, 1951), p. 133.

[5] This is the usual interpretation of Malthus' position, but his
final stand—as reported correctly by the Webbs, in the quotation on
p. 86 above—was precisely the opposite.

which type of such control we should choose. . . . The
sterile rejection of population theory, at least on the part
of socialism, is definitely out of place, for the two are not
in principle incompatible. . . . Only a transformation of
society can extirpate the misery and vice that today
damn nine-tenths of the world to a lamentable existence;
but only a regulation of population growth by the most
moral means possible, probably the use of contraceptives,
can forestall the recurrence of this evil.[6]

Thirty years later, the mature Kautsky wrote another work
on the same subject, taking issue with the Revisionist wing of
the party. He himself had begun as a Revisionist, he confesses
in the preface; "as a callow young fellow who understood
nothing of Marxism, I saw it as my most important task to
revise it." In his later, more orthodox exposition of Marx's
views on how population growth functions in a capitalist
economy, there is nothing very new. The most interesting
chapters are on population and socialism. In spite of the fact
that farmhands are "veritable fanatics" in their craving for
small plots of their own, the socialist state would succeed in
absorbing them, though not by expropriation, into its much
more efficient collectivized agriculture. Thus, for "at least a
century" after it broke the capitalist dams to technological
progress, socialist society would be able to expand food production "much faster than any possible population growth."
True, mortality would fall "enormously," since many of its
specific causes would be eliminated together with the profit
system; but fertility would also decline as the new woman
took an interest in "the possibility of enjoyment and creativity
in nature, art, and science." In fact, one might suppose that
with so many distractions from family life, depopulation
rather than overpopulation would ensue. This fear, however,
is groundless, for the anxieties that inhibit childbearing in a
capitalist era would also have been removed. In short,

[6] Karl Kautsky, *Der Einfluss der Volksvermehrung auf den
Fortschritt der Gesellschaft* (Vienna: Bloch und Hasbach, 1880),
pp. 166–192. See also Ludwig Quessel, "Karl Kautsky als
Bevölkerungstheoretiker," *Neue Zeit*, 29:1, No. 16 (January 20,
1911), 559–565.

socialist society will be perfect, as defined; for whenever population growth varies from the optimum, "public opinion and the conscience of individuals will make women's duties clear."[7]

Throughout these polemics, the most important argument is a simple statement of faith: neo-Malthusianism, like Malthus' theory itself, is reactionary; "the principle of population is the root and source of all the essential errors of all sociology."[8] Socialism will bring a "period of general happiness, in which our present mortification of the flesh (Selbstkasteiung) will be unknown."[9]

How much did this not quite unanimous opposition to birth control among theorists influence the actual behavior of German Social Democrats? It was not merely, it must be noted, a doctrinal dispute among the party intellectuals: the whole membership participated, for example, in a mass meeting in 1913 "against the birth strike."[10] Class differences in Western fertility, ordinarily explained by the greater religious or cultural traditionalism of the lower classes, may well have been also a consequence of the fact that socialism, the main antitraditionalist ideology of these classes, included a ban on the use of contraceptives. Especially in Germany, where the Social Democratic Party was both large and well established among the working class, this may have been a factor of considerable importance.

*Britain.* Such early advocates of neo-Malthusianism as Robert Dale Owen and John Stuart Mill called themselves "socialists," but this was not yet a very specific designation. In the second half of the nineteenth century the loose radical-

[7] Kautsky, *Vermehrung und Entwicklung in Natur und Gesellschaft* (3rd ed.; Stuttgart: Dietz Nachfolger, 1921), Chaps. 15–16; the first edition had been published in 1910. See also Kautsky, *The Economic Doctrines of Karl Marx* (London: Black, 1925), Part 3, Chap. 5.

[8] Wilhelm Hohoff, "Der Malthusianismus," *Neue Zeit*, 40:7 (November 11, 1921), 177–183; 40:9 (November 25, 1921), 204–210, at p. 209.

[9] Max Schippel, *Das moderne Elend und die moderne Übervölkerung: Zur Erkenntnis unserer sozialen Entwicklung* (Stuttgart, 1888), p. 254.

[10] Lewinsohn, *op. cit.*

ism generally associated with the Chartist movement or Benthamite utilitarianism separated into several divergent strands. One of the most important figures of the neo-Malthusian movement was George Drysdale, founder of the original Malthusian League and author of *The Elements of Social Science,* a book of some 600 finely printed pages which went through thirty-five English editions and was translated into at least ten languages. Drysdale's extensive and sympathetic exposition of classical economic theory bound neo-Malthusianism not only to Malthus but to the whole school of thought that Marx and other socialists opposed. Advocacy of birth control was also an important element of Free Thought; the 30,000-member National Secular Society, headed by Charles Bradlaugh, was for a period the main organization propounding it.[11] But neo-Malthusianism was "the especial *bête noire* of the Socialists, land reformers, and other advocates of redistribution and democratic control" and was thus "disliked by the laboring classes which it was especially intended to help."[12] The reason, in the view of Marie Stopes, was that "the intense anti-socialism of the Malthusian League antagonized the great mass of the working people."[13] These two partisan accounts, while opposed on where to lay the blame, agree that in England the birth-control and socialist movements were adversaries. The organizational competition was often combined with ignorance of the opponent's position, and on both sides the debate was conducted with intolerant fervor.

As was pointed out in the previous chapter, the Webbs are an exception to the generality that socialists who attack Malthus do not understand what he has written. For these out-

[11] F. H. Amphlett Micklewright, "The Rise and Decline of English Neo-Malthusianism," *Population Studies,* 15:1 (July, 1961), 32–51. The best book-length study, though out-of-date in some respects, is Norman E. Himes, *Medical History of Contraception* (Baltimore: Williams & Wilkins, 1936).

[12] C. V. Drysdale, *The Malthusian Doctrine and Its Modern Aspects* (London: Malthusian League, 1917), p. 4. The author was long a president of the second Malthusian League, founded immediately after the Bradlaugh-Besant trial by his father, Charles R. Drysdale, who was the brother of George Drysdale.

[13] *Early Days of Birth Control* (London: Putnam, 1923), p. 28.

standing scholars of English socialism, the main question was not the increasing number of people but the decreasing quality of the genetic stock. They used the records of a sickness-benefit society to show that among this considerable sample of the provident (mostly skilled workers and small shopkeepers) the birth rate had fallen more than twice as fast as in the population as a whole.[14] Sidney Webb spelled out the implications in a pamphlet published by the Fabian Society:

> It looks as if the birth-rate was falling most conspicuously, if not exclusively, not among the wealthy or the middle class, as such, but among those sections of every class in which there is most prudence, foresight and self-control. . . . This very fact emphasizes the character of the "selection" that is going on. And to the present writer, at any rate, it is the differential character of the decline in the birth-rate, rather than the actual extent of the decline, which is of the gravest import. . . . In Great Britain at this moment [1913], when half, or perhaps two-thirds, of all the married people are regulating their families, children are being freely born to the Irish Roman Catholics and the Polish, Russian and German Jews, on the one hand, and to the thriftless and irresponsible . . . on the other. . . . This can hardly result in anything but national deterioration; or, as an alternative, in this country gradually falling to the Irish and the Jews. Finally, there are signs that even these races are becoming influenced. The ultimate future of these islands may be to the Chinese![15]

This is, in several respects, a remarkable passage. Webb not only dismisses as nonsense the theory (perpetrated by Bebel and, in later years, by Josué de Castro[16]) that the decline in fertility was the accidental effect of diet or another feature

[14] Sidney and Beatrice Webb, *Industrial Democracy* (London: Longmans, Green, 1919), pp. 637 ff.
[15] Sidney Webb, *The Decline in the Birth-Rate* (Fabian Tract No. 131; London: Fabian Society, 1913), pp. 7–17.
[16] Josué de Castro, *Geography of Hunger* (London: Gollancz, 1952).

of modern life. He also saw that contraceptive devices are decisive only in the context of the will to use them; all too many analysts, including world-famous demographers, took it for granted that birth-control means would be used whenever they became available. The method by which Webb tested his hypothesis was ingenious, and for that date a great advance over any empirical study. The passage is also remarkable, however, for its less than fervent opposition to ethnocentrism. This analysis of population policy was certainly superior to Kautsky's or Bebel's, but in their negative evaluation of the small-family system, the Webbs reverted to the socialist norm.[17]

As late as 1925, the British Labor Party took an ambivalent stand toward planned parenthood. In that year the Department of Health had banned birth-control information in its clinics, and a Party Conference refused to protest. "The subject of birth control," it declared, "is in its nature not one which should be made a political party issue, but should remain a matter upon which members of the Party should be free to hold and promote their individual convictions." According to the sympathetic interpretation of G. D. H. Cole, "the reason for this attitude was, of course, the presence in the Labor Party of strong religious (especially Roman Catholic) groups hostile to family limitation."[18] Unless he wishes to suggest that the party was utterly opportunist, the reason was also that on this issue its own tradition did not demand a principled stand.

*Holland.* The Dutch Neo-Malthusian League has a special

[17] This negativist attitude was reflected even in their *Soviet Communism,* generally the high point in Western socialism's credulous enthusiasm for Stalinism. It passed on to its Western readers the official Soviet position on such matters as the forced-labor camps, the treason trials of the 1930s, and the significance of the democratic guarantees in the Stalin Constitution, but, in contrast to many other admirers of the Soviet system, discussed birth control and abortion (in only five pages out of a 1000-page book) with more circumspection. See Sidney and Beatrice Webb, *Soviet Communism: A New Civilisation?* (3rd ed.; London: Longmans, Green, 1944), pp. 669–674.

[18] G. D. H. Cole, *A History of the Labour Party from 1914* (London: Routledge & Kegan Paul, 1948), pp. 200–201.

importance in the history of the movement. In its early years it was the model for the rest of Europe (to this day, a pessary —invented by the German physician W. P. J. Mensinga—is often termed a "Dutch cap"). Its early growth was disrupted by a struggle for power between socialist and nonsocialist members. The socialists won control in 1919, and the founder of the League, Dr. J. Rutgers, had to tender his resignation as chairman. Subsequently some individual socialists—such as F. M. Wibaut, the Amsterdam councilor, and W. A. Bonger, the famous criminologist—became strong advocates of birth control; but the Social Democratic Workers Party, speaking through official spokesmen like Dr. L. Hoyermans, used orthodox Marxist arguments to oppose neo-Malthusianism.[19]

In postwar Holland, political factionalism has affected socialists' attitudes toward the Netherlands Society for Sexual Reform (the present name of the Neo-Malthusian League). Its president, W. F. Storm, resigned from the Labor Party to protest the so-called police action against Indonesian nationalists, which the Right wing of the party supported. The Communists, on the other hand, attacked the neo-Malthusians as "Trotskyist" and "reactionary."[20]

*France.* This ambivalence was also to be seen among French socialists, the radical party of a country where some kind of birth control had become a virtually universal practice by, say, 1914. There were numerous attacks on family limitation in *Mouvement Socialiste,* a party magazine. Since neo-Malthusianism was logically opposed to revolutionary ideas, one socialist pamphlet argued, it was objectively counterrevolutionary.[21]

In 1908 a neo-Malthusian publishing house, *Génération Consciente,* was founded, and it began to fire a heavy counterbarrage of pamphlets at the socialists.[22] In these years just

[19] See various issues, particularly during 1922, of *De Socialistische Gids, De Nieuwe Tijd,* and *De Vrijdenker.*

[20] See in particular *De Waarheid,* May 26, 1951.

[21] R. Vargas, *Que devons-nous penser du néo-Malthusianisme?* (Montpellier, 1909).

[22] For example: Dixelles, *Entre prolétaires;* Victor Ernst, *Socialisme et Malthusianisme;* Alfred Naquet and G. Hardy, *Néo-Malthusianisme et socialisme.*

before the First World War, neo-Malthusians made a particular effort to appeal to the antimilitarist mood of the socialists. Marinont recalled, for example, that when Napoleon was told that one of his campaigns had cost 100,000 men, he answered, "One night in Paris will make good the loss." Bringing Lysistrata up-to-date, the author proposed foiling the warmakers by a "belly-strike."[23] *La grève des ventres* was also the title of a pamphlet by the anarchist Fernand Kolney, who argued that communism was possible only if population growth was controlled.

*United States.*[24] The small and relatively insignificant socialist movement in the United States was largely derivative from its counterpart in Europe. Bebel, the leader of the opposition in the Reichstag, was perhaps the best known European socialist, and his *Woman* eventually circulated in three different translations. Native socialists were concerned to distinguish their party from the communistic free-love utopias that flourished in New York State and the Middle West, and this effort sometimes resulted in what can only be termed prurience. Charles Kerr, for instance, the publisher of Marx's *Capital* and many other socialist books, himself wrote *Morals and Socialism*, which passed over the question of sexual ethics as too individual a matter for philosophic treatment. In *The Sorrows of Cupid*, by Kate O'Hare, one-time international secretary of the Socialist Party, the reader was taught that the capitalist system deprived many of the pleasures of early marriage and a solid family life with a numerous progeny. A similar message was expounded in John Spargo's *Socialism and Motherhood*. From such attitudes party members would hardly have pushed for birth-control clinics, but they generally did not oppose neo-Malthusianism either. Possible reasons are that the small Socialist Party was largely based in the middle class, and that the anarcho-syndicalist International Workers of the World (IWW) represented an anti-Marxian (and hence potentially pro-Malthusian) influence. Margaret Sanger's living room was a rendezvous for Bill Haywood, leader of the IWW; Alexander Berkman, the Russian anarch-

[23] Léon Marinont, *Socialisme et population.*
[24] See Sidney Ditzion, *Marriage, Morals, and Sex in America: A History of Ideas* (New York: Bookman, 1953), Chap. 8.

ist; John Reed, already a darling of the radical literary world; and similar types. The contrast with German Social Democracy or even the English Fabians is manifest.

*Summary.* These preliminary notes[25] do no more than challenge the notion that socialism and neo-Malthusianism have been allies in seeking parallel aims. Even when we emphasize the convergences between the two movements—the similarities in the theories of Marx and Malthus noted in the previous chapter, the anomalous young Kautsky who tried to incorporate neo-Malthusian ideas into orthodox Marxism, the atypical Webbs who read Malthus before discussing him—we must conclude that, by and large, the divergent factors were stronger.

When the advocates of family-planning adopted the name of neo-Malthusians (or even Malthusians), choosing to ignore Malthus' principled opposition to contraceptives, they linked their movements to his weaknesses as well as to his strong points. That neo-Malthusians depended so much on the *Essay* for their arguments meant that, among Marxists, Marx's emotional rejection of Malthus was more easily, however illogically, transferred to such men as Bradlaugh. An orthodox Marxist believed that when the capitalist system was supplanted by a planned economy, population pressure would disappear, and that before that fundamental transformation took place, the limitation of family size would not improve matters substantially. An orthodox Malthusian believed that human ills, including war and poverty, derived largely—or mainly—from population pressure. A compromise view, that improvement was possible both by establishing more efficient institutions and also by restricting population growth to the resources available, would seem to be so reasonable that the continuing opposition cannot be accounted for by mere doctrinal rigidity.

Once the various socialist parties and neo-Malthusian leagues had been established, this rigidity was hardened, of course, by organizational rivalry. Just as socialists who be-

[25] After a slightly more ambitious survey, Eversley concluded that "the socialist attitude towards population awaits fresh analysis." D. E. C. Eversley, *Social Theories of Fertility and the Malthusian Debate* (Oxford: Clarendon, 1959), p. 160.

lieved in the right of women to vote generally opposed the suffragists' efforts to establish this right, so even those who supported birth control in the abstract often fought the specific organizations espousing it. But the first question is how this organizational competition arose, why socialist parties did not themselves include the cause of planned parenthood in their program rather than often fighting it.

We cannot find the explanation by abstracting the organizational fight into a struggle between conservative and progressive, or between bourgeois and working-class forces. To term Malthus a "conservative"—a man who wanted to institute free universal education at the beginning of the nineteenth century—is to abandon any meaning in the word. Nor have neo-Malthusians generally been opposed to institutional changes; in family matters, socialists have usually been more traditionalist. The typical Social Democrat, as much the solid family man as his petty-bourgeois counterpart, often had the same puritanical aversion to birth control. When Bebel, for example, discussed it, he did so without ever mentioning it by name; and the very meaning of some of his passages is obscured by this excess of delicacy. The Social Democratic Party also wanted, simply for political reasons, to limit its deviation from majority views to issues that it deemed crucial. One purpose of Bebel's book, thus, was to discredit the widely held belief that socialists were libertines who favored free love—and birth control.

If the principled difference between the two movements has to be summarized into a dichotomy, a better one is individualist vs. what might be termed "groupist" or, in political terminology, liberal vs. socialist. According to Marx, an individual could not typically improve his situation by his own efforts; he could only join an organization of his social class and, working with the laws of History, help to establish a new society. Latter-day Marxists have softened this harsh analysis; trade unions, for example, are no longer regarded only as training organizations for the final struggle against capitalism but also, or primarily, as means of effecting real gains within bourgeois society. But it is still only the class organization, the party or the trade union, rather than the individual, that can implement change. Malthus and neo-

Malthusians, on the contrary, have stressed much more the responsibility of each man for his own fate and thus the possibility of transforming society by an accretion of individual improvements. It was in this sense that neo-Malthusianism was declared to be counterrevolutionary; for the individual worker's "illusory" hope that he might improve his state by himself would impede the development of workers' organizations and thus postpone the "real" conquest of misery by socialism. The Stalinist dictum of "the worse, the better" (or, in German, *Nach Hitler, wir*) is not altogether heretical Marxism.

The neo-Malthusian argument that appealed most to the pre-1914 socialist parties was the call for *la grève des ventres*. Inconsistently, party agitators demanded of the workers that they deny the capitalists' cannon their fodder without yielding their orthodox Marxian opposition to neo-Malthusianism in any other respect. Generally advocates of planned change, many socialists preferred to ignore the element of human will so evident in the modern decline of fertility and to explain the middle class's control of family size by a hypothesis that —in the case of Bebel, for instance—sounded farfetched even when he offered it. Many other socialist and progressive analysts were reluctant to hypothesize that the decline in family size had been based fundamentally on the desire for fewer children, effected through improved contraceptives.[26] Marx's opposition to Malthus' *program* of increasing individual responsibility had become a dogmatic blindness to a *fact* of nineteenth-century social history—that middle-class parents gradually came to view their role in rational rather than traditional terms.

[26] For instance, Enid Charles believed that the decline in family size was due to increased privacy (over the Victorian period) of "so many marriages," "the widespread habit of excessive washing, most common among the prosperous and educated, less common in Catholic countries, in rural communities and among the poorer classes," and similar factors that are interesting at least for their novelty among professional demographers. *The Menace of Under-Population: A Biological Study of the Decline of Population Growth* (London: Watts, 1936), pp. 172, 182–183.

# THE EVOLUTION OF
# SOVIET FAMILY POLICY

In any society the family has three main functions: to perpetuate the population, to maintain cultural continuity from one generation to the next, and to determine the place of each newborn infant in the social structure. In static societies these three functions are in balance, but in one undergoing rapid change there is a tendency toward imbalance that subjects the family to constant strain.

In totalitarian societies particularly, conflicting pressures increase the stresses upon the family. On the one hand, the totalitarian state always attempts to validate its existence by denying the legitimacy of the society it has supplanted, and it cannot tolerate the strong emotional bond between the old and the new inherent in the father-son relation. Nor can such a regime accept the principle that the son shall inherit, even temporarily, the father's place in society, for a fundamental characteristic of totalitarianism is that each person's status is determined solely by his relation to the ruling power. These pressures are reflected in various decrees and in institutions like the Nazis' *Hitlerjugend* (Hitler Youth), the avowed purpose of which was to break down the family and weaken its influence.

On the other hand, a totalitarian regime finds the family something of a necessary evil, for the expansionist aims demand a rapidly growing population. This opposite pressure is reflected in other decrees strengthening the family and granting state subsidies to encourage families of large size and in slogans like the Nazis' *"Kinder, Kirche, Küche"* (Children, Church, Kitchen). The only way out of this contradiction would lie in devising some alternative institution to take over the functions of the family, but all the attempts to do this have failed.

In the Soviet Union, the Party has responded to this characteristic dilemma of totalitarianism by a gradual shift of emphasis in its family policy. During the period from the 1917 Revolution to the First Five-Year Plan, the major stress was placed on breaking down intergenerational continuity in order to attract more young people away from their conservative parents to the revolutionary Party. From the early 1930s on, however, the regime began once more to encourage continuity between father and son, since by this time, some of the postrevolutionary generation could be counted upon to support Communism. The return to a stronger family, moreover, was necessary as a way of replacing the millions who died as victims of the forced collectivization of agriculture and, later, as casualties of the war of 1941–45. Thus, in broad terms, the Soviet regime shifted from a family policy calculated to help establish its rule within Russia to one designed to furnish the larger population requisite to a strong internal economy and, especially, an effective foreign policy.[1]

## Down with the Family

During the first fifteen years or so of Soviet rule, the two full family codes plus a number of separate decrees gradually developed a generally consistent and complete family policy.[2] All legal inequalities between the sexes were abolished. Not only bigamy and adultery but even incest were dropped from the statutory list of crimes. Religious marriage was no longer recognized by law, and there seems to have been an official effort to reduce even the civil registration of marriages to a formality of no importance. De facto marriages were recognized as legally equivalent to those effected by civil ceremony, and such "nonregistered marriages" numbered perhaps

[1] There was a parallel progression in Soviet primary education—first a policy that loosened every bond and facilitated infiltration and then, after the new personnel had taken over, a strict tightening of control.

[2] The codes were dated October 17, 1918, and November 19, 1926. Both are translated in Rudolf Schlesinger, *Changing Attitudes in Soviet Russia: The Family in the USSR* (London: Routledge & Kegan Paul, 1949), pp. 33–41 and 154–168.

a quarter of a million by 1936, when the law was changed. Divorce could be had simply and cheaply at the wish of either partner, and at least among the small minority directly influenced by the Party line it was frequent.

That the early decrees were predominantly negative reflects their principal purpose: to hasten the disintegration of the patriarchal family of tsarist Russia. In Bukharin's words, "this formidable stronghold of all the turpitudes of the old regime" was the most pervasive and therefore, perhaps, the most powerful brake on the forward course of the revolution; it had to be removed. Political expediency guided the Soviet family policy of this period more than the abstract dogma of Engels' *Origin of the Family*, Bebel's *Woman*, and other Marxist classics.

While the Party actively sought to weaken family ties, it was not much concerned with sexuality. The Party line, insofar as there was one, was to avoid extremes: as Lenin put it, "neither monk nor Don Juan." Though he added also an admonition against "the intermediate attitude of the German philistine," this was perhaps the closest Western analogue to the ethical norm of the leading Bolsheviks.[3] Devoted to their Party duties, they typically led respectable personal lives and censured, with something like puritanical fervor, the occasional Lunacharsky who amused himself with a ballerina.

There were both Left and Right deviations from the Party line on sex. On the Left, Alexandra Kollontai was the principal advocate of a free, "glass of water" sex life. She usually presented her atypical views in the relatively safe form of fiction. In her *Love of Three Generations*, for example, she had the heroine, Shenya, declare: "I change my lovers according to my mood. At the moment I am pregnant, but I do not know who my child's father is, and moreover I do not care." On the Right, on the other hand, Professor Zalkind of Sverdlov University championed a rigid sex code which called for absolute premarital continence and condemned birth control and abortion. "Sex must be entirely subservient to class," he declared, and "the purely eugenic question of the revolu-

[3] Klara Zetkin, *Reminiscences of Lenin* (London: Modern Books, 1929); cited in Schlesinger, *op. cit.*, p. 77.

tionary Communist cleansing of humanity through posterity must be the only consideration in the choice of the beloved."[4]

In Party circles formal social curbs on sexuality were lax. Not so, however, the controls on reproduction. In spite of the assiduously propagated legend to the contrary, the right of parents to decide for themselves on the spacing and number of their children was never established as a Soviet norm. Opinion on the matter within the Party was divided, and policy therefore ambivalent, but in the dominant official view:

> Birth control [was] . . . a bourgeois panacea for social ills, which could have no place in a socialist society. [The Communists] interpreted the question from the point of view of a conscious limitation of the race rather than of permitting women to choose for themselves whether they wished to give birth to an endless succession of children.[5]

Such Soviet officials as advocated legal access to contraceptives did so not because they favored neo-Malthusianism per se, but rather because they considered the inevitable alternative under the prevailing conditions of Soviet life—an increase in abortions—the greater evil.[6] In any case, contraceptives were not generally available, even in the cities. By official regulation, what meager supplies there were had to be held at the state-run medical clinics, to be called for on each occasion when they were needed.[7] With the physical scarcity compounded by such bureaucratic controls, one can well believe that a "widespread prejudice" developed against the use of contraceptives.[8]

[4] See Jessica Smith, *Woman in Soviet Russia* (New York: Vanguard, 1928), pp. 129–131.

[5] *Ibid.*, p. 186.

[6] See, for example, the comments of D. I. Yefimov, People's Commissar for Health of the Ukrainian Soviet Republic, and Professor K. Bogolepov, of Leningrad University, quoted in Schlesinger, *op. cit.*, pp. 183, 259.

[7] Alice W. Field, *Protection of Women and Children in Soviet Russia* (New York: Dutton, 1932), p. 98.

[8] Maurice Hindus, "The Family in Russia," in Ruth Nanda Anshen, ed., *The Family, Its Function and Destiny* (New York: Harper, 1949), p. 113.

Abortion, consequently, was the more common mode of limiting family size, even though the state policy toward this was unambiguously hostile. Abortions were legalized only in order to facilitate their rigid control. A woman desiring an operation was required to go before an official committee, which tried to convince her that it was her duty to society to give birth to the child. In cases of first pregnancy, requests were denied except when supported by urgent medical considerations. In cases other than first pregnancies, as indicated by the 1927 statistics for Moscow, 40.8 percent of the authorized abortions were for medical reasons, 57.1 percent for economic reasons, and only 2.1 percent on all other grounds.[9] Such "frivolous" pleas as, for instance, the unmarried status of the mother or the parents' belief in a planned family were not acceptable.[10]

If an applicant was reluctant to accept a committee's negative decision, some doctors made it a practice to require her to watch other women undergoing the operation. Since abortions were performed without anesthetic, this was a sight that usually produced a sudden awareness of her social duty.[11] According to the director of the abortion department of the Moscow Institute for the Protection of Mothers and Infants, the Soviet Union was "the country in which abortion is least practiced."[12] Under such a system it is easy to see why this might have been the case.

## Wanted: A Substitute

In the early years of the Soviet state, then, there was a conscious effort to break down the family structure by various

[9] Field, op. cit., p. 83.

[10] Discussing the abrogation of the decree permitting abortions (which took place in 1936, not in 1946, as he says), Hindus remarks that thereafter "physicians had to steel themselves against the cries of despair of unmarried girls, who threatened suicide if they had to go through with childbirth" (op. cit., pp. 119–120). The implication that the new decree changed policy in this respect has no factual basis.

[11] Field, op. cit., pp. 91–92.

[12] Fannina W. Halle, Woman in Soviet Russia (New York: Viking, 1933), p. 144.

legal means—elimination of the differentiation in law between legitimate and illegitimate births, removal of adultery and incest from the category of crime, and judicial indifference to whether the support of a child born out of wedlock was charged to the biological father or to some other man (especially when the latter happened to have more money). At the same time, the state was concerned that the current generation should more than reproduce itself, and it therefore restricted abortions and controlled the use of contraceptives.

But these parallel efforts to de-emphasize the traditional family and yet assure a high birth rate posed the problem of how the physical care and socialist upbringing of children were to be accomplished. The dilemma is also seen in Nazi policies. One of Himmler's titles was Reich Commissar for Strengthening German Folkdom (or RKFDV), and he and his assistants proposed a number of means of improving—from the Nazi point of view—Europe's racial composition.[13] SS-men were given weekend leaves in order to impregnate women that the Party selected for their racial characteristics, and this effort to bypass the family, though not successful, is important as an indication of the regime's intent. In the words of Martin Bormann, a favored lieutenant of Himmler, "after the war, those women who have lost husbands, or who do not get husbands, should enter a marriage-like relationship with preferably one man, from which should result as many children as possible." The stipulation "after the war" was made, of course, only to prevent a drastic decline in morale: if the plan had been made public immediately, "not every soldier forthwith would desire that in event of his death his wife or his betrothed should beget children by another man."[14]

During the transitional phase in the evolution of Soviet

[13] See Robert L. Koehl, *RKFDV: German Resettlement and Population Policy, 1939–1945* (Cambridge: Harvard University Press, 1957).

[14] Oron J. Hale, "Adolf Hitler and the Post-War German Birthrate: An Unpublished Memorandum," *Journal of Central European Affairs*, 17:2 (July, 1957), 166–173. The whole memorandum is a remarkably interesting document, particularly for the intricate mixture of Nazi racism with such "progressive" ideas as, for instance, that the legal distinction between legitimate and illegitimate births must be abolished.

family policy, tentative and partly contradictory steps were taken to resolve this dilemma—on the one hand, toward reviving the family but remolding it in accord with socialist concepts; on the other, toward evolving alternative institutions to take over the family's functions in rearing the young. As a step toward a new family concept attuned to Soviet ideals, an attempt was made in Party circles during the middle 1920s to develop "socialist" marriage and other family ceremonies, described by one author in these words:

> The bride and groom sit on a red-draped platform, attended by fellow union members and representatives of the women's organization. The head of the factory committee is master of ceremonies. The pair pledge themselves to work mutually to raise the production of the factory, and suitable speeches are made, followed by an entertainment or refreshments. This ceremony is followed in due course of time by the Octobrina, in place of the old christening. . . . The child is dedicated to the Soviet state, and instead of being named for one of the saints is christened "Lentrozina" for Lenin, Trotsky, and Zinoviev, or "Era" if it is a girl; or "Rem" for Revolution, Electrification and Moscow, "October Twenty-fifth," or some other appropriate name, if it is a boy.[15]

How effective such secular ceremonies might have become in developing a new family concept is difficult to say. No ritual is effective as a means of social control until after a certain tradition has been established, and before this could happen in this case the regime's policy had changed.

While these new ceremonies were evolving the regime also began to establish state-run crèches and kindergartens as substitutes for the parents in caring for children. Lenin had described such institutions as "the simple, everyday means, involving nothing pompous, grandiloquent or ceremonial,

---

[15] Smith, *op. cit.*, pp. 93–94. Cf. Ella Winter, *Red Virtue: Human Relationships in the New Russia* (New York: Harcourt Brace, 1933), p. 152: "An amusing illustration of changing conditions in the USSR is the child whose parents enthusiastically named him Lentrozin for Lenin, Trotsky and Zinoviev. . . . Only the first syllable of the boy's name is good Communism now."

which can in actual fact emancipate women and abolish their inequality with men as regards their role in social production and public life."[16] Progress in translating this vision into actuality, however, was slow. Even in Moscow, the showplace of the nation, fewer than one-tenth of all infants were being cared for in the crèches as late as 1931, and the standards of these makeshift institutions were no more adequate than their number.[17]

For the two million waifs left by the war of 1914–18 and the subsequent civil war, Communist orphanages provided a further substitute for the family, enabling the state to instill in them the proper deference to the Party. Conservative family influences were also combatted through the youth adjuncts of the Party and, more broadly, through the newly established schools, which the regime set up as political training grounds for the new generation. "The school apart from life, apart from politics," Lenin had said, "is a lie."

The Party did not stop at trying to curb the family's influence on the child; it sought to use the child to influence his parents. To make the malleable youngster the Party's advocate in the home was hardly conducive to harmonious family relations. One sympathetic observer of the period wrote:

> The way in which children, especially the Pioneers, are urged to educate their parents, to persuade them to learn to read and write, clean their teeth, and give up going to church, is not always pleasant and is very prejudicial to family life.[18]

All of these early attempts to transform marriage and the family, however, were more important as indications of the orientation of Soviet policy than for their immediate effect. In a country torn by war and revolution, civil strife, and

[16] V. I. Lenin, "A Great Beginning" (1919), quoted in A. Krasnopolsky and G. Sverdlov, *The Rights of Mother and Child in the USSR* (Moscow: Foreign Languages Publishing House, 1953), p. 39.

[17] Field, *op. cit.*, p. 111.

[18] Klaus Mehnert, *Youth in Soviet Russia* (New York: Harcourt Brace, 1933), p. 222.

famine, the decrees of far-off Moscow were barely heard in the hamlets, and certainly not rigidly enforced. Even before the revolution the old family structure of tsarist Russia was already beginning to disintegrate under the impact of the pre-1914 industrialization; the process was hastened by the war and often completed by the civil war, when this was fought, so to speak, within the family. The low level of the economy and particularly the miserably inadequate housing were far stronger as disintegrative influences than any official decree. Still, the Party's efforts to reshape family life would undoubtedly have had profound effects in the long run, had it not been for an intervening shift in policy.

## The Family Revitalized

The shift, which began in the mid-1930s, was toward tightening rather than weakening family bonds. In order to stimulate marriages, the stigma was removed from romantic love of the old-fashioned Western bourgeois variety. Whereas the heroine of a 1930 Soviet novel would win her husband by fulfilling her factory production norm, a few years later her successor was showing less concern with abstract five-year plans and more with her own personal appearance. According to *Pravda*, reflecting the new line:

> We endorse beauty, smart clothes, chic coiffures, manicures. . . . Girls should be attractive. Perfume and make-up are a "must" for a good Komsomol girl. . . . Young people must gather and dance.[19]

If marriage was encouraged, divorce—which had been easy in the early period—was now actively discouraged by a succession of increasingly restrictive measures. First came a regulation requiring that each divorce be entered on the person's internal passport; next, sizable fees were introduced; and finally, in 1944, all but political reasons were eliminated as absolute grounds for divorce. Except in such cases, a

[19] Quoted in Nicholas S. Timasheff, *The Great Retreat: The Growth and Decline of Communism in Russia* (New York: Dutton, 1946), p. 317.

couple seeking a divorce was required first to go before a People's Tribunal, which was not empowered to grant the divorce but merely to try to effect a reconciliation. Only then could the parties take their case before a Superior Court, where the motives and allegations of husband and wife were weighed and a divorce was either granted or denied. The fact that the court based its decision entirely on ad hoc arguments enhanced its discretionary power and thus the ability to enforce the current Party policy.[20]

The renewed emphasis on the family was reflected, in a negative sense, in a modification of Soviet law that made the entire family of a criminal responsible for his offense. In many cases, the families of persons arrested in the great purges of the 1930s perished with the "criminals," presumably because it was feared that family resentment would generate new disloyalty to the regime.[21]

The changes in family policy culminated in a 1944 decree, the character of which is evident from its full title—"Decree on increase of state aid to pregnant women, mothers with many children, and unmarried mothers; on strengthening measures for the protection of motherhood and childhood; on the establishment of the title of 'Mother Heroine'; and on the institution of the order of 'Motherhood Glory' and the 'Motherhood Medal.'"[22] By this decree the distinction between civil and unregistered marriages, and hence between legitimate and illegitimate children, was re-established. Unmarried persons and parents of only one or two children were subjected to special taxes, while Stakhanovite mothers received progressively larger subsidies according to the number of children. A woman who had borne and raised ten or more

[20] Cf. G. M. Sverdlov, *Some Problems of Judicial Divorce*, quoted in Schlesinger, *op. cit.*, p. 378.

[21] Cf. Zbigniew K. Brzezinski, *The Permanent Purge: Politics in Soviet Totalitarianism* (Cambridge: Harvard University Press, 1956), pp. 82–84, 110.

[22] Full text in Schlesinger, *op. cit.*, pp. 367 ff. See also Sverdlov, *Soviet Legislation on Marriage and the Family*, summarized in *Soviet Studies*, 2:2 (October, 1950), 192–201; W. Parker Mauldin, "Fertility Control in Communist Countries: Policy and Practice," Milbank Memorial Fund, *Population Trends in Eastern Europe, the USSR, and Mainland China* (New York, 1960), pp. 179–215.

children was entitled to the highest award—the title of "Mother Heroine," carrying a lump payment of 5,000 rubles plus 300 rubles monthly for four years.

While the regime justified the system of family allowances in terms of social welfare, the device of progressive premiums was, as Schlesinger has pointed out, primarily intended as "an incentive to the production of enormous numbers of children."[23] In line with this intent, the already stringent restrictions on abortion were replaced by a flat prohibition except when they were necessary to save the mother's life.[24]

### Soviet Comments on "Malthusians"

When the change in family policy was completed, the Soviet press started an attack on the advocacy of planned parenthood, "the man-hating ideology of imperialists."[25] Even one accustomed to the scurrility of Bolshevik polemics must find the outrageous distortions and bizarre associations something of a new departure. The flow of these animadversions, particularly heavy up to 1953, the year of Stalin's death, subsided somewhat in quantity during the subsequent decade, but with little change in content or tone. The report of the main Soviet delegate to the United Nations Population Conference in Rome, 1954, is typical. He passed over most of

[23] Under the 1944 decree, by Schlesinger's estimate, a mother of six or more children could acquire an income sufficient to live modestly during her childbearing years. She always "had a great incentive to cover the expense of bringing up her older children by having new ones" (*op. cit.*, p. 397).

[24] Despite the previous limitations, the number of abortions had increased to such an extent that, in some places, they equaled or even surpassed births. Thus, 371 abortions were recorded for every 100 live births in Moscow during 1934. See Frank Lorimer, *The Population of the Soviet Union: History and Prospects* (League of Nations; Princeton: Princeton University Press, 1946), pp. 127–128. This increase was undoubtedly due to the hardships imposed by the enforced collectivization, which reached its height in 1930, and to the famine of 1932–33.

[25] A. Y. Popov, *Sovremennoe Mal'tusianstvo—Chelovekonenavist-nicheskaya ideologiia imperialistov* (Moscow: Gosudarstvennoe Izdatel'stvo Politicheskoe Literatur, 1953).

the topics on the agenda to concentrate on the single one that, in his terms, divided the East from the West.

> The outstanding peculiarity of the conference . . . is the striking manifestation of the struggle between two trends in the underlying questions of theory and practice of population statistics: the reactionary one, connected with neo-Malthusian ideas, and the progressive one, led by the delegates of the Soviet Union and the People's Democracies.[26]

While these writings cannot be readily classified, several themes are recurrent, as illustrated in the following examples.

*Personalities.* Bertrand Russell "calls for immediate atomic bombing of the peace-loving peoples and advises the rulers to see to it that 'the death rate is high.' "[27] He preaches "the raving fascist idea of breeding a special breed of people especially adapted to atomic warfare."[28] Darwin's *The Next Million Years* is "a bouquet of the reactionary Malthusian ideas which justify the bestial imperialist policy of aggressive wars and extermination of peoples."[29] "The American racist Margaret Sanger, who offered to help formulate a birth-control program" in Japan, thus agreed with a man who had allegedly "proposed compulsory reduction of the population."[30] "Abraham Stone, a specialist in sterilization, is traveling around the countries of Southeast Asia working out plans

[26] Report of T. Ryabushkin, translated in *Soviet Studies,* 7:2 (October, 1955), 220–230. It is hardly probable, however, that "the distinguished English economist, Colin Clark," and the other Catholic delegates who attacked planned parenthood would have agreed that they were "led" by the Communists.

[27] G. Alexandrov, "American Imperialists' Ideology is Cannibals' Ideology," *Pravda,* June 7, 1952; translated in *Current Digest of the Soviet Press,* July 19, 1952.

[28] Popov, *op. cit.,* p. 122.

[29] D. Troshin, "In Captivity to Subjectivism—On Preachers of Reactionary Ideas in Natural Science," *Pravda,* November 16, 1953; translated in *Current Digest of the Soviet Press,* December 30, 1953.

[30] O. Skalkin and A. Filippov, "Designs and Deeds of American Neo-Malthusians," *Pravda,* November 20, 1952; translated in *Current Digest of the Soviet Press,* January 3, 1953.

to reduce the population of these countries by 'scientific methods.' "[31]

Many more books of a Malthusian character have appeared in the last five years than in the entire preceding 150 years. Malthusian propaganda has been heard from false scientists like Vogt, Cook, Pendell, Pearson and Harper, Russell and Barker; from writers like Aldous Huxley and Paul Rebus; from ministers, politicians, diplomats, etc. . . . Masquerading as scientists and philanthropists, these lackeys of American monopolies openly advocate cannibalism and try to justify the demoniacal plans for the mass extermination of peoples.[32]

The "progressive forces" struggling against this "Malthusian obscurantism," on the other hand, are also a curious array. They include R. R. Kuczynski, identified as "a German demographer" (he was until his death perhaps the leading British demographer); Burgdörfer (the leading population official of Nazi Germany); Josué de Castro, who has revived August Bebel's theory on the relation between food and fecundity; Anton Zischka, a journalist who has written a book on overseas countries for Europeans considering emigration; Lucas, "a British ichthyologist"; Communist or fellow-traveler scientists like John Bernal or Palme Dutt; and Maurice Thorez.[33]

*Fascism.* "In their black business of deceiving the masses, the American warmongers have borrowed the criminal methods of the Hitlerite fascists. Slander, falsehood, hypocrisy, demagogy, zoological racism, cannibalistic Neo-Malthusian-

---

[31] A. Tamarin, "Fanatical Delirium of Contemporary Malthusians," *Literaturnaya Gazeta,* May 10, 1952; translated in *Current Digest of the Soviet Press,* June 28, 1952. As a matter of fact, Dr. Stone, one of the leaders of the American planned-parenthood movement, was invited by the government of India through the World Health Organization (WHO) to investigate the possibilities of reducing fertility in Indian villages. Since the Catholic countries in WHO threatened to resign if he advocated birth control by contraceptives, he had to agree to propose limiting births only by the rhythm method.

[32] Popov, *op. cit.,* pp. 5–6.
[33] *Ibid.,* Chap. 7.

ism, the flouting of all norms of human honor and morality —all these were part of the arsenal of the Hitlerite fascists, all these have been put to work by the American imperialists in the service of their predatory aims."[34] The United States is called the successor to Nazi Germany; neo-Malthusianism is termed "part of the arsenal of the Hitlerite fascists"; "the neo-Malthusians openly merge with the Hitler brand of racism."

Actually, fascist countries have all attempted to increase their populations both by family subsidies and by bars to contraceptives. Some democratic countries have also instituted either positive or negative incentives to larger families, but the United States far less than others.

*Racism.* "Malthusianism is very closely knit with racism, bourgeois nationalism, cosmopolitanism, and other hideous forms of imperialist ideology."[35] "The misanthropic ideas and practices of racist lynchers, geopoliticians and neo-Malthusians, who demand the extermination of millions of people, are being disseminated more and more widely in the U.S.A."[36]

> The American obscurantists are particularly concerned about the densely populated countries in Asia and the Far East, considering them testing grounds for their inhuman experiments.[37] What this "concern" means may be seen from the example of Korea, Viet Nam, Malaya, Burma, the Philippines, Egypt, Morocco, Tunisia, and other countries, where the American imperialists and their British and French partners are terrorizing and slaughtering multitudes of entirely innocent people.[38]

When an Indian scholar like Dr. Sripati Chandrasekhar arrives at the same conclusion as Western demographers and

[34] "Expose the Warmongers' Ideology," *Pravda,* June 4, 1952; translated in *Current Digest of the Soviet Press,* July 19, 1952.

[35] Popov, *op. cit.,* p. 23.

[36] "Policy of Fascism and War," *Izvestia,* January 14, 1953; translated in *Current Digest of the Soviet Press,* February 21, 1953.

[37] Skalkin and Filippov, *op. cit.* Cf. Popov, *op. cit.,* p. 130.

[38] Tamarin, *op. cit.* The perfect continuity between the two sentences indicates that both authors have been following the Party line correctly.

advocates birth control for India, he is chided for his errors in much milder language.[39]

*Sterilization.* Generally neo-Malthusians are condemned not for their advocacy of birth control, but for the fact that some of them advocate sterilization. They allegedly associate with lynchers and proponents of germ warfare. "A direct link exists between human sterilization, the lynching of Negroes, and the waging of germ warfare in Korea. All these reflect the cannibalistic policy of the American pretenders to world domination."[40]

*Cannibalism.* We have it on the authority of Khrushchev himself that "birth control is a cannibalistic theory."[41] What began as a polemical metaphor has become a necessary element of the standard description of neo-Malthusianism, to be repeated in every article.

*Cosmopolitanism.* "Malthusians have proposed that an international organization on birth control be created in order to reduce population by 'humane' and 'scientific' means. . . . In essence, this demand boils down to a demand that national sovereignty should be abrogated and that the international organization (which, directly or indirectly, would be put under the control of the United States) should be given the right to force one or another state to reduce its population by 'scientific' means. . . . This is how postwar Malthusian 'theorists' have tried to propagandize for cosmopolitanism and national nihilism."[42]

*War-mongering.* Contrary to the "lying booklet" of the "American professor-demagogue," Frank Lorimer—that is, the

[39] For example, by Alexandrov, *op. cit.*: In his book, *Demographic Problems of India and Pakistan* (Paris: Dunod, 1950), "Chandrasekhar, who notes that more than ten million persons die each year in India and 40 out of 100 do not survive the age of 5, directs his wrath not against the British imperialists who brought India to unheard of poverty and are guilty of the death of hundreds of millions of Indians by starvation in the course of several generations, but against the people of India themselves, who multiply 'too rapidly' and pleads for birth control! . . ."
[40] Skalkin and Filippov, *op. cit.*
[41] United Press dispatch, January 8, 1955.
[42] Popov, *op. cit.*, p. 129.

289-page study sponsored by the League of Nations[43]—"in the USSR the policy of developing the welfare of one state by crushing other states has been liquidated forever. . . . The Soviet socialist state has no need of external expansion or of colonial aggrandizement."[44] The "Malthusians' ravings," on the other hand, are no more than an "ideological preparation of the rear echelon of the imperialist countries for a new world war."[45] "Bloody wars, the atom bomb, and other means of mass extermination of peoples, the devouring of nation by nation—such are the contents of the blood-thirsty ravings of present-day Malthusians."[46]

> By annihilating hundreds of thousands of women and children with the aid of bacterial, chemical and napalm weapons, the Malthusians want to prove that the number of people in the world is "excessive" and is subject to forcible reduction.[47]

## Why the Change?

The usual explanation of the shift in Soviet family policy after the early 1930s has been, to borrow the words of Maurice Hindus, that "conservatism, in the sense of respect for the acceptable heritage of the past, as well as for the fruitful achievement of the present, was edging radicalism out of the picture."[48] This has been the dominant interpretation put

[43] Lorimer, *op. cit.* Popov's quotations give no page reference, and I have not been able to find a passage in Lorimer corresponding to the following alleged quotation: "There is no doubt that a tempestuous population growth will develop in the Soviet Union. The big question for the rest of the world is whether it will succeed in restraining this expansion to the limits of Soviet borders" (Popov, *op. cit.*, p. 138).

[44] *Ibid.*, p. 138.

[45] *Ibid.*, heading of Chap. 5.

[46] *Ibid.*, p. 133.

[47] V. Korionov, "In Himmler's Footsteps," *Pravda*, August 16, 1952; translated in *Current Digest of the Soviet Press*, September 27, 1952.

[48] Hindus, *op. cit.*, p. 117. This was not, however, the author's main emphasis in a work he wrote at the time of the turn, *The Great Offensive* (New York: Smith & Haas, 1933).

forward by Soviet apologists, and it was also the essential theme of such profoundly anti-Stalinist works as Timasheff's *The Great Retreat* and Trotsky's *The Revolution Betrayed*.

In retrospect, such an explanation seems somewhat wide of the mark. While it is difficult to find a single adjective to describe Stalinist society, "conservative" scarcely is the *mot juste* to characterize the stupendous goals of the five-year plans, the collectivization of the peasants at the rate of one million a day (with five to six million discards), the Moscow show-trials, the *Gleichschaltung* of the arts and sciences, and the territorial expansion in Europe and Asia.

If one can speak of a "conservative" period in Soviet history, when the revolution was "betrayed" in a great "retreat," it was rather the period of the New Economic Policy, or NEP (1921–28), when the Party granted a temporary respite to small producers and petty merchants. This truce with capitalism was ended by the wholesale collectivization of agriculture and the First Five-Year Plan, which Stalin himself termed "a profound revolution . . . equivalent in its consequences to the revolution of October 1917."[49] The new family policy, though often justified by the Party on the basis of bourgeois and even tsarist precepts, was an integral part of this second Soviet revolution, and it can be understood only as a response to the new needs with which this upheaval confronted the regime.

Essentially two factors underlay the revitalization of the family. The first was the huge population loss resulting from the collectivization program, which later was multiplied by World War II. According to the 1926 census, 71.7 million of Soviet Russia's 82.7 million occupied civilians were engaged in agricultural production. The fundamental transformation effected by the First Five-Year Plan was to bring this dominant sector of the economy under complete state control. The

[49] [J. V. Stalin], *History of the Communist Party of the Soviet Union* (*Bolsheviks*) (New York: International Publishers, 1939), p. 305. "The distinguishing feature of this revolution," he added, "is that it was accomplished *from above,* on the initiative of the state, and directly supported *from below* by the millions of peasants who were fighting to throw off kulak bondage and live in freedom on the collective farms."

expropriation of peasant holdings was a prerequisite to the superrapid industrialization, for it furnished the state with the necessary capital and with a cowed labor force.

The cost in human lives, however, was fantastic. Unyielding opponents of the collectivization drive were branded as "kulaks" or, when they were too obviously not well-to-do peasants, as "kulak-followers"—or even, as in the case of such an urban intellectual as Bukharin, as persons with a "kulak soul." According to a 1930 report by Molotov, the kulak section of the population, including their families, totaled 6 or 7 million.[50] This was the number of persons ousted from their land and not permitted to enter the new collectives.[51] In the words of an American Communist journalist's eyewitness account, they constituted a new social class of "pariahs without any rights which need be respected, and without any knowledge as to what they might do to be saved."[52]

How many of these fled to the cities, how many were sent to the forced-labor camps that were established during the First Five-Year Plan, and how many lost their lives in the process or in the consequent famine of 1932–33, it is impossible to determine precisely. One authoritative study estimated that between 5 and 5.5 million Soviet citizens disappeared between the censuses of 1926 and 1939.[53] Stalin's own estimate of the loss of human life as a result of collectivization was 10 million.[54]

Additional population losses during the war of 1941–45 were estimated by one authority at an excess mortality of 12

[50] *International Press Correspondence*, 1930, p. 373.

[51] As Stalin put it, "It is ridiculous and fatuous to expatiate today on the expropriation of the kulaks. You do not lament the loss of the hair of one who has been beheaded. There is another question which seems no less ridiculous: whether the kulak should be permitted to join the collective farms. Of course not, for he is a sworn enemy of the collective farm movement. Clear, one would think." "Problems of Agrarian Policy in the USSR," in *Selected Writings* (New York: International Publishers, 1942), pp. 162–163.

[52] Anna Louise Strong, *The Soviets Conquer Wheat* (New York: Holt, 1931), p. 81.

[53] Lorimer, *op. cit.*, pp. 133–137.

[54] See Winston Churchill, *The Hinge of Fate* (Boston: Houghton Mifflin, 1950), p. 408.

to 19 million, plus a birth deficit of 8 million.[55] These night-marish figures, however, now appear to have been conserva-tive. The clearest evidence of the enormous mortality comes from the sex ratios published as part of the 1959 census. Among those aged 32 years and over, there were only 599 males per 1,000 females. Actually, the whole of the Soviet era has been building up a male deficit, as one can see from successive census figures (including those from the only tsar-ist census):

| | |
|---|---|
| 1897 | 700,000 males short |
| 1926 | 4,900,000 males short |
| 1939 | 7,200,000 males short |
| 1959 | 20,800,000 males short |

Not all types of extraordinary mortality are included in these statistics (famine, for example, does not generally re-sult in an unbalanced sex ratio), but they are a rough index of the deaths from war, terror, and forced labor. The alloca-tion between the war of 1941–45 and the terror of the prior period can be estimated from the successive census figures, from the sex ratios of particular age-groups in 1959, and from independent data on military mortality. The number of men who served in World War II was only about 20 million, and if we assume that half were killed—a generous estimate, even allowing for the known slaughter—then a deficiency of almost 11 million is still to be accounted for by other causes.

To these extraordinary deaths one must add the extraor-dinary nonbirths—those that would have taken place under "normal" circumstances but did not. The total depletion from terror and war, as these affected both fertility and mortality, was of the order of 80 million—about 25 million during the civil war and the establishment of the Bolshevik rule, at least 10 million during the social revolution of the 1930s, and some 45 million during World War II. These figures are ob-viously estimates, but they are so monstrously large that one

[55] Warren W. Eason, "Population and the Labor Force," in Abram Bergson, ed., *Soviet Economic Growth: Conditions and Perspectives* (Evanston, Ill.: Row, Peterson, 1953), pp. 101–125.

could cut them in half, or by two-thirds, and still arrive at the same conclusion—that every Soviet institution had to be adapted to this catastrophe. Postwar policies with respect to forced labor, the armed forces, and education reflect, at least in part, the effort to use the remaining limited manpower as efficiently as possible.

## Need for Stability

The first need that the shift in family policy reflected, then, was to replace these manpower losses. The second was to restore stability to Soviet society, which the second revolution of the late 1920s and early 1930s had broken down into a dangerously fluid mass. The social structure of the country had undergone tremendous upheavals and the need for consolidation and stabilization could also be met in part by the new family policy.

By the mid-1930s the new generation of parents had lived through nearly two decades of Soviet society. For many of them the élan of the early revolutionary years had been a personal experience, not wholly erased by subsequent difficulties and disappointments. Such parents presumably would not try to instill in their children's minds a faith in the displaced institutions of tsarism, which they knew principally through Soviet propaganda. On the contrary, many of them could probably be counted on to inculcate Russian patriotism and loyalty to the Soviet regime in the youngest generation; and the regime needed whatever stability a retightening of family bonds might afford it.

Of course, Soviet policy is not completely a rational adaptation to practical needs. The Party planners may start a change in policy as a rational response to such needs, but in their impetuous effort to make the country swallow the new line immediately, completely, and enthusiastically, they generally overshoot the original mark. Totalitarian systems have no built-in feedback mechanism to check this tendency, and their course is typically marked by spasmodic reversals from one extreme to the other. This characteristic of the system has been no less manifest in Soviet family policy than in other policy spheres.

By a realistic appraisal, however, the shifting policy line of the government has probably had less profound effects on the Soviet family than the more constant social conditions.[56] Urbanization, which began before the revolution, became a powerful surge under the impact of collectivization and industrialization and is still continuing at a rapid rate. As elsewhere, this transformation has produced smaller, looser families—a tendency reinforced in the Soviet Union by the persistent shortages of food, consumer goods, and particularly housing. Despite their recent upward tendency, general living standards in the USSR remain at a lower level than before the end of the NEP in 1928.

Though there has been no significant modification in the basic character and objectives of Soviet Communism, the present leadership in the Kremlin has condemned the oppressive and inflexible policies of the Stalinist era and indicated its own more rational approach by a slight degree of liberalization. The Great Thaw has achieved—to borrow Dwight Macdonald's metaphor—the temperature of northern Greenland. Should this trend continue, it will be reflected in Soviet family policy, and certain changes already effected may be interpreted as indicative of the probable direction. Under a 1954 decree, abortion was once more legalized under certain conditions.[57] That this was clearly not intended to lower the birth rate, however, is indicated by the continued frenetic denunciations of neo-Malthusians that we have noted. Pregnant women are now entitled to be paid while on maternity leave, the length of which has also been extended, since April 1, 1956, from 77 to 112 calendar days. Divorce remains expensive and difficult to obtain.

Neither the political nor the social milieu of the Soviet system has been conducive to the eventual evolution of Western family norms. When the policy was ostensibly "liberal," parents were not given the right freely to determine what size family they would have. When it became "conserva-

[56] Cf. Kent Geiger and Alex Inkeles, "The Family in the USSR," *Marriage and Family Living*, 16:4 (November, 1954), 397–404.
[57] See Mark G. Field, "The Re-Legalization of Abortion in Soviet Russia," *New England Journal of Medicine*, 255 (August 30, 1956), 421–427.

tive," religious and other traditionalist norms did not set the pattern of family life. Whatever the coating, the basic ingredients of the pill remain the same. The shifts in Soviet family policy, however significant in incidentals, have always been in line with the fundamental purpose of maintaining Party strength within the USSR and maximum Soviet power in the international sphere. With respect to these fundaments, there has been no "great retreat," nor is any indicated for the future.[58]

[58] A study of the Soviet family, the first book-length analysis in English since Schlesinger's, appeared too late to be used here: David and Vera Mace, *The Soviet Family* (Garden City, N.Y.: Doubleday, 1963).

# THE POPULATION OF EUROPE

Europe west of the Soviet Union comprises only about 5 million square kilometers, or less than 4 percent of the world's total area. That it is reckoned a continent rather than the western portion of Eurasia is due less to geography than to history. For this extension of the earth's largest land mass, by global standards no more than a largish peninsula, was the cradle of one of the world's great civilizations, crucial of course to Europeans and their overseas descendants but increasingly so also to other peoples as well. Almost all the forces presently transforming Asia, Africa, and Latin America —whether electricity or nationalism, whether Marxism or public sanitation—are developments of cultural elements that originated on the world's smallest continent.

Europe, exclusive of the Soviet Union, has a total population of about 440 million, or less than 15 percent of the world's total. It includes 26 nations at least as large as Luxemburg, plus half as many smaller principalities and territories. The four largest countries—the United Kingdom, West Germany, France, and Italy—are very roughly equal in population, each with approximately 50 million inhabitants; and the smaller units range down to Andorra, with about 8,000 persons, and Vatican City, with only 1,000. Not only in size but also in wealth and power, in level of culture and degree of political freedom, the range is great from one country of Europe to another. Yet underlying this diversity is also a certain uniformity, which defines the continent and sets it off from the rest of the world. Commentators on India have often introduced their subject by pointing out that in many respects this subcontinent of Asia is as heterogeneous as Europe. One might turn the simile about and suggest that in many respects Europe is as much a single unit as India. In reviewing the economic and cultural factors that have shaped

Europe's population, thus, we shall have repeated occasion to note both how one European country or region contrasts with another and, on the other hand, how often these differences shrink when they are put against the worldwide range.

## The Balance of Births and Deaths

Before the development of modern industry, Europe was already distinguished from the other great civilizations by the control that its family system imposed on the rate of population growth. In classical India or China, for example, marriage was all but universal and typically took place at puberty or shortly thereafter. In Europe a quite different pattern evolved, varying from country to country but with certain characteristics common at least to the Western region. Guilds generally did not permit apprentices to take a wife until they had finished their training, and this regulation meant that a substantial portion of the urban population had to postpone marriage for a considerable number of years after it was physiologically possible. In agriculture, numerically the most important sector of the late medieval and early modern economies, farmhands were almost members of a farmer's family, and thus were under no social or economic pressure to marry early. Men were induced to put off assuming parental responsibilities until they had acquired the means to care for a wife and children. This meant in many cases that they never married, but lived as fully accepted members of a household headed by an older brother, who because he had inherited the family plot was able to be a "husband" (which means, literally, *householder*).[1] As a result of this personally onerous but socially effective system of birth control, Europe's population generally did not press as heavily on the subsistence available to it as in the Asian civilizations; compared with China or India, Europe was relatively free of great famines. And at the beginning of the modern era, the continent was still relatively sparsely populated.

With the rise of European science and industry, one after another the main causes of early death were brought under

[1] See below, p. 182, n. 23.

control. Traditional agricultural practices yielded to greatly improved methods, and such food-deficiency diseases as scurvy became medical rarities. Vaccination against smallpox, discovered at the end of the eighteenth century, made it possible to eliminate this dread disease. When drinking water could be transported through iron pipes, public authorities could finally segregate it absolutely from sewage and thus control cholera and all the other scourges spread by excrement. From Louis Pasteur's hypothesis that each of the infectious diseases is carried by a microscopic organism to their virtual elimination as causes of death took, in the most advanced countries, only half a century.

Just before the First World War, the high correlation between industrialization and effective control of mortality was evident. In Northwest Europe—that is, the British Isles, the Low Countries, Germany, Switzerland, and Scandinavia—only 15 persons died each year per thousand of the population; in France, Italy, and the western portion of Austria-Hungary this death rate was about 20; and in Spain and the Balkans it was about 25. Since that time death rates have steadily fallen—apart from the two world wars—throughout Europe, and this regional variation all but disappeared. Merely the acquisition of an urban-industrial culture, once the major travail of the transition was past, was invariably accompanied by a substantial decline in mortality; but improvements beyond this point depended not on industrialization per se but rather on how effectively its benefits were distributed among the whole population. Of the countries of Northwest Europe, thus, those with the fullest and most efficient social services have achieved the most effective death control. In his book on the population of Europe, Kirk took Holland's record as the optimum and compared it with the rest of the continent, assuming that the age structure was the same in all countries. By this standard, 35 percent of the mortality in the rest of Europe was "excess" in 1939, that is, unnecessary if the medical techniques available had been fully used.[2]

[2] Dudley Kirk, *Europe's Population in the Interwar Years* (League of Nations; Princeton: Princeton University Press, 1946), pp. 180–182.

A more common measure of a country's all-round ability to combat death is its infant mortality rate. Under the most primitive conditions—typically before accurate statistics are collected—the rate is well over 300 per thousand live births. We can illustrate the remarkable decline from this figure by looking at Sweden, whose record is comparable to that of the Netherlands. During the second half of the eighteenth century the rate in Sweden fluctuated around 200 infant deaths per thousand live births. During the nineteenth century it fell slowly but consistently, reaching 100 by 1900. Since that date the decline has been faster, down to about 15 in 1960. In about six generations, thus, Sweden's infant mortality was cut by 92.5 percent.

Several generations ago, the greatest demographic difference between industrial and nonindustrial nations, also on a world scale, was in their mortality. Public sanitation and modern medicine, whose effects were transforming the populations of Europe and its major overseas extensions, were only beginning to spread to most of the countries of Asia, Africa, and Latin America. While this contrast still remains, since about 1945 the worldwide variation in mortality has been reduced greatly. With the discovery of antibiotics and powerful insecticides, and with their global distribution through international agencies, every country has been able to bring epidemic diseases under more effective control. Since the less developed nations have proportionately many infants and children, as *their* mortality was reduced the death rates of the whole populations also fell tremendously. In industrial countries, and also in those European countries at the periphery of its industrial core, the diseases of advanced ages—cancers and heart ailments, in particular —rank among the most important causes of death, while for the rest of the world these are still relatively insignificant. When in effect old age is the principal cause of death, countries with relatively few elderly persons are especially favored.

For the five-year period 1956–60, on the average only 11 persons in Europe died annually for each thousand in the population. In historical terms this is an astoundingly low figure. Even more remarkably, while Europe's death rate fell to this new low, the difference shrank between it and that of the rest of the world. For the same five-year period Asia's average death rate was only 22 and that of Africa only 25, so that for the world population the rate during this period was 18 per thousand, or a figure that a generation ago was close to the best that had been achieved in the most advanced countries.

Now that the control of early death is becoming characteristic of the whole world, fertility once again marks the greatest difference between Europe and other continents. As we have seen, there were built into the traditional family of preindustrial Europe institutional checks to uninhibited procreation. When large numbers of young people moved to the growing towns and thus escaped from the villages' censorious eyes, it may be that these bonds were broken and that fertility went up from its traditional level. Malthus may have been harking back to this norm of parental responsibility when he propounded late marriage as the prime means of escaping the dire effects of overpopulation. His counsel, obviously enough, was not readily accepted; what is surprising is that the behavioral norm he recommended spread as much as it did.

Especially among the middle classes—that is, those who were most likely to improve their life chances by postponing the formation of their family—the age at marriage rose steadily during the first half of the nineteenth century. In England between 1840 and 1870, for instance, the average age at marriage of clergymen, doctors, lawyers, merchants, manufacturers—in short, aristocrats and "gentlemen" of all types—was almost precisely 30 years.[3] In Ireland, as the extreme case of this European pattern, postponement of marriage was not restricted to the gentry but became the universal standard. In 1946, or just before the new postwar trend, the average age at marriage was 33 years for males and 28 for females; and about one person out of four was still single at age 45. As compared with many underdeveloped countries, where females especially marry shortly after puberty,

[3] J. A. Banks, *Prosperity and Parenthood: A Study of Family Planning among the Victorian Middle Classes* (London: Routledge & Kegan Paul, 1954), p. 48.

or even with such overseas countries of European culture as the United States, where the median age at marriage for females is 20, present-day Europe is anomalous. Throughout the continent marriages below the age of 15 are almost nonexistent, and even those below the age of 20 are atypical. The European countries where in 1960 the modal age at marriage for females was as high as 25 to 29 years included the following: the United Kingdom, France, Belgium, and Switzerland; Ireland and the Netherlands; Norway and Sweden; Portugal, Spain, Italy, and Greece. Over a wide range of European cultures, thus, the norm is still operative that a man should marry and bear children only after he has established the means of caring for his wife and offspring.

That in so many European countries people marry relatively late is all the more remarkable since by and large effective contraceptives are generally available. The Protestant churches and "respectable" middle-class persons fought against legal contraception for a period, but this opposition was overcome almost half a century ago, and that of the Nazi and Fascist parties vanished with the end of their regimes. The Catholic ban on contraceptives is truly effective only in Ireland and perhaps in Spain; and the Communist ban applied intermittently in the Soviet Union and Mainland China has not been a significant factor in Eastern Europe. Contraceptives are more widely available in the West, but in most of the "People's Democracies" abortions are legal and the number performed is considerable.

If we look at the historical trend in fertility, the first thing we see is that the pattern is essentially similar to the one in mortality: the lower birth rates started in Northwest Europe and spread south and east together with the urban-industrial culture. Within this general pattern, however, a number of countries stand out as exceptions. In France, thus, the average family size began to fall very early—some time in the eighteenth century, while the country was still a monarchy and before it was in any degree industrialized. By the time of the First World War, the French birth rate was the lowest in Europe; and as fertility dropped in other nations, particularly during the depression-ridden 1930s, many European demographers and statesmen thought that their countries were following the French path to literal perdition. In the late 1930s the lowest birth rates (that is, below 17.5 per thousand) were in a strange assortment of countries in addition to France: England, Belgium, and Switzerland; Norway, Sweden, and Estonia; Austria and Czechoslovakia. Many of these countries, as well as Fascist Italy, Nazi Germany, and some others, tried in various ways to induce young people to marry and have larger families; but the effect of these pronatalist measures was in most cases close to nil.

The revival of natality came during and immediately after the Second World War, when there were shortages of housing and sometimes even of food—when, that is to say, material conditions hardly favored family life. Fertility rose enough to make nonsense of the dire forecasts of Europe's depopulation, but still only to a level that was low by global standards. For the five years 1956–60—the same period for which we earlier compared mortality—the average annual rate for the whole world was 36 births per thousand population, and for Africa it was 47, for Asia 41, for North America 34. Europe had only 19 births per thousand population, or by far the lowest rate among all the continents. In only a few countries was the 1960 birth rate higher than 20—namely, Ireland and the Netherlands, which have been demographic anomalies for a century or more, Poland and Yugoslavia, Portugal and Spain; and even among these, the rate was barely as high as, say, in the United States.

The natural increase, thus, has gone through the cycle known as the demographic transition. At the beginning of the modern era many children were born, but a large proportion died before reaching maturity, and Europe's population grew slowly. Then, one after another, the causes of early death were brought under control, while for several generations Europe's fertility remained more or less constant or, it may be, even rose slightly. The consequent increase in population was tremendous.

Before that complex transitional period commonly known as the industrial revolution, Europe's cities—those that were then in existence—were no more than small towns. According to a list that the medieval historian J. C. Russell compiled from a wide variety of sources, in the thirteenth to the sixteenth centuries representative town populations ranged from 78,000 (Venice at its height) down to what we would term hamlets.[4] These urban centers were important administratively and culturally, but the proportion of the population living in them was never more than a few percent of the total. These urban aggregates became large cities only when, with the rise of manufacturing, they acquired an important new economic function. They grew largely by the in-migration of peasants' sons and daughters, whose numbers increased faster than the opportunities that the countryside afforded them.

Almost all of the migration within each European country was ultimately a movement not only to cities but to the largest cities. In England the dominant flow was to the Midlands or to London, in France overwhelmingly to Paris, in Sweden to Stockholm, in Austria-Hungary to Vienna, or, if not, to Budapest, and so on. The exceptions to this pattern were countries with important regional differences, such as in language (Switzerland, Belgium, Spain), or in religion (Germany), or in economic development (Italy); and here the same kind of urbanization took place within a smaller unit. And much of the international migration within Europe was another version of this movement of country people to industrial jobs. Irish, Scots, and Welsh went to England, Poles to Germany and France, Italians to France; the typical movement was from the rural periphery to the industrial center.

During the same period that Europe's cities were filling up, the continent poured forth an emigration of a size and importance unique in world history. Of the estimated 67 million persons who migrated across an ocean between 1800 and 1950, some 60 million were Europeans. They and their descendants founded great new nations in North and South America and in Oceania, and in various spots in the rest of the world they established important outposts of their industrial civilization. The first source of this emigration was

[4] J. C. Russell, "Late Ancient and Medieval Population," *Transactions of the American Philosophical Society*, Vol. 48, Part 3 (June, 1948), Tables 63–65.

Northwest Europe—the British Isles, Germany, and Scandinavia—where industrialization and the concomitant population increase began. Then, as mortality fell in Southern and Eastern Europe and these populations grew at a faster tempo, different countries became the dominant sources of emigration. At the high point of this so-called "new" migration, just before the First World War, some 400,000 left Italy in a single year, and well over half that number departed from each of Austria-Hungary, Russia, and Spain plus Portugal. The tide was stemmed by the war and broken by postwar restrictive legislation in both emigration and immigration countries.

Before 1914 migrants were ordinarily economically motivated; after that great watershed, migrations were largely or wholly political in their origin. The peace treaties following the First World War established a number of new states in Central and Eastern Europe, and in the subsequent period the League of Nations sponsored population exchanges designed to reduce the size of Europe's many ethnic enclaves. Migration from Communist Russia and from Fascist Italy, previously two of the dominant sources of both intra-European and especially overseas migrants, was prohibited, or, more precisely, was redirected to Soviet Asia and the Italian colonies in Africa. From Hitler's accession to power in 1933 to the beginning of the Second World War six years later, the Jewish population of Germany fell by more than half, presumably mostly because of emigration, partly because of successful evasions of the official count. A considerably larger number of ethnic Germans migrated to Germany, which in the depression of the 1930s now had a labor shortage.

All of these political migrations, however significant compared with past history, were dwarfed by the displacements concomitant with the Second World War. Even if we exclude the Soviet Union, the site of the largest movements, the migrations involved a very considerable percentage of Europe's population; the exact figures are of course not known. The large number of refugees from battle areas was greatly augmented when belligerents on both sides undertook the "strategic" bombing of nonmilitary targets. The Nazis rounded up

Jews from all their conquered areas and shipped them to
death-camps. Many thousands of German settlers followed
the Nazi armies in their victorious march eastward and then
rushed headlong back before their retreat. Germany imported
about 5 million forced laborers to supplement the 2 million
prisoners of war working in that country, so that by the end
of the war aliens constituted a fifth of the German labor force.
In the postwar period those Jews and other displaced persons
who survived generally left Germany, and were replaced by
ethnic Germans expelled from Czechoslovakia, the western
regions of postwar Poland, and various other German enclaves. West Germany has absorbed more than 7 million of
these refugees, and East Germany more than half that number. To every open door, or door that could perhaps be
opened, there have come political refugees—from the Soviet
Union, Fascist Italy, Fascist Spain, Nazi Germany; the list
continues to Hungary of 1956, but does not end there. Especially since 1945, this political push from Europe has been
matched by an overseas political pull—the increased efforts
of Australia, Canada, and other countries to accelerate the
influx of desirable immigrants. The movement typical of
Europe in its liberal heyday, when passportless persons left
under their own momentum to seek, if not their fortunes,
then better working conditions, is gone.

The effect of emigration on Europe's population is difficult
to calculate. It is likely that the departure of some 60 million
persons, by relieving the economic pressure that largely
stimulated the exodus, actually quickened the continent's
population growth. This population increase also stimulated
Europeans to reduce the size of their families; and by the
interwar years, as we have seen, the notion was widespread
that this decline in fertility would continue to literal depopulation. In the postwar perspective, we can see rather
that Europe's death control and its birth control are both
excellent, so that by world standards its growth has been
extremely low. During the 1950–60 decade, when the world
as a whole increased by an annual average of 18 per thousand, for Europe this was only 8 per thousand. The population explosion, that common metaphor so ominous for Asia

and Latin America, applies to very few countries of Europe, and to these in a different sense.

As we noted, Europe's total population of 440 million now constitutes less than 15 percent of the world's total. According to a forecast by the United Nations, in the year 2000 this percentage is likely to be 10 or less.[5] The decline of Europe's population, no longer imminent in absolute terms, is a safe prognosis relative to that of the rest of the world. However, one should not accept too readily the notion that Europe is therefore less well off. The very rapid population growth of India, of China, of Central America, does not constitute an economic, social, or political advantage to those countries; but the contrary. The rational balance of births and deaths that Europe has achieved is a sign of moral health and economic and political strength; it is an example that one day the rest of the world must learn to follow.

[5] U. N. Department of Economic and Social Affairs, *The Future Growth of World Population* (Population Study No. 28; New York, 1958).

# FIRST IMPRESSIONS (1954)
## OF DUTCH SOCIETY

Strolling down one of Amsterdam's side streets in the early evening is like walking through a series of living rooms. The family groups clearly visible from the sidewalk are as stylized, and just about as public, as wax figures in a store window—the man smoking a pipe and reading his paper, the wife across the room sewing or knitting, the several children bent over their schoolbooks, the dog napping in the right foreground. American or British suburbs approximate the smug dullness of this petty bourgeois idyl, but not, I think, its self-containing peace.

A hundred facts, ranging from the low illegitimacy and divorce rates to the results of public-opinion polls, might be cited to illustrate the continuing dominant role of the family in Dutch society. Night life, except for tourists, hardly exists even in Amsterdam: one spends the evening at home, with one's wife and children. Almost all newspapers come out in the afternoon and are sold mostly through subscription: they are read at home, quietly, after dinner. Dutch is the only language I know of that has a specific word for the unit of man, wife, and children—*gezin*—in addition to *familie*, which means what sociologists call the "extended family" in English.

Since no casual visitor is likely to get an invitation to a Dutch home, he will usually not appreciate the importance of the family in Dutch culture. The tourist hurrying through fills his mind with trivia: florin and guilder mean the same thing, dogs are not "curbed," sidewalks are scrubbed every Friday, Amsterdam's mail boxes are on the rear of the trolleys that go to the central post office. Even if he stays long enough to delve beneath these superficialities, however, he will probably get a very lopsided impression of Holland. For, as in every country whose national income is based in part on tourists, the "attractions" to which his attention is directed are contrived to satisfy his expectations.

Thus, windmills do pepper the landscape, even if less thickly than on Delft china; but the last of these windmills was built more than a century ago, and most of them no longer grind grain or pump water. Now the government maintains them as "national monuments," and unpicturesque Diesel engines do the work. No foreigner leaves Amsterdam without a tour of Marken and Volendam, two "fishing villages" whose picturesquely garbed inhabitants fish little but, speaking good English, French, or German, sell glimpses into their quaint pasts. The Alkmaar cheese market, to which every tourist agency runs special buses, is so overrun with camera'ed foreigners that it is a distinct achievement to get an unencumbered photo of the costumed Dutch carrying cheeses to the seventeenth-century weighing-house. Wooden shoes are still the standard footwear of the peasant and fisherman, and it is not likely that they will ever be replaced: they act like, as well as look like, small canal-boats, and on the often soggy ground they do more cheaply what rubber boots do elsewhere. In the cities, however, they are a rarity outside tourist shops. In one community, the last clog-carver works in a shop window and is paid his wage by the novelty manufacturers' association. It is sad to watch the world become more and more standardized, which in Western Europe means more and more Americanized; but is it really better to have folk customs artificially maintained, or revived, largely for their dollar value?

Tulips, on the other hand, and flowers in general, are as much a part of the life of the people as the well primed tourist expects. The bulb fields and the competitive exhibits of the various growers are more exciting even than their commercial description. In the smaller towns, the standard middle-class home is a one-family house, two rooms deep, opening front and back on gardens. In Amsterdam, Rotterdam, and The Hague, flowers often decorate homes, restaurants, museums, movies, bridges, squares, urinoirs, and even the bombed-out areas not yet rebuilt. At every second corner along the avenues there is a flower peddler who sells twenty perfect rosebuds for the equivalent of 40 cents, to take an expensive example.

Physically at least, the western half of the country is a replica of the picture postcard. There are canals everywhere, as one expects, but nothing about them denotes the remarkable fact that they are flowing upward into the sea. The dikes that hold the sea back are also more interesting to read about than to look at. They are not walls, but embankments, with roads and sometimes houses on them. (No one who has ever seen one could be taken in by the fanciful story of Peter and his heroic thumb, but one community, aware of his popularity among tourists, has erected a statue in his honor.)

That Amsterdam is one of the most beautiful cities on the Continent is in part because its adaptation to modern life has not yet obliterated the old city. Its canals, gracefully curving in concentric rings around the central square, are lined with seventeenth-century houses, each different and yet all in the same harmonious style. Today, these one-time patrician residences house institutions and business offices; there is a fascinating medley, or cacophony, of old and new—fine old mansions used as warehouses; a frontage often without sidewalks and with a truly medieval disregard of building lines, made dangerous for pedestrians by rumbling trucks; a passenger barge with blaring horns advertising the Liberal candidate. The houses are thriftily built, squeezed together like spectators watching a parade, with steep, narrow staircases going up like ladders. Windows are many, small, white-rimmed; in more recent buildings, they have an infinity of shape, size, and position, often giving a fillip to otherwise uninspired architecture.

A truer symbol of present-day Holland than the windmill, and really a less commonplace one, is the bicycle. In Holland, the bicycle is not an independent vehicle, but one member of a school of fish, a swarm of gnats. A dozen bikes, or a hundred, move down the street in flexible unity, encompassing a stopped trolley, impatiently pausing at the infrequent traffic lights, thinning out when the speedsters get a chance to show their mettle, thickening again as the traffic grows heavier—but moving always as a whole, with a life of its own. There was an ordinance prohibiting riders from taking more

than one child passenger on a bicycle, but it was withdrawn
in response to indignant protests. There is a brass band, with
every member on a bike; it proclaims itself, correctly I am
sure, as unique in the entire world. There is an escalator,
undoubtedly also unique, constructed large enough to hold
bikes and their riders. Groups of all kinds cycle together—
the young man with his girl sitting side-saddle behind; another couple each on a bike and holding hands; a mother
going shopping with her youngest in a little seat on the han-
dlebars, her next youngest in a little wicker chair at the back;
a family going on an outing strung out one behind the other,
with the youngest children distributed over several bikes; the
delivery bicycle or tricycle in its hundred variations. When,
at five in the evening, all these groups coalesce into a purpose-
ful homeward-bound stream, it is an adventure for even a
native of Manhattan to cross the street. In his charming
*Letters from Holland,* Karel Čapek discusses the dangerous
ubiquity of bikes and ends with a speculation on the effect
they may have had on the Dutch national character:

> Now that [the bicycles] cannot get their own back on
> me, I don't mind declaring quite openly that I didn't like
> them, because to my mind it is somewhat unnatural for a
> man to be sitting and stepping forward at the same time.
> The practice of stepping forward while seated can ulti-
> mately affect the pace of a nation's development. It be-
> comes possible to tread slowly and nevertheless to get
> along quickly. You realize this when you see how far the
> Dutch have gone, although they tread at about the same
> rate as a slow-motion film. But I, arm-swinging pedes-
> trian that I am, will not interfere with their bicycles; let
> every nation follow its star by the methods which it
> understands.

## The Dutch "National Character"

Holland has more studies of national character than anyone
will ever read. A generation ago, under the very powerful
influence of S. R. Steinmetz, Dutch social scientists turned
from the then current armchair philosophizing and began to

develop an empirical school of their own, called sociography. A sociographic study attempts to relate all the data concerning a given locality in a meaningful way—geographical factors, the characteristics of the population, social history, economics, culture, folklore. At its best, as when a good sociologist writes about the region where he was born, it can combine personal intimacy with scientific detachment in a way seldom otherwise achieved. But at the usual level of doctoral dissertations, these studies are as sterile, in my opinion, as most of the empirical work being done in the United States. While it is a useful exercise for a student to study in detail a small unit of society—a portion of a province, a village, sometimes even a single parish—too often this conditions the range of his thought. Dutch social scientists tend to speak either of "man" or of the inhabitants of this or that particular area, and there is a marked paucity of work about the present-day Netherlands as a whole: no satisfactory social history, no study of its population, no economic history.

The usual description of the Dutch national character is "petty bourgeois." In one of his essays, Otto Jespersen related this estimate to the extraordinary frequency of the diminutive ending in the Dutch language. Even in scientific discourse, not to mention ordinary conversation, the diminutive is almost as frequent as in an old-fashioned English-speaking nursery. Jespersen concluded that the Dutch are a petty-bourgeois people living in a small country with small ideas. While this is certainly deducing too much from too little, it seems to me that the often dubious study of national character can reasonably be approached through language, particularly through the study of essentially untranslatable words. A list of words unique to Dutch would include, among many others, two that one hears very often: *netjes,* which combines the meanings of nice, cute, clean, pleasant, proper—a Dutch social scientist who visited the United States remarked on her return that she found America "hygienic but not *netjes*"; and *deftig,* by which upper-class businessmen are often described —seriously before the war and today sometimes ironically— and which means dignified, elegant, fashionable, aristocratic, distinguished, stately, proper. In Dutch, the word *schoon,* like its German cognate *schön,* can mean beautiful, but as a development from the national passion for housecleaning, its usual current meaning is clean, or clean-beautiful.

Another way to approach the question of national character is through the results of public-opinion polls. Based on the results of these polls: 18 percent of the Dutch people believe that one can foretell the future through the stars, palm-reading, and other methods; 7 percent have had telepathic experiences (with respect to occultism in general, Holland seems to be the Southern California of the Continent); 28 percent go to at least one concert a year, 48 percent to at least one play; 40 percent were reading books at the time they were questioned (compared with 21 percent in the United States, 55 percent in England); 30 percent read the Bible regularly, including only 3 percent of the Catholics; 68 percent would like to have blue eyes; 47 percent of the tenants consider their rent cheap; 53 percent of the women wear nylons; 47 percent of the women do not approve of mixed bathing (this is a recurrent issue in the press; it is forbidden in some parts of the country); 85 percent of all homes have a spring cleaning; 24 percent regard the United States as an example to follow, 8 percent Russia, 58 percent no country; 45 percent approve of world government; 38 percent think English ought to be the world language, 29 percent Esperanto (instructions in public telephone booths are printed in five languages, including Esperanto).

A generation ago, all college students in the Netherlands were required to study six languages, and Greek was dropped from the general curriculum only after a considerable campaign. Simultaneous instruction in English, French, and German is now begun at the age of thirteen or fourteen, and college freshmen are given reading lists including books in all three languages as a matter of course. The professor of one course in modern history that I visited in Amsterdam, trying to give an impression of pre-1914 Europe, illustrated his points by reading passages in their original from Stefan Zweig and H. G. Wells. In the better bookstores, books are arranged by subject matter rather than language. Stenographers are expected to be able to take dictation in at least two, and preferably three, foreign languages. On the other hand, the smattering that all educated people have of these three languages seldom rises to a real command; and even in government or university publications the written English is usually poor.

Dutch culture is not only "petty bourgeois" but Christian. How pervasive religion remains in the lives of the people can be appreciated in almost any feature of Dutch society, from the incidental to the most basic. A serious discussion on any subject is likely to get under way by exchanging information on the participants' religious faiths; this sets the line and determines whether certain fundamentals can be assumed or must be included. A meal at someone's home begins with what a German-born acquaintance called "the Dutch moment," during which each person, before he begins eating, surreptitiously observes whether the other is first going to pray. In restaurants of any class, one sees people praying; at the luncheon break during the annual convention of the Netherlands Sociological Society, the chairman asked for a moment of silence so that those members who wanted to could pray. Trolley posters admonish young girls to maintain their chastity and tell readers to speak freely of God but not to take His name in vain.

At any hour of any day, one can turn on the radio and hear "Let us pray." There are two radio stations in Holland, both government-owned, and program time on them is divided among the various radio societies—Catholic, several Calvinist, Labor, and Liberal—in proportion to their support among listeners. Each society issues its own magazine featuring its own programs and its own message; a periodical that listed all the programs, with the propaganda of none of the groups, was forced by the courts to cease publication. The various program directors compete for the listener's attention with some of the same high-pressure methods that any American finds familiar, but with the difference that they plug their faiths rather than their sponsors' soap or corn flakes.

The division of all Dutch life along religious lines begins with the segregation of children into Catholic, Calvinist, or secular schools. Typically, a Dutch child plays only with children of his own faith, and he learns early that the *andersdenkende*—those with another point of view—are queer. When he grows up, his friends are of the same religion, he marries in his own faith, joins the party and trade union associated with his church, reads his church's newspapers and periodicals, often even buys in stores owned by those of his faith. The Dutch, it has been said, have as many dikes in their mental life as in their countryside.

Why should a people in the geographical center of Northwest Europe have clung so tenaciously to traditions that elsewhere have been disappearing? In a world increasingly socialist, Holland has retained many of the old petty-bourgeois norms in not only its ideology but also its day-to-day life. In a world more and more secularist, Holland has remained a stronghold of traditional Christian faith, both Catholic and Protestant. The causes of these differences lie deep, and to explain them is not simple. The whole of Dutch history, from the very foundation of the state, is relevant.

## Persistence of the Past

Modern Holland was born in an eighty-year war of independence against Catholic Spain. From the beginning, nationalism and Protestantism were like opposite sides of the same coin; the relation between church and state was like that between left and right hand. The amazing victory against Philip's mighty empire was followed by the truly incredible growth of Holland's wealth and culture. This small people, living on the mud flats at the mouths of the Rhine and Meuse, developed its herring fleet into the world's largest merchant marine. With the fabulous wealth of Java and a near-monopoly of the spice trade, Holland became the most prosperous nation of the seventeenth century, competing with Louis XIV's France and outshining Britain. Peter, later Tsar of all the Russias, who traveled to Haarlem to learn shipbuilding, was only the most famous of the thousands of foreign artisans who came to Holland to learn their trade. Dutch canals and brick-paved roads were the marvel of all Europe. In spite of her niggardly natural resources, Holland built a universal culture to the heights of Rembrandt, Grotius, Spinoza, Huygens, van Leeuwenhoek—to name the giants among the scores of others who graced seventeenth-century Holland.

Religion may have been the base of this rich culture, the prime reason for its extraordinary growth. When Max Weber tried to show that what he termed the Protestant Ethic had been a necessary precondition to the development of modern capitalism, he could have found no better example of this thesis than Calvinist Holland. According to Calvinist doctrine, each man is predestined to salvation or to eternal damnation. Nothing he can do can change his fate, but (according to the doctrine as it developed after Calvin) his status on earth can be taken as a sign of what his lot after death will be; for does not God favor His elect in this world as well as the next? That is to say, the full religious fervor of a pious people became a stimulus to commerce and other secular activity. It may have been the Protestant Ethic that made the seventeenth century Holland's Golden Era.

In the eighteenth century, however, Holland suffered a gradual decline from this peak, first in trade, then in other sectors of the economy, finally in her entire culture. The very fact that Holland's success in commerce had been so phenomenal inhibited the rise of industry: the burghers who had become wealthy in trade would not invest in factories. Thus, once the decline set in, it was never again possible to approach the splendor of the Golden Era. Britain's culture is built on its Victorian base, the nineteenth-century fruition of her industry and empire; France's is derivative from the rationalism and revolutionary élan of the eighteenth century; but Holland still harks back to the seventeenth century. This means that "the heroic struggle" of Protestant Holland against Catholic Spain is not merely one echo of a faded tradition but a part of living national sentiment.

The rationalist, materialist, secular emphasis of Western culture developed in eighteenth-century France, and the doctrines of the French Revolution (in a diluted and distorted form) were spread over Europe by the medium of Napoleon's armies. Mercantile Holland, however, was a modern country before the French Revolution: there were no serfs to be freed, as in the Germanies, no Inquisition to be outlawed, as in Spain. Since the function of Napoleon's armies in Holland was not to bring the Rights of Man, it may be that the principal effect of the eighteen years of oppressive occupation was to reinforce the House of Orange, the Netherlands Reformed Church, and every other element of social traditionalism.

When her independence was restored in 1815, Holland was at the lowest point in her modern history. Half the town population were on the dole; most of the other half were little better off. Infant mortality ranged from one-third to one-half; life expectancy was estimated at 34 years. Misery was drowned in gin. Thousands died in cholera epidemics. In these same years, a number of ministers seceded from the Netherlands Reformed Church, which had been the state church and remained the church of the ruling class. Though Calvinist in origin, the Reformed Church was insufficiently Calvinist in doctrine and attitude for part of its lower-middle-class membership. In its social content, this schism was the Dutch counterpart of the 1830 revolutions on the Continent or the Chartist movement in England. As in all the series of complicated schisms and unions over the following 120 years, the break with the parent church was formally based on religious differences, but each time some whose theology should have led them to secede chose to remain because of the higher social status associated with the Reformed Church. Thus, the group of quarreling, more rigid sects—which can be designated collectively as the Orthodox Calvinists—have had an influence quite disproportionate to their relatively small numbers. Their unyielding traditionalism in social and political questions has echoed in the conscience of the more orthodox wing of the main church, which has acted in turn as a bridge to the center of Dutch social and political power.

Around the middle of the nineteenth century, there were two contending forces, almost too amorphous to be called parties: the Liberals and the Conservatives. The Conservatives were reactionary in the literal sense of the word, but did not agree among themselves how far back they wanted to go. They gradually lost power to the Liberals, who began to split into left and right wings and then into smaller groupings, principally over the issue of how far and how fast suffrage should be extended. There was a political vacuum and no industrial proletariat to fill it, for modern industry only began to develop in Holland after 1870. The vacuum was filled by a coalition between Orthodox Calvinists and Catholics, both underprivileged groups just beginning to rise from their torpor.

For two centuries after the Dutch nation was born in the war against Catholic Spain, the large Catholic minority were second-class citizens. The constitution of 1848 gave Catholics equal suffrage, and during the several following decades the Catholic community sought new means of self-expression. Newspapers and literary journals were started by the dozen, manifestoes were written, Catholic historians dug into sources and wrote learned tomes to break the link between *Protestant* and *nation*. In this ferment, after several false starts, a Catholic State Party was founded by Herman Schaepman, a poet-priest turned politician. During the same period, Abraham Kuyper—an Orthodox Calvinist minister, founder and editor of a daily, author of several hundred books and pamphlets—founded the Anti-Revolutionary Party, which consciously and explicitly held up the Old Testament in opposition to eighteenth-century rationalism and the principles of the French Revolution.

Slowly, persistently, fighting against the prejudices within their own groups, Schaepman and Kuyper built the foundation of a future coalition. The first important cooperation was in what the Dutch call "the school fight," the 75-year struggle to get and widen state support of religious schools. In 1886, after the largest extension of suffrage to date, the two parties won an important victory and formed the first Calvinist-Catholic cabinet. There was a Liberal comeback, but from the 1890s to World War II, with minor interruptions and variations, Holland was ruled by this coalition. It eventually combined many of the progressive features of socialist parties elsewhere—wider suffrage, full rights to trade unions, social legislation—with measures designed to maintain Holland no longer as a Protestant but as a Christian nation.

While every important area of social life has been shaped by this Christian government, the first, education, remained the most important. The first coalition government got state subsidies for both Catholic and Calvinist parochial primary schools; and over the years, in a struggle that has influenced Holland's political life more than any other, the subsidies were gradually increased in size and extended over wider and wider areas. Free primary education, attacked as unfair competition to religious schools, was finally abolished; and today pupils must pay at the same rate in all schools, with the deficit in all made up by the state. One of the last big fights took place when Kuyper founded a university and his party pushed through a bill subsidizing institutions of higher learning. In 1918, there was a grand "pacification"—a compromise by which the religious parties voted for female suffrage and the Liberals and Socialists accepted government subsidies for religious schools as inviolable. The hope that this would end the school fight was fulfilled, however, only in the sense that the secularists no longer had the forces and spirit for more than minor skirmishes. In 1952, for example, government subsidies were extended to special Catholic and Calvinist trade schools, against only nominal opposition.

## Religion, Politics, and Population

The socialist movement had been started in the 1870s by a group of German émigrés, and for some fifty years it followed the pattern of the German Social Democrats—the discussions around Revisionism at the turn of the century, the split into a more moderate Right and a more orthodox Left (although in Holland the Left was in many respects less Marxian than anarchist), even a one-day mock revolution in 1918. During the interwar period, however, the socialist leaders gradually turned more and more to the British Labor Party as their model, particularly in the effort to seek a broader base than merely the industrial proletariat. This transition was completed by the cooperation of underground groups during the Nazi occupation, and the socialists emerged from that experience with a new name, the Labor Party, and a new philosophy. Their key concept was "the breakthrough": they wanted to shatter the old religious parties and realign the electorate into the mass of workers, farmers, intellectuals, and middle class, all organized into the Labor Party, versus a small conservative minority. These tactics failed completely. A comparison of the results of the last prewar and the first postwar elections shows how little difference five years of war and occupation made in party affiliation. The new Labor Party was supported by the same percentage of the electorate as the several prewar socialist and progressive groups that had united to form it, but by no more.

The central feature of every postwar government in the Netherlands has been a Catholic-Labor coalition, and no government on any other basis would be stable. The weakness of Labor politics is aggravated by the fact that, in the center, the Catholics are in the strategic position: if pushed to it, they could conceivably unite with enough of the parties on the Right to form a weak cabinet, but for the Laborites the choice is coalition with the Catholics or out of the government. Thus, while the change from Calvinist-Catholic to Catholic-Labor as the typical coalition has reflected a real shift to the Left, it has brought about fewer changes than one might suppose. Particularly in those areas in which the Church has special interests—religion, education, family welfare, public morals—the Catholic party calls the tune, and the Laborites dance to it as cheerfully as they can.

Postwar Dutch politics has been dominated by the contrast between the constricted economy and the rapidly growing population. Not only did the country suffer very heavily from the war and Nazi occupation (and, more recently, from flood damage), but it lost the Indies, which used to contribute one-sixth of the Dutch national income. On the other hand, the population has grown from five million in 1900 to more than ten million today. This remarkable growth has resulted from a very low mortality, the effect of excellent social services available in every village, and a fertility so high as to have become one of demography's important unsolved puzzles.

One of the reasons for Holland's high fertility is so simple that it defies analysis: the Dutch like children. If in the United States the national ideal of feminine beauty is the adolescent girl with perfectly regular features and high breasts; if in France it is the somewhat more mature, more experienced woman; in Holland it is the young mother, comely rather than beautiful, simple and dutiful rather than brilliant. The repetitive pictures of Queen Juliana with her several daughters—crossing the street with a baby in her arms, amateurishly skiing with an older girl, sitting at home with her husband

and family—are at least as effective, I think, in maintaining the traditional family ideal as in fulfilling their more conscious purpose, to symbolize national unity. Several of the young intellectuals I met, precariously beginning their careers, were willing to make extraordinary sacrifices in order to begin their families immediately; and with them the question was not the unavailability of contraceptives, as often in the country-side, or moral qualms against using them, as among the more devout Calvinists and the Catholics, but one of taste. The American concept of being able to "afford" a baby, one of them told me, is barbaric.

The birth-control movement in Holland has a semilegal status. The national law designed to hamper its growth is reinforced, particularly in the Catholic South, by more stringent local ordinances. Nevertheless, legal restriction is a less effective impediment than the general sentiment that respectable people do not discuss birth control, in any terms or in any context: even the several conferences on population problems that I attended refused to hear the neo-Malthusian point of view. When the official journal of the Netherlands Medical Association published one short article on birth control in December, 1949, it was showered with cancellations and denunciatory letters, in some of which the physician-correspondents displayed gross ignorance of even the medical aspects of contraception. Medical students in general are taught nothing of birth control; and even in Amsterdam, the least hidebound of the universities, it was only recently, after a long, uphill fight, that the local head of the planned-parenthood society was given permission to conduct free private classes for medical students interested enough to attend. Nevertheless, particularly since the war, the Netherlands Society for Sexual Reform, as it terms itself, has grown rapidly, and it now has more than 50,000 members. More than that—virtually all members of all groups now practice some birth control; the question is only whether honestly or hypocritically, whether with effective or ineffective means.

The sanctioned solutions of the growing population pressure are, over the long run, industrialization and, for the more immediate future, emigration. The intense interest in emigration, evident in all media of public expression, would in any case have developed a large outward movement; and this has been reinforced by the government, which has made a series of bilateral agreements with several countries and has organized and subsidized the passage of emigrants. During the eight-year period 1946–53, there were more than 180,000 such sponsored emigrants, principally to Canada and Australia. However, the total postwar emigration from the Netherlands has been only about one-fourth of the natural increase in the population.

The inherent difficulties of an industrialization program in a country with few natural resources, a relatively immobile labor force, and no established market for industrial products, cannot be overcome easily; and in the Netherlands they have been aggravated by the ambiguous attitude of many policymakers towards industrialization. All groups recognize that industry is necessary, but many fear its social consequences no less than they look forward to its economic benefits. The sociological journal of the Netherlands Reformed Church has conducted a series of surveys to try to determine to what extent industry has resulted in increased secularization. Catholic discussions of the issue often emphasize spreading industry through a countryside rather than concentrating it in towns, in an effort to maintain the social values of the village. While it is impossible to gauge the precise effect of these religious qualms, certainly they are not unrelated to the complaint, often heard in Holland, that industrialization is proceeding too slowly.

The rapid population growth has been at disparate rates in the various religious groups. In particular, the Catholic minority, about a third of the total population in 1900, is now almost 40 percent; and in the youngest sector of the population the proportion is higher. Catholic and other periodicals continually speculate about what will happen when the figure reaches 51 percent. Quite apart from whether this will happen and, if so, when, the discussion does much right now to exacerbate religious tensions. It must be emphasized that Dutch Catholics retain much of the pugnacity developed in their struggle for full civil status; they have none of the easygoing liberalism to be found among some of their French or Belgian coreligionists.

The hatred of Germany and Germans among the Dutch is, so far as I could judge, more widespread and intense than, for example, in France. When I first arrived in the country and spoke Dutch still with a strong admixture of German words and idiom, I was treated by passers-by and minor officials like a pariah—an unusual but edifying experience for a dollared American in Europe. Nevertheless, many people are responsible enough to see that it is necessary to seek out what good survived the Nazis in Germany, to try to develop it and cooperate with it. It is difficult, if not impossible, to remember with full vividness every horrible detail of Nazi atrocity, and yet to seek a mode of common existence with some of the Germans who participated in it; and that the Dutch attempt to do *both* shows at least glimmerings of the imagination that the present situation demands.

# FAMILY SUBSIDIES IN THE NETHERLANDS

That Holland is a demographic anomaly in Northwest Europe has long been recognized by social scientists. Its natality has been consistently the highest in this culture area, and its mortality (except for the war years) has generally been at one of the lowest rates in the world. The consequent increase in the population is startling, especially when compared with that of Northwest Europe as a whole, as in Table 1.

TABLE 1. POPULATION INCREASE IN THE NETHERLANDS
AND THE REST OF NORTHWEST EUROPE, 1850–1950

|  | Mean Population (thousands) | Percentage Increase |
|---|---|---|
| Netherlands | | |
| 1846–1850 | 3,058 | |
| 1896–1900 | 5,026 | 64 |
| 1946–1950 | 9,784 | 95 |
| Rest of Northwest Europe[a] | | |
| 1846–1850 | 107,611 | |
| 1896–1900 | 149,251 | 39 |
| 1946–1950 | 189,993[b] | 27 |

[a] Eire, United Kingdom, Norway, Sweden, Denmark, Germany, Belgium, Luxemburg, France, Switzerland.

[b] For 1947–50, population figures were available for West Germany only; these were adjusted on the assumption that the ratio to the population of all of Germany remained the same as in 1946. However improbable this may be, the difference will not affect the total sufficiently to invalidate the comparison.

SOURCES: R. R. Kuczynski, *The Measurement of Population Growth: Methods and Results* (London: Sidgwick & Jackson, 1935), supplemented by United Nations *Demographic Yearbooks* and *Monthly Bulletins of Statistics.*

In the general upswing of the birth rate during and after the war, Holland's reached a maximum of 30.2 in 1946, almost half again as large as that of any other country in Northwest Europe. Now that the cohorts born in the middle 1940s are beginning to enter the labor market, this will increase by 50,000 to 75,000 persons per year—a disturbingly large figure for a country of this size.

Holland's economy, in contrast to its population, deteriorated sharply from its prewar position. The Netherlands East Indies, which used to account for fully one-sixth of Holland's national income, is now independent Indonesia. Every element of the Dutch economy, from rolling stock to manpower, was depleted by the German occupation; and the difficulty of the postwar reconstruction has been aggravated by the general maladjustments of the European economy. The contrast between the rapidly growing population and the war-damaged economy stripped of Indonesia created an almost tangible population pressure. At all levels of social intercourse, the public became acutely aware of this. The government is attempting to alleviate it by sponsoring expensive industrialization and emigration programs, which to date have been only partly successful.[1]

It is against this background that Holland's family-endowment policy is administered. Under such circumstances, whether family subsidies affect the birth rate is a decidedly relevant question; and this is the principal subject of this paper. Secondly, Holland affords an example of the interaction between Socialist and Catholic family policies, and of the consequent tendency of family subsidies, once they have been instituted, to grow in size and importance.

## Underlying Social Philosophies

Advocates of a family-endowment policy have been motivated by one or more of four general considerations:

(1) Catholic philosophy: The natural unit of society is not the individual but the family, and wages should therefore be paid at least in part according to family needs, rather than individual worth.

(2) Egalitarianism: Since in general there is a negative

[1] See below, pp. 310–314.

correlation between income and family size, family subsidies help effect a more equitable distribution of income.

(3) Social welfare: The children of large families are often those who most need assistance.

(4) Population: To the extent that the secular decline in the birth rate has been caused by economic factors, it can be checked by family subsidies.

These four principles are ranked in order of decreasing importance, from a fundamental norm to a contingent expedient of unproved value. In general, therefore, the strongest advocates of family subsidies have been Catholics, especially those most in accord with the doctrines of Leo XIII and in countries (particularly France) with especially low natality. Fascist countries (and, since the middle 1930s, the Soviet Union) have also uniformly adopted some mode of family endowment, particularly because of the assumed value to the nation of a rapidly growing population. Socialists and liberals, on the other hand, have been less consistent. In Anglo-Saxon countries, they have sometimes been among the most vigorous proponents of a family wage (for example, Eleanor Rathbone in Britain, Paul Douglas in the United States); but the historic role of Continental socialist parties and their affiliated trade unions has been forthright opposition, petering down in recent years to acquiescence.

Socialists are caught between two contradictory tenets, the underlying ideology of "To each according to his needs" and the trade-union slogan of "Equal pay for equal work." In general, family subsidies are paid at the expense of the wages of unmarried workers—either directly, when the total wage fund remains equal, or indirectly, through the inflationary pressure created by an increase in income with no corresponding increase in production. This conflict of interest tends to weaken union solidarity, especially since employers' contributions to family subsidies have often been gained in place of other union demands. Moreover, unless administrative safeguards are established, various abuses are possible: undue interference in the worker's family life, discrimination against married workers, and others. Thus, in the decade following the First World War, when family-endowment programs got under way in most countries, socialists and trade unionists opposed them. In Limoges, CGT members went so far as to refuse to accept benefits after the system had been established; in Berlin, members of the metalworkers union threatened to leave the organization unless the system was effectively opposed. However, it became increasingly difficult, particularly during the depression, to align this stand with fundamental socialist principles; for one could hardly find a more direct translation of "To each according to his needs" into social action than a law regulating workers' pay according to the number of minor children they had to support. Fundamental opposition to family subsidies, therefore, tended to give way to differences over administration and other details.

In Holland,[2] the family-subsidy principle began as a wholly Catholic concept. The Minister of Labor during the depression following the First World War, P. J. M. Aalberse, was a Catholic economist of progressive views. At his initiative, the government established the Supreme Labor Council (*Hoge Raad van Arbeid*) to give it information and advice on economic and social questions, and this Council stimulated a rapid extension of Holland's social legislation.[3] Articles by Aalberse in the *Catholic Social Weekly* advocating family subsidies were supported by such larger works as *The Regulation of Pay Rates according to Catholic Sociology* by Professor J. D. J. Aengenent. Such organizations as the Union of Parents and Heads of Families and the Roman Catholic League for Large Families helped circulate these views more widely. The first application of these concepts was also under Catholic auspices: the successive groups of government em-

[2] Most of the facts concerning this early development, but not their interpretation, are from an unpublished manuscript by H. H. Heringa, "Sociale organisatie en reorganisatie," Amsterdam, 1950. See also Hugh H. R. Vibart, *Family Allowances in Practice* (London: King, 1926), especially pp. 36–41.

[3] Among its 44 members, representing employers, labor, and the government, the balance of power was held by twelve social scientists representing "the public." Measures adopted during this period included a workmen's compensation act (1921), supplemented by special accident-insurance laws for seamen and farm laborers; old-age pensions (1919); increased doles to the unemployed—as well as an extension of the 40-hour week to 48 hours.

ployees to get family subsidies—post-office employees, teachers, railroad employees, government mineworkers, etc.—received them as a result of the Catholic bloc's persistent fight for the principle in Parliament; and the first private employers to sign union contracts under which they paid bonuses for children were Catholic owners of textile mills in the South.

Dutch socialists were strongly opposed to this trend, for the reasons noted above. Moreover, this division was to be expected in terms of rational self-interest, for Catholics tended to have the largest families and the secularist urban intellectuals and skilled laborers who led the Socialist Party the smallest ones. Socialists attacked the family subsidy as a premium for breeding. De Walle, a socialist pamphleteer, termed the Union of Parents and Heads of Families a "Union of Reactionaries." In 1921, the secularist trade-union federation (NVV) called a special "Anti-Family-Subsidy Congress." In spite of the vigorous language in which it was voiced, however, this opposition was evanescent, for principled criticism of family subsidies was compromised, as has been noted, by the contradiction with socialist ideology. Practical criticisms, on the other hand, had the paradoxical result of extending and strengthening the system. The mineworkers union objected, for example, on the ground that mine owners, who paid part of the subsidy, tended to give preference to single men, and this made it harder for married men to find employment. More generally, socialists regarded all needy families as entitled to special benefits, not merely those of certain government employees or certain workers. While the intent of these arguments was to advocate other modes of social welfare or of income redistribution (particularly differential income taxes), they were easily diverted to support the Catholic effort to extend and rationalize the family-endowment system. From 1925 on, all persons employed by the state were paid in part according to the number of children they had; and the proportion of all workers covered by union contracts who received family subsidies increased from 12 percent in 1920 to 27 percent in 1938.[4]

[4] L. P. van der Does, *De economische beteekenis der sociale verzekering* (Deventer: Kluwer, 1946), p. 104.

In 1937, C. P. M. Romme, one of the Catholic Party's principal leaders and then Minister of Social Affairs, introduced a bill extending family subsidies to all workers, and the socialists supported it except for differences on administrative details. Principled opposition came only from the liberals, who denounced giving government support to this "morality of the unreasoning animal," and from some of the Orthodox Calvinists, who oppose insurance of any kind as an affront to God.[5] It went into effect on January 1, 1941, but the differences between the Catholic and the socialist principles underlying it did not affect its development until after the war. By Romme's interpretation, the purpose of his bill was to aid families with more than the average number of children; thus, subsidies began with the third child and increased progressively for children of each higher order of birth.[6] For the socialists, on the other hand, the purpose of the bill was less to help large families than all families, and at the end of 1946, the law was amended in this sense.

Neither the Catholic principle of progression nor the so-

[5] W. F. de Gaay Fortman and A. C. M. van der Ven, *Handleiding voor de toepassing der kinderbijslagwet* (Alphen-aan-den-Rijn: Sansom, 1941), pp. 22–32. P. Zandt, the leader of a splinter preserving Calvinist principles in fossil form, announced in Parliament that he could support the bill only if he could be sure it was not insurance; while the socialist Van der Waerden was opposed to subsidies on principle but would support an insurance bill. It was a measure of Romme's parliamentary adeptness that he was able to satisfy both. The bill passed the Second Chamber by 66 votes to 22 and, after a delay occasioned by the fall of the government, passed the First Chamber by 27 to 7. It was signed by the Queen and became law on December 23, 1939, but during the five months before the German invasion there was no time to put it into effect. However, "after the German army was replaced by a [German] civilian administration, it developed that these authorities desired to have the law put into effect quickly." There were slight differences between Romme's bill and a "decree of the Führer," and the authors discuss whether the Dutch or the German text was the final authority (*ibid.*, pp. 34–37).

[6] Romme is in this respect a mild Malthusian. Malthus was in general opposed to laws that shifted the burden of support from parents to the community, but he was for allowances to families with six or more children, for these would give needed assistance to the parents without encouraging improvident marriages.

cialist one of virtually equal subsidies for all children has any necessary relation to the total amount paid out in subsidies, but the effect of the successive compromises between these two positions has been to raise this total substantially, for each new amendment has been made with the highest current figure as the base. Table 2 shows the amounts paid under the original law and at three subsequent dates.

TABLE 2. AVERAGE SUBSIDIES, IN DUTCH CENTS PER WORKING DAY, PAID IN THE NETHERLANDS FOR EACH CHILD OF EACH BIRTH ORDER, 1945–63

| Birth Order | 1945 | 1947 | 1952 | 1963 |
|:---:|:---:|:---:|:---:|:---:|
| 1 | 0 | 40 | 44 | 83 |
| 2 | 0 | 40 | 46.5 | 90 |
| 3 | 13 | 40 | 47 | 90 |
| 4 | 20 | 42.5 | 51.5 | 123 |
| 5 | 24 | 44 | 54 | 123 |
| 6 | 27 | 45 | 56 | 138 |
| 7 | 29 | 46 | 57 | 138 |
| 8 | 30 | 46 | 58 | 138 |
| 9 | 31 | 47 | 58.5 | 138 |
| 10 | 32 | 47 | 59 | 138 |

Sources: F. J. H. M. van der Ven, "Terug naar Romme!" *Economie,* 16:5 (February, 1952), 197–203; communication from the Centraal Bureau voor de Statistiek, June 11, 1963.

Other revisions of the law in line with the socialists' arguments in 1937, such as its extension to cover illegitimate children and the small self-employed class,[7] have also been additions rather than substitutions. Thus, the cost of the program, which Romme estimated at ƒ15 million, had grown to more than ƒ225 million by 1950 and to ƒ616 million by 1961,[8] or by considerably more than can be accounted for by the postwar population growth and inflation.

[7] But see also Centrum voor Staatkundige Vorming, *Proeve van een ontwerp van wet op het verlenen van kinderbijslag aan zelfstandigen* (The Hague: Katholieke Volkspartij, 1948).

[8] At the official exchange rate a guilder is worth about a quarter of a dollar, but its purchasing power is generally higher for most commodities.

## Subsidizing Population Growth?

In this context, the key question concerning family subsidies is their effect on fertility, and this is not one that can be answered definitely. Most of the discussion in other countries, including such an excellent work as David Glass's book on population policy,[9] is not directly relevant, because of the important differences between Holland and the rest of Western Europe in this respect. Once parents have come to view their role largely in rational terms, it is generally impossible either to revive traditionalist attitudes towards childrearing or to pay them enough to make up for their financial loss.[10] In such countries as France and Sweden, therefore, where family subsidies were introduced after a sharp decline in average family size had taken place in order to *raise* fertility to its previous level, their effect was probably small. In Holland, however, the family-subsidy law was less remedial than preventive: its purpose was to help *preserve* the traditional system of family norms still prevailing. As an incentive, subsidies are generally regarded as ineffective, but as a counter to economic deterrents, they may strongly reinforce other, nonrational incentives.

Under such circumstances, the size of the subsidy need not be great for it to be effective. According to a sample survey made by the Central Bureau of Statistics in 1950, the average subsidy paid to industrial workers amounted to 13 percent of their weekly wage for an average of 2.4 minor

[9] D. V. Glass, *Population Policies and Movements in Europe* (Oxford: Clarendon Press, 1940).

[10] In the United States around 1930, middle-class "parents spent between $9,180 and $10,485 in rearing a child through the age of eighteen. Dividing this figure (say, $10,000) by 18, and multiplying by the number of children in the country, we can calculate the total annual amount a nation would need to spend to cover cash expenditures made on children. For the United States it would be around $23,990,079,540, or more than six times the total governmental expenditures in 1930. . . . *At least* this amount would be required if genuine economic rewards for having children were given." Kingsley Davis, "Reproductive Institutions and the Pressure for Population," *Sociological Review,* 29 (July, 1937), 289–306.

children.[11] Since the amount of subsidy paid is the same for all classes, it is proportionally much higher for low-income families, or those with the highest fertility. Thus, in the middle 1950s a person with a monthly income of ƒ640 received a subsidy equal to 6 percent of this for three children, while someone with an income of ƒ160 got 24 percent; for seven children, the equivalent proportions were 17 and 67 percent.[12] Moreover, the average cost of bringing up a child *decreases* with the number of children,[13] while the amount of the subsidy *increases* with the birth order of the child.[14]

Moreover, the family subsidy is only the most direct of the many rational advantages of parenthood. To some degree, any social-welfare program tends to shift the financial burden of raising a family from the parents to the community, and in Holland this tendency has been reinforced by scaling various advantages or disadvantages according to family size. Even to list all these would require a special study, but several examples will suffice to give some notion of their range. In 1946, men with five or more children, including reserve officers, were exempted from military service. In June 1950, the government provided interest-free loans to persons repatriated from Indonesia, ranging from ƒ1,200 for a married couple wiith no children to ƒ3,000 for one with eight children. In April 1952, the cost of schooling was reduced to three-quarters of the usual rate for the third child, and to half of the rate for the fourth and subsequent children.

[11] Centraal Bureau voor de Statistiek, *Statistiek der lonen,* 4:2 (July–September, 1951), 35–84.

[12] D. J. M. Knibbeler, "Heeft de kinderbijslag in Nederland invloed op de gezinsgrootte?" *Mens en Maatschappij,* 28:3 (May 15, 1953), 153–174.

[13] According to a survey of employees and government clerks made in 1951, the average weekly outlay per child amounted to ƒ9.69 when there were 1.4 children, ƒ8.97 with 1.8 children, ƒ7.49 with 3.4 children, and ƒ6.9 with 5.4 children. Centraal Bureau voor de Statistiek, *Nationaal Budgetonderzoek,* "Enkele uitkomsten over het eerste kwartaal 1951," p. 14.

[14] In order to prevent the fostering of very large families, Douglas suggested that, on the contrary, subsidies should cease after the fourth or fifth child, or should be provided in a diminishing scale. Paul H. Douglas, *Wages and the Family* (Chicago: University of Chicago Press, 1925), p. 256.

Taxes are steeply graduated: in the various income brackets, bachelors pay more than the highest married person's rate, which falls sharply with the size of the family.[15] The principle is observed also in private industry: in February 1952, when the mammoth Philips plant reduced the working week to 40 hours, pay was cut to that for 42 hours for single men, while for married breadwinners it remained at the 48-hour rate. More important than any of these examples, or of the similar more or less incidental cases that could be added, are the facts that all increases in pay are now made through general contracts arranged jointly by the employers, trade unions, and government, and that these contracts are usually based in part on the concept of a "just wage." As one example, a general increase in February 1950 can be cited:

> *Married* workers, of either sex, below 23 years of age, with *two or more children;* and *breadwinners,* of either sex, below 23 years of age, belonging to a *family of at least four persons,* and whose normal earnings constitute at least two-thirds of the *total income of the family,* including any government subsidies and pensions, are entitled to a 5 percent increase in salary (provided it has not already been increased to 105 percent of the salary as of January 1, 1950, in accordance with prior regulations or increases).[16]

Whether the cumulative effect of these measures is to keep Dutch fertility high cannot be shown one way or another—first, because the determinants of fertility are very imperfectly understood; secondly, because in any case it would probably be impossible to isolate the effect of these measures. Actually, however, no one doubts their effect, but advocates of the family-subsidy program now tend to stress either that

[15] Cf. B. J. M. van Spaendonck, "Verhoging van de kindertoeslag als noodzakelijke maatregel voor de vermindering van de spanning tussen lonen en prijzen," *Economie,* 12:3/4 (December, 1947–January, 1948), 117–137.

[16] *Keesings Historisch Archief,* Vol. 7, p. 8619. The added italicization emphasizes the range of criteria by which wage rates are now usually set; note that neither skill nor productivity is mentioned.

its avowed purpose is not to raise the fertility rate or that the supposed causal relation cannot be proved.[17]

A pamphlet issued by the Catholic Social-Ecclesiastical Institute, for example, distinguished sharply between family and population policy. Zeegers and Godefroy write: "Catholic family policy is based on principles of natural right and, especially, of social justice, which apply *always and everywhere*. The aims of population policy differ according to time and place."[18] While the differentiation may be valid, its relevance is slight. Among some Catholic publicists, there is a conscious desire to have the larger natural increase among Catholics continue until they become a majority in the Netherlands,[19] and the authors' wholly unobjectionable demonstration that this is unlikely to happen within the next seventy to eighty years could indicate only over how long a range some policies are set. In any case, even if the *purpose* of family subsidies is indeed only to further social justice, their *effect* on the birth rate may be to stimulate fertility. "Since the family subsidy," the authors argue, "covers only a portion of the outlay that must be made for the child's food, clothing, recreation, and education, an increase in the size of the family must always lower its relative standard of living. Thus, family subsidies can never act as an incentive to procreation."[20] This would be true only of economic men; the acts of real persons are influenced but not necessarily determined by monetary factors. Moreover, this very discrepancy between the costs of bringing up a child and the extra income acquired

[17] For example, Knibbeler, *op. cit.*

[18] G. H. L. Zeegers and J. Godefroy, *Demografie en gezinspolitiek* (Katholiek Sociaal Kerkelijk Instituut; The Hague: Pax, 1953), p. 30.

[19] So important a man as Romme, then parliamentary leader of the Catholic People's Party and editor of one of the largest Catholic dailies, wrote that "full Catholic emancipation" can be achieved only when "our people will have become Catholic in the vast majority" (*De Volkskrant*, October 25, 1951). It is not necessary to postulate, as Zeegers and Godefroy do, that non-Catholics have projected their irrational fears as Catholic aims.

[20] Zeegers and Godefroy, *op. cit.*, p. 69. Incidentally, it is remarkable to find the allegation in this context that an increase in family size "must always" lower its relative welfare.

for this has been the principal argument in the continuous, and largely successful, effort to increase subsidies.

Before the war, when population pressure was not a problem, the relation between subsidies and fertility was freely admitted. Kohlbrugge, for example, advocated a graduated tax system (thus, not even family subsidies but their milder negative equivalent) on the ground that it would "encourage" a high fertility rate.[21] Bomans declared that socialists "fight with all their strength against the system of family subsidies, which they scornfully term a *'fokpremie'* [premium for breeding]; this is understandable, for they see in it, and rightly, a brake to neo-Malthusian practices."[22] Sometimes current proponents of the family-subsidy system, even while they deny that it tends to increase fertility, accuse those who disagree with their program of trying to "depress" the birth rate because of their principled opposition to the large family.[23] Similarly, the extension of subsidies to mothers of illegitimate children has been opposed on the ground that this would increase extramarital fertility.

Dutch socialists, thus, now accept family subsidies as a legitimate element of social security, and the repeated Catholic-Labor compromises have resulted, paradoxically, first in the extension of the system to all wage earners and then in a continual increase in the amount of the subsidy. Superficially, the Catholics have won, but their victory may have unanticipated consequences highly deleterious to their fundamental aims. The principal bond uniting the human family is neither romantic love nor moral and legal sanctions, but the joint parental task of caring for the children. Communal assistance to children in need strengthens the family, but when the state begins to take over the father's economic function, the family is thereby weakened.

In the 1920s the Dutch feminist Mrs. Mansholt-Andreae

[21] J. H. F. Kohlbrugge, *Practische sociologie,* VI: *Sociale nooden,* II: *Sexueele en geestelijke problemen* (Groningen: Wolters, 1929), 73-74.

[22] J. B. Bomans, *Het gezinsloon en de groote gezinnen* (Haarlem: Spaarnestad, 1919), p. 23.

[23] E. J. Hoogenstraaten, "Gezinspolitiek," *Katholiek Staatkundig Maandschrift,* 5:7 (September, 1951), 246-252.

advocated what she termed a "motherhood wage" (*moeder-loon*)—that is, a direct remuneration by the state to mothers for the social work done in giving birth to children and bringing them up to be healthy and responsible citizens, to be made independently of the husband's wage or of his employment or unemployment.[24] By most of the arguments used to support family subsidies, this was a better system: it makes little sense in social-welfare terms, for example, to deprive a family of the subsidy when a man loses his job. In Mrs. Mansholt's eyes, the "motherhood wage" had the added advantage of increasing the wife's economic independence, so that the force impelling a woman to remain with her husband for financial reasons would be less strong. Dutch policy is tending in this direction. The persistent pressure to reduce the gap between the cost of raising a child and the amount of the subsidy may continue to effect increases. Zeegers and Godefroy attempt to estimate the cost of extending the system from wage earners to the whole of the population,[25] and if this goal is reached, the present link between the husband's wage and the mother's income will necessarily be weakened, if not broken. As Kingsley Davis has put it, the logical outcome of such pecuniary measures is a change in reproductive institutions:

Undoubtedly, as many people fear, some families at the bottom of the social scale (and perhaps others) would find this a delightfully easy method of earning a livelihood. Now see what would happen. The Government would meet this situation by commanding that persons who live by producing children must prove their fitness. It would thereby produce, gradually and probably unwittingly, a new profession—the profession of child-rearing. It would take only one step more to introduce required training for the professional child-rearers, thus elevating both the standards and the social status of this occupational group. With training there would come specialization. The different subsidiary functions in the creation of new citizens would be taken over by

[24] Cf. Vibart, *op. cit.*, pp. 150–154.
[25] Zeegers and Godefroy, *op. cit.*, pp. 54–60.

specialized groups within the profession. Some women would merely *bear* children, others would care for them physically, others would educate them. Thus, by a gradual evolution unforeseen at the start, the use of monetary rewards for having children would lead to a system in which the father's role is assumed by the state, the mother's role by professional women paid by the state for their services. A new kind of reproductive organization compatible with modern society would have been substituted for the family.[26]

[26] Davis, *op. cit.*

# THE DEMOGRAPHIC TRANSITION
# IN THE NETHERLANDS

Demography ought to be one of the happiest meeting-grounds of sociologists and historians. Studying the population of any society is typically begun with a social analysis —comparing the fertility, say, of one class with that of another. And in this case such an analysis is much less likely to be static than is usual in other branches of sociology, for both the flow of life from one generation to the next and the succession of censuses suggest, and sometimes demand, a historical framework. Actually, however, demography has not benefited from very much interpenetration of the two disciplines. Most of the historians seriously concerned with population have concentrated on the period before the advent of reliable statistics, and their demographic expertise has not ordinarily been at a high level. And sociologists have usually been content with that roughest and most simplistic of models, the theory of the demographic transition, the bare bones of which have all too seldom been rounded out with historical detail.

In the theory of the demographic transition, the population growth of an area undergoing modernization is divided into three stages: (I) a more or less static population at high levels of fertility and mortality; (II) a period of constant fertility and falling mortality, with a consequent rapid increase in population; (III) a more or less static population at more efficient levels of birth and death control.

The last decade or so has seen a relatively large number of excellent studies, which in sum may eventually revise our ideas of population trends in the early modern period. Perhaps the most important change being made in the conception of the demographic transition is in the refinement of the original thesis that it applies equally well to all countries undergoing modernization. It has by now become obvious that there are more differences than similarities in the population development of, say, nineteenth-century England and twentieth-century India. Several writers have suggested that among Western cultures overseas countries like the United States and the British dominions, whose empty lands were filled in large part by immigration, constitute a special subclass. And population growth in even so homogeneous a culture area as Western Europe has differed significantly from one country to another, so that a true picture of its demographic past will have to be based on many more national or even local historical studies, to be synthesized at some future date into a more complex, but more accurate, over-all model.

In this essay I wish to bring to the attention of their English-speaking colleagues some of the interesting and important work that Dutch sociologists and historians have been doing in population analysis, and to suggest a few of the general theoretical implications of their findings. That the population history of the Netherlands is anomalous is of course well known, but some of its specific features seem also to be variations on Western themes. If the relation between population growth and modernization is to be better understood, we must learn how to maintain a delicate balance between the specific facts of the historian and the generalizing function of the sociologist.

## Population Growth

In the theory of the demographic transition, one postulate is that the population growth was wholly a natural increase; and before we apply this theory to any specific historical case we must ask whether the net migration actually was insignificant. This was the case in the Netherlands during the nineteenth and twentieth centuries, to the extent that one can tell from the inadequate statistics.[1] But what of earlier centuries? When the Republic of the United Netherlands was established in the sixteenth century, it became a haven for

[1] See William Petersen, *Planned Migration: The Social Determinants of the Dutch-Canadian Movement* (Berkeley: University of California Press, 1955), Chap. 3.

refugees from Catholic Europe, first of all Calvinists from the reconquered Spanish Netherlands (now Belgium) and Jews from Spain itself, later French Protestants and East European Jews. No accurate record was kept of this immigration,[2] nor of the emigration that partly balanced it. That the Spanish Jews and the Huguenots had a great impact on Dutch commerce and industry is not a good clue to their numbers, particularly when these are taken as a percentage of the national population rather than of the relatively few towns where the immigrants mainly settled. Whether the zero net migration that the model demands was true of the Netherlands is not known, but it is reasonable to assume that it was.

Estimating internal migration is no less difficult, and the problem cannot be wholly bypassed. The best of the early data refer principally to the urban population, and in order to use them for our purpose we must try to distinguish between the natural increase of the towns and the net migration to them. During the three centuries or so preceding the first national census, the towns' population increased greatly,[3]

[2] For example, Amsterdam maintained a "dénombrement de tous les Protestants réfugiés" from 1681 to 1684, but discontinued it just before the revocation of the Edict of Nantes and the consequent much larger migration. During these three to four years, almost 2,000 persons were listed. See the discussion in J. G. van Dillen, "Omvang en samenstelling van de bevolking van Amsterdam in de 17e en 18e eeuw," *Bijdragen en Mededelingen der Dialecten-Commissie van de Koninklijke Nederlandse Akademie van Wetenschappen te Amsterdam, 14, Bevolking en taal van Amsterdam in het verleden* (Amsterdam: Noord-Hollandsche Uitgevers Maatschappij, 1954), 1–24. During the eighteenth century, many of the Sephardic (so-called "Portuguese") Jews left Holland, and were replaced by Ashkenazi Jews from Germany and Lithuania; see Ernst Baasch, *Holländische Wirtschaftsgeschichte* (Jena: Gustav Fischer, 1927), pp. 251–252.

[3] Around 1500, which is almost as far back as the first records will take us, the largest city, Utrecht, had fewer than 20,000 inhabitants. Five or six others—in order of size, Leiden, Delft, Haarlem, Amsterdam, Gouda, and Dordrecht—had more than 10,000 each, and a half dozen others something under this figure. About 1550, Amsterdam and Utrecht each had about 35,000, four other cities about 20,000, eight others between 12,000 and 15,000. Shortly after 1600, Amsterdam had over 100,000 and was the largest city in the Low Countries, Leiden and Haarlem were each

but certain of the data suggest that this was the consequence mainly of large in-migration.[4]

Sometimes it is possible to check this impression by relating the population growth of the towns to that of the countryside by the use of provincial censuses. In the case of Holland Province, for example, we can compare the urban and rural sectors in 1622[5] and in 1795, as shown in Table 1.

almost half as large, three other towns had more than 15,000. In the late seventeenth and eighteenth centuries, the urban growth was slower, and in some regions there was even a considerable decline from about 1750 on. See Roger Mols, *Introduction à la démographie historique des villes d'Europe du 14ème au 18ème siècle* (Gembloux: Duculot, 1954–55), Vol. 2, pp. 520–523; Leonie van Nierop, *De bevolkingsbeweging der Nederlandsche stad* (Amsterdam: Binger, 1905); W. S. Unger, "De oudste Nederlandsche bevolkingsstatistiek," *Economist*, 62 (1913), 745–764; Leonie van Nierop, "De aanvang der Nederlandsche demographie," *Economisch-Historisch Jaarboek*, 5 (1919), 192–208.

[4] Of the men inscribed in Amsterdam's marriage registers, for instance, 51 percent were born outside the city during the first quarter of the eighteenth century, 55 percent in 1750, 60 percent in 1791 (*ibid.*). These very high proportions cannot be taken, however, as in-migration rates. The migrants were undoubtedly mostly young adults and thus disproportionately represented among bridegrooms, and whatever out-migration from the city took place usually escaped being recorded. In any case, Amsterdam was not typical of Dutch cities, nor is it today. See also Leonie van Nierop, "Het zielental van Amsterdam in het midden van de 18e eeuw," *Amstelodamum*, 38 (1951), 151–154, where data of the same type are used to argue that the city's natural increase during the eighteenth century was nil, so that both the growth and the later decline were the consequence of migration.

[5] The census of 1622 was taken to prepare for the levy of a special head tax, and earlier analysts have for this reason rejected it out of hand. But Van Dillen, who has made the most detailed study of this count, believes that the underenumeration typical of fiscal censuses was less serious than in most others, because in this case the administration was exceptionally efficient. The province was divided into 23 localities, each under a special commissioner who directed the precinct officials in the towns and the sheriffs in the countryside, and both of these latter groups were required to take a special oath of office. Moreover, even at this early date, the tax was a progressive one, adjusted to both the payer's income and the size of his family. J. G. van Dillen, "Summiere staat van de in 1622 in de Provincie Holland gehouden volkstelling," *Economisch-Historisch Jaarboek*, 21 (1940), 167–189.

The increase of 16 percent over 175 years means an average of less than 0.1 percent per year, but this figure can be accepted only with three reservations: (1) If we substitute for the two actual census counts the larger figures including underenumeration as estimated by Van Dillen, the increase would be by 25 rather than 16 percent. (2) The calculation of the trend between the two censuses by simple subtraction blurs the fact that the growth curve for both towns and countryside rose during the seventeenth and early eighteenth centuries and fell off sharply from about 1750. (3) Neither the towns nor especially the rural regions of Holland Province were typical of the Netherlands as a whole.

TABLE 1. POPULATION OF HOLLAND PROVINCE, 1622 AND 1795[6]

|  | Towns | Countryside | Total |
|---|---|---|---|
| 1622 | 397,882 | 269,698 | 667,580 |
| 1795 | 518,561 | 258,005 | 776,566 |
| Percent increase | +30 | −5 | +16 |

This last point is worth expanding. In their generalizing function, sociologists tend to structure any analysis of town and country in the early modern period into a fairly rigid functional division between agricultural and nonagricultural localities, and thus between *Gemeinschaft* and *Gesellschaft*. The historical example of Holland Province suggests that in any particular case this can be a gross oversimplification. Its rural economy, according to De Vooys, included the following quite heterogeneous and sometimes dynamic elements: (1) *Agriculture.* In some areas this sector of the economy and the population based on it were relatively static. But in the so-called Westland—the strip along the coast south from The Hague, which to this day is the center of commercial horticulture—the intensification of agriculture afforded a base for population increase during the seventeenth and eighteenth centuries. (2) *Peat-cutting.* With the depletion of the peat

[6] A. C. de Vooys, "De bevolkingsspreiding op het Hollandse platteland in 1622 en 1795," *Tijdschrift van het Koninklijk Nederlandsch Aardrijkskundig Genootschap,* 70 (1953), 316–330.

bogs in South Holland, peat-workers were replaced by a smaller number of agriculturists, resulting in a population loss in this region. (3) *"Suburban" commerce and handicrafts*, particularly in the environs of Amsterdam and Rotterdam. Here the population fluctuated together with that of the cities. (4) *Fishermen and marine workers* living in both coastal and inland villages north of the IJ River. The virtual disappearance of their means of subsistence resulted in a considerable out-migration and decline in the population in the second half of the eighteenth century.

That the urban population of Holland Province increased by 30 percent over the designated period while the rural population fell off by 5 percent was undoubtedly due in large part to migration, both between these sectors and from other provinces to Holland's cities. But in view of the atypical features of Holland Province, it is well to check this conclusion with data from Overijssel, a generally agricultural province with some early industry. In Table 2 the population growth of this province is shown separately for the three largest towns and, below, for the smaller towns and the countryside of the three socio-economic areas of Salland, Twente, and Vollenhove.[7] Note that before the nineteenth century the rate of increase in the three large towns was well below the average for the whole province, and that by and large the growth curves of the small towns and the countryside tended to move together. These figures suggest that rural-urban migration was not so important a factor in urban growth as in Holland Province, and perhaps Overijssel was more representative of the country as a whole. It may be indicative that for the period since 1795, the growth curves of this province and of the Netherlands are almost identical.[8]

[7] B. H. Slicher van Bath, *Een samenleving onder spanning: Geschiedenis van het platteland in Overijssel* (Assen: Van Gorcum, 1957), pp. 70–71. The overlap of 16 years between columns 2 and 3 is intentional: it is not possible to fix precisely the date when the retardation in population growth began. The early population figures in this work are based on the plausible manipulation of a wide variety of local statistics. While the methodology is an interesting topic in itself, to discuss it here would take us too far afield.

[8] See the graph in *ibid.*, p. 81.

TABLE 2. REGIONAL POPULATION INCREASE IN OVERIJSSEL, 1675–1849

| | Percent Increase in Population | | | |
|---|---|---|---|---|
| | 1675–1723 | 1723–1764 | 1748–1795 | 1795–1849 |
| Overijssel | 37.6 | 35.9 | 9.5 | 60.4 |
| Three largest towns (Zwolle, Deventer, Kampen) | 20.7 | 15.8 | 3.1 | 65.8 |
| Other towns in | | | | |
| Salland | 44.1 | 36.6 | 12.4 | 24.3 |
| Twente | 33.4 | 74.9 | 7.0 | 58.2 |
| Vollenhove | 37.5 | 4.0 | 13.4 | 60.3 |
| Countryside of | | | | |
| Salland | 31.1 | 34.9 | 17.1 | 69.0 |
| Twente | 72.5 | 58.1 | 8.4 | 42.0 |
| Vollenhove | 41.6 | 24.6 | 9.7 | 75.7 |

According to the estimate of Slicher van Bath, the population of Overijssel at the specified dates was as follows:

| | | |
|---|---|---|
| 1475 | 52,660 | Earliest estimate possible; not reliable. |
| 1675 | 70,678 | Earliest fairly reliable estimate. |
| 1795 | 134,104 | First national census. |
| 1840 | 197,694 | First reliable national census. |
| 1957 | 748,337 | A recent estimate from population registers. |

This steady and increasingly rapid growth does not include short-term fluctuations. A more detailed analysis[9] permits the population increase from 1675 to 1930 to be divided into four periods, with the average annual rates of growth as follows:

| | | |
|---|---|---|
| 75 years | (1675–1748) | 0.75 to 1.0 percent |
| 60 years | (1748–1811) | zero to 0.5 percent |
| 80 years | (1811–1889) | almost 1.0 percent |
| 40 years | (1889–1930) | 1.3 rising to 1.7 percent |

Do these data take us back to the hypothetical Stage I of the demographic transition? The so-called static population characteristic of this stage typically fluctuates around a horizontal mean, and it would seem that this cycle is to be seen in Overijssel between 1675 and 1811. The average growth during this period, however, was not zero; and this suggests that these 136 years constitute rather a transition from Stage I to Stage II. If the upswing from 1675 to 1748 was faster than that of an ordinary Stage I cycle, as may well have been the case, this was presumably because the premodern prosperity was enhanced by the new factors that eventually would effect a steady increase in numbers. In the second half of the eighteenth century, a time of economic depression, the population growth slowed down and for the leanest thirty years was not much more than zero. Here again we can reasonably hypothesize that the figures reflect two overlapping curves—a decrease in population that would have resulted from a Stage I depression, canceled by Stage II factors favoring population increase.

It seems reasonable, lacking precise data, to apply this scheme to the population history of the whole country. Ac-

[9] *Ibid.*, p. 56.

cording to one estimate—or better, guess—the number of inhabitants of the present area of the Netherlands in 1540 was 882,400.[10] To specify this figure to the nearest hundred is certainly unwarranted, but it may well be correct to the nearest hundred thousand. From the middle of the sixteenth to the middle of the eighteenth century, then, the population probably grew from less than a million to something over two million, and during the second half of the eighteenth century it probably remained nearly static. The growth since the date of the first national census, as shown in Table 3, falls within

TABLE 3. POPULATION GROWTH IN THE
NETHERLANDS, 1795–1960

| Year[a] | Population (–000) | Percent Average Annual Increase During Preceding Period |
|---|---|---|
| 1795 | 2,097 | — |
| 1829 | 2,613 | 0.72 |
| 1839 | 2,861 | 0.91 |
| 1849 | 3,057 | 0.67 |
| 1859 | 3,309 | 0.80 |
| 1869 | 3,580 | 0.79 |
| 1879 | 4,013 | 1.14 |
| 1889 | 4,511 | 1.18 |
| 1899 | 5,104 | 1.24 |
| 1909 | 5,858 | 1.39 |
| 1920 | 6,865 | 1.45 |
| 1930 | 7,935 | 1.46 |
| 1940 | 8,923 | 1.18 |
| 1950 | 10,200 | 1.35 |
| 1960 | 11,577 | 1.35 |

[a] As of December 31 of the designated year, except for 1849 (November 19) and 1869 (December 1). Figures from 1795 to 1930 are from the census; thereafter from the population registers.

[10] J. C. Ramaer, "De middelpunten van bewoning in Nederland voorheen en thans," *Tijdschrift van het Koninklijk Nederlandsch Aardrijkskundig Genootschap*, 38 (1921), 1–38, 174–214. The estimate was based on counts of the number of *dwellings* in various towns and in the whole of Holland Province, but more than half of the total constitutes the unmeasured rural sector of the other provinces.

Stage II of the demographic transition, and even within the early phase of this stage, before the long-run growth rate has begun to decline. From 1795 to 1870 the annual increase averaged about 0.75 percent, and since 1870 it has been around 1.25 percent. In the Netherlands, there is not only no indication of the "incipient decline" in population characteristic of Stage III, but hardly any sign of an incipient deceleration of the present rapid rate of growth.

That the population increase characteristic of modern times began in the seventeenth century or earlier is in accord with the usual macroscopic estimates. Both Willcox and Carr-Saunders took 1650 as their starting date and posited a subsequent continuous growth both of the world's population and, more specifically, of Europe's.[11] In a historical analysis of one particular country's population, however, the probability that the increase in numbers began so early demands a re-examination of the usual thesis that its cause was wholly, or almost wholly, the decline in mortality.

## Mortality

One can trace the course of Holland's mortality by fairly reliable statistics only since the middle of the nineteenth century. Attempts have been made to devise estimates from burial records of earlier centuries, but the data are so poor that they cannot yield even satisfactory local rates. De Haas has compiled from a number of contemporary sources the expectation of life at various ages from 1825 to date.[12] In Amsterdam, expectation of life at birth rose slowly from about 35 years in 1825 to about 38 years in 1845. For the whole of the country, this index was about 38 years in 1845 and only 40 years in 1875; but from that date on the rise has been

[11] Both sets of figures are given in United Nations, *The Determinants and Consequences of Population Trends* (New York, 1953), p. 11.

[12] H. K. de Haas, "De bevolkingsgrooten gedurende de laatste eeuw," *Nederlandsch Tijdschrift voor Geneeskunde*, 94 (July 8, 1950), 1972–77. For the period 1825–45, the calculation is based on Lobatto's study of the population of Amsterdam, which undoubtedly differed somewhat from the rest of the country in its mortality.

much faster and, apart from World War II, without interruption.

As Table 4 shows, the remarkable decline in the Dutch death rate over the past century has been, more precisely, only since around 1880.[13] The thirty years preceding that date saw little change, either in the decennial averages or in the extremes of the considerable variation from year to year and from one province to another. The same trend can be noted in infant and child mortality, which in this period constituted a large fraction of the general death rate.[14] The

TABLE 4. CRUDE DEATH RATES IN THE NETHERLANDS, 1850–1957

| | Decennial Average | Range of Annual Rates from Low to High | |
| --- | --- | --- | --- |
| | | National | Provincial |
| 1850–59 | 25.5 | 22.3–31.0 | 17.7–40.4 |
| 1860–69 | 24.9 | 22.9–28.7 | 17.7–39.8 |
| 1870–79 | 24.4 | 22.2–28.4 | 18.0–39.0 |
| 1880–89 | 21.3 | 19.7–23.6 | 16.5–26.4 |
| 1890–99 | 18.7 | 16.9–21.0 | 13.8–18.9 |
| 1900–09 | 15.6 | 13.7–17.9 | 12.6–16.6 |
| 1910–19 | 13.5 | 12.3–17.5 | 11.2–20.0 |
| 1920–29 | 10.6 | 9.6–12.3 | 8.9–14.8 |
| 1930–39 | 8.8 | 8.4– 9.6 | 6.8–11.0 |
| 1940–49 | 9.9 | 8.1–15.3 | 7.0–17.6 |
| 1950–57 | 7.55 | 7.3– 7.8 | 6.6– 9.0[a] |

[a] This is the range of what might be termed the normal death rate. In the new province of the Northeast Polder, with an almost total absence of elderly people, the death rate was only 1.7 in 1951. In Zeeland in 1953, after the main dikes broke and several of the large islands were flooded, the death rate rose to 11.4.

[13] The figures are calculated from the convenient compilation in A. Polman, *Ontwikkeling en huidige stand van de sterfte in Nederland en België* (The Hague: Vereniging voor Demografie, 1951).

[14] Infant mortality fluctuated around an almost constant mean from 1840 to 1880, and the age-specific rates for children and adolescents began to fall only in the 1870s. For a good discussion illustrated by a striking graph, see J. H. de Haas, "Van strijd tegen sterfte naar strijd voor gezondheid," *Wetenschap en Samenleving*, 13 (May, 1959), 59–63.

reasons for the decline from the relatively high plateau on which the death rate rested in the middle of the last century are, of course, no mystery. Both specific cures for various diseases and highly significant improvements in the environment began to be developed with accelerating speed in the last decades of the nineteenth century. That is to say, the application of the most efficient means of death control effected not a transition from a static to a growing population, but the quickening of the rate of growth from 0.75 to 1.25 percent per year that, as we have noted, also took place in the 1870s.

Was the considerable population growth before the introduction of modern medicine and public health also the consequence, either wholly or mainly, of a prior decline in mortality? And, if so, how can we account for this fall in the death rate? While it is not possible to answer these questions directly from mortality statistics, at least plausible hypotheses can be suggested from known institutional changes and their probable effect on the death rate.

The conclusions that McKeown and Brown reached in their important paper on mortality in eighteenth-century England are relevant also to other European countries of that period.[15] They divided the possible causes of a reduction in mortality into three broad classes, as follows:

(1) Specific preventive or curative therapy. In the Netherlands as in England, most treatments of the various important causes of death can be discounted for a period earlier than the middle of the nineteenth century. It is a moot question whether fever hospitals, for example, helped restrict contagion by the semiquarantine they imposed or raised the death rate by the fact that virtually all persons who entered them would be infected.[16] So long as bleeding was the first treatment for illness, the contribution that physicians made to their patients' health was minimal; so long as some-

[15] Thomas McKeown and R. G. Brown, "Medical Evidence Related to English Population Changes in the 18th Century," *Population Studies*, 9 (November, 1955), 119–141.

[16] Indeed, the hospital that Herman Boerhave (1668–1738) established in Leiden set a new standard for cleanliness and care of patients, but however important it was as a training center, the fact that it had fewer than two dozen beds tells how little effect it can have had on the conquest of the mortality of that time.

thing like half of surgical patients died of infection, it can be questioned whether surgeons saved more patients than they killed. "It might safely be said," McKeown and Brown conclude, "that specific medical treatment had no useful effects at all, were it not for some doubt about the results of the use of mercury in syphilis, iron in anemia, cinchona in malaria, and inoculation against smallpox."

(2) A change in the balance between the virulence of the infective organism and the resistance of the host. In specific instances—for example, the transformation of scarlet fever from a frequently fatal disease to a relatively trivial complaint —this was probably the decisive factor. The general effect of such changes on the long-term trend in the death rate, however, was undoubtedly slight.

(3) Improvements in the environment. By the partial elimination of the other two classes, this would seem to be the major cause of any important decline in mortality before about 1850. It is difficult to analyze these improvements, not only because data of all kinds are less numerous and less accurate before that date, and because the relation between environmental changes and presumably consequent declines in mortality are typically vague, but because it is hardly possible to speak of "improvements" in Dutch living conditions during the century from 1750 to 1850.

It was during this period, a hundred years of almost unrelieved economic depression, that the first systematic studies were made relating mortality in the Netherlands to the environment. As early as 1770, the Academy of Sciences was sufficiently interested in this relation to offer a prize for the best answer to the question, "What human diseases derive from this country's physical conditions?"; and the competition stimulated a larger number of persons to do statistical research.[17] They and their counterparts in other countries laid a necessary base for the rapid advances in understanding during the past century.

[17] See Van Nierop, "De aanvang," *op. cit.* An interesting commentary on these works is given in two articles by A. C. de Vooys, "De opkomst van de medische geografie in Nederland," *Geografisch Tijdschrift,* 4 (1951), 1–8; "Een regionale statistiek uit het begin der 19e eeuw," *ibid.,* 1 (1948), 110–114.

There is very little in these early statistical studies to suggest a rise in the standard of living. Take the matter of food supply, one of the more important environmental influences on mortality. The Netherlands of the seventeenth century was ahead of the rest of Western Europe in its agricultural techniques. In the eighteenth century, thus, the first stimulus to the transformation of the English countryside—improved drainage and fertilizers, new crops, better breeding of farm animals—was an imitation of Holland. There can be little doubt that in both seventeenth-century Holland and eighteenth-century England the better and more varied diet of the populace resulted in better health. But for the latter decades of the eighteenth century and the first half of the nineteenth, the Dutch data recount mostly inadequacy, often misery. In the 1840s, when the potato blight spreading across Europe invaded the Dutch fields, the endemic deficiency developed into a near-famine. "Food consumption, at least in the cities, was just as low as in Ireland."[18]

The variation in infant mortality can also be explained in part by diet. In some regions and among the upper classes generally, babies were breast-fed. But where mothers had to work, they fed their infants on bread soaked in water with a little milk or even gin. When the babies cried, they were given a bit of rag in which a piece of chewed bread with sugar had been tied. "This murderous thing," as De Vooys terms it, went by a variety of local names, but everywhere it was more infectious than nutritious.

Living conditions of the poor, particularly in the cities, were deplorable. Often a family of eight shared one bed. Almost one-tenth of the population of Amsterdam lived in damp cellars. According to various urban samples, infant mortality ranged from one-third to one-half. The correlation between size of township and the rate of infant mortality was positive

[18] I. J. Brugmans, *De arbeidende klasse in Nederland in de 19e eeuw* (*1813–1879*) (The Hague: Nijhoff, 1925), p. 155. See also A. C. de Vooys, "De sterfte in Nederland in het midden der 19e eeuw: Een demogeografische studie," *Tijdschrift van het Koninklijk Nederlandsch Aardrijkskundig Genootschap*, 68 (1951), 233–271; P. Geyl, *Geschiedenis van de Nederlandse stam* (*1751–1798*) (Amsterdam: Wereld-Bibliotheek, 1959), Vol. 3, pp. 59–61 and passim.

until the 1880s; then, with the more rapid improvement of urban health facilities, the correlation was reversed during the following twenty years.[19]

One reason for the high rates of urban mortality, both infant and general, is that many Dutch cities are in Holland Province, most of which is below sea level. This fact was certainly relevant to their state of health before the full development of modern engineering. The average death rates for 1841–60 ranged from above 32 per thousand population in the low-lying townships of Holland Province and Zeeland, to below 22 per thousand in the high-lying townships in the East. The segregation of sewage from drinking water was especially difficult in the western provinces, and there were recurrent outbreaks of cholera until the 1860s. What was termed "swamp fever" (*moeraskoorts*) was actually a group of diseases, which each year ran through a seasonal cycle—influenza and malaria in the spring; in June and July diarrhea among infants, often linked to typhus or bacterial dysentery, whose incidence increased in the fall; and at the end of the year the various respiratory diseases. The drinking water in Zeeland was particularly poisonous: on one occasion in the 1780s, of 1,040 Swiss troops stationed in Sluis, only 12 or 13 could stand on their feet after just one month.[20]

In short, there is good circumstantial, though not decisive statistical, evidence to support the thesis that, at least for some social classes and regions, the death rate rose from the average of, say, 1650–1750 to that of 1750–1850. So long as public-health measures were relatively primitive, the congestion of the cities increased the danger of contagion; and under such circumstances the growth of cities would tend to increase mortality. There was probably also a decline in the living standards and especially the diet of the mass of the people. Extant accounts of seventeenth-century food habits are concerned principally with the well stocked tables of the bourgeoisie, but in this relatively prosperous period even the

---

[19] Centraal Bureau voor de Statistiek, *Sterfte van kinderen beneden het jaar in elke gemeente van Nederland* (The Hague, 1910).

[20] Callenfels, as cited in De Vooys, "De sterfte in Nederland," *op. cit.*

poor probably ate better than their more numerous counterparts in the 1820s and 1830s, certainly better than in the
1840s.

If there was any decline in general mortality, then, it was
probably quite small. Was it great enough to account for the
increase in population—taking only the period measured by
national censuses—from roughly 2.1 million in 1795 to almost
3.1 million in 1850? Or is there not a prima facie case here
for the probability that fertility rose?

### Fertility

In the conventional model of the demographic transition,
it is assumed that Stages I and II were characterized by a
more or less constant fertility at close to the physiological
maximum. The population growth during Stage II—the consequence thus, wholly or almost wholly, of the fall in mortality
—pushed parents to adopt the small-family system, which
was based on a new rationalist attitude toward conception
and the various contraceptive means invented or popularized
during the nineteenth century.

While this model has a certain rough validity, there is
little evidence on the face of it to support some of the details.
Reproduction up to the physiological maximum is not the typical practice among either primitive peoples or preindustrial
civilizations. Conscious family limitation did not have to wait
for mechanical and chemical contraceptives; it can be effected by coitus interruptus, abortion, or infanticide—methods
as old as human history.[21] The average size of the family,
moreover, depends not merely on the parents' will but on the
variety of cultural and religious norms governing the age at
marriage, the proportion of adults that marry, the remarriage
of widows, the frequency of marital intercourse, and the like.

The conscious regulation of family size in late medieval
and early modern Europe was in part accomplished by

[21] Cf. A. M. Carr-Saunders, *The Population Problem: A Study in
Human Evolution* (Oxford: Clarendon, 1922); see above, p. 59.

coitus interruptus, in part by abortion and infanticide.[22] A more significant check to fertility, however, had been gradually inculcated: the principle that a man might not marry until his living was assured.[23] In some cases, this norm was spelled out in detailed regulations of particular institutions. In other cases, it was strong enough to govern family formation without being specified in written laws. The principal check to unlimited procreation in the Dutch countryside of several centuries ago, the stem family, is a good example of the second type.

In the Netherlands as in all Germanic countries, the sib remained an important legal body until the late Middle Ages.[24] And in many parts of the Dutch countryside, both it and the stem family function still as meaningful social organizations. Until rather recently a discussion of the latter could have been based on nothing more than the impressions

[22] The opposition of the Catholic Church to these latter practices was vehement and specific enough to suggest that they were common. Five means of controlling family size were specifically forbidden—inducing sterility by drugs or incantations, aborting the fetus by violent exercise, killing the infant at birth, refusing to nurse one's child, and accidentally sleeping on it. See J. C. Russell, *British Medieval Population* (Albuquerque: University of New Mexico Press, 1948), p. 160. As late as the seventeenth century, when Vincent de Paul established the charitable order associated with his name, one impetus to his act was to furnish foundling hospitals as a functional substitute for the continuing high rate of infanticide.

[23] This process in England is suggested by the etymology of the two words, *husband* and *anilepiman*. The word *husband* derives from two words meaning "house" and "dwell," and its original meaning (still preserved in *husbandman* and *husbandry*) was a householder, a man who had a home. The Middle English word for an unmarried man was *anilepiman* ("only man"). These two terms, one referring to property and the other to marital status, gradually became associated as opposites: *anilepiman* came to mean a man who had no living and therefore could not marry, and *husband*, a man who was able to care for a family and therefore could get (or, eventually, was) married. George C. Homans, *English Villagers of the 13th Century* (Cambridge: Harvard University Press, 1941), Chap. 10.

[24] See G. A. Kooy, *Het veranderend gezin in Nederland: Een sociaal-historische studie* (Leerdam: Ter Haar & Schuijt, 1957), Chap. 3 and especially p. 41.

of folklorists, plus a few incidental jottings by social scientists; but since the war the three-generation household has suddenly become a "social problem," to be studied by social workers, churches, and government agencies. This new interest has culminated in Kooy's excellent sociological analysis,[25] based in part on a questionnaire survey of the Achterhoek (literally, "back corner"), an agrarian region in the province of Gelderland, but relevant also to other areas where a strong organization of the stem family still persists, and to a historical analysis of the Dutch countryside as a whole.

In its typical form, the household of the stem family can be described as follows.[26] One of the sons (or where there are no sons, one of the daughters) is designated as the sole heir to the family farm, either explicitly in a legal document or implicitly by the tradition that all accept. When he marries, his bride comes to live under his parents' roof. In principle, the heir's brothers and sisters leave the farm; in practice, they often remain, unmarried uncles and aunts with a status between that of family members and servants. Variation in the present-day expression of this tradition is illustrated in Table 5.[27] The normal household consists of two families of successive generations (lines 1 and 2, plus some other families, probably, in which both grandparents had died). Attached to this nucleus, however, there may be an unmarried sibling of the heir or his wife (line 3), or a more distant relative (line 5), or servant or farmworker, also unmarried (line 6). Note how seldom the property is shared by two families of the same generation (line 4). The restriction that this system imposes on fertility is patent. The main desideratum, that from generation to generation the farm remain undivided in the same family, is safeguarded, but to this principle is sacrificed the normal family life of a considerable proportion of the adult population.

[25] G. A. Kooy, *De oude samenleving op het nieuwe platteland: Een studie over de familiehuishouding in de agrarische Achterhoek* (Assen: Van Gorcum, 1959).

[26] *Ibid.*, pp. 35–36.

[27] Calculated from Table 6, *ibid.*, p. 33. This pattern was influenced in this case by a severe housing shortage, the consequence in part of war damage.

TABLE 5. PERCENTAGE DISTRIBUTION IN PATTERNS OF
JOINT RESIDENCE IN TWO REGIONS OF THE ACHTERHOEK

|  | Graafschap | Lijmers |
|---|---|---|
| 1. Two families of successive generations | 49.9 | 38.6 |
| 2. Family with one grandparent | 27.5 | 27.0 |
| 3. Family with an unmarried uncle or aunt | 8.6 | 18.2 |
| 4. Two families of the same generation | 0.1 | 0.4 |
| 5. Family with a more distant relative | 4.2 | 7.4 |
| 6. All other patterns | 9.7 | 8.4 |
|  | 100.0 | 100.0 |
|  | (3,918) | (740) |

Because of their frustration, this pattern has been inherently unstable under modern conditions. Whenever a change in circumstances makes it possible, the unmarried hangers-on of these joint households rush to set up their own homes and establish their own families. Thus, several times in Holland's recent history there has been an explosive rise in the fertility of certain areas or certain social classes:

(1) The extension of arable land by reclamation has had the paradoxical effect of aggravating population pressure. For the settlers on the polders being built out of the former Zuider Zee are mostly younger sons of farmers, many of whom in their prior status would have been unable to marry. And in the new settlements, in part because of the preponderance of young adults, the birth rate has on occasion been more than 70 per thousand population![28]

(2) During the last quarter of the nineteenth century artificial fertilizers were introduced in the sandy regions of the East and South, and the greatly improved productivity of the soil made it possible to divide up family farms into viable units of smaller acreage. For two or three generations, it was possible in this way for a much larger proportion of young

[28] This situation is discussed at greater length in Petersen, *op. cit.*, pp. 103–108. See also Sjoerd Groenman, "L'assèchement du Zuiderzée et le problème de la population aux Pays Bas," *Population*, 7 (October–December, 1952), 661–674; "Zuiderzee gronden en sanering van de kleine boerenbedrijven," *Landbouwkundig Tijdschrift*, 64 (January, 1952), 5–14.

adults to marry and procreate. And today these regions generally have the highest fertility rates in the country, for it has been difficult both to re-establish the traditional pattern of family limitation by the nonmarriage of some adults, and to overcome the opposition of the various churches to family limitation by the use of contraceptives.[29]

(3) The joint household and the limitation on human fertility that it implies disappeared earlier where agriculture was based on the naturally more fertile clay soil. This process has been analyzed in detail by Hofstee, particularly for the Oldambt, a region in northeast Groningen Province. Until the eighteenth century, the farm laborers there lived almost as members of the farmer's family, sleeping in the same house, eating at the same table, working together during the day, talking about common interests in the evening. From about 1775 on, this patriarchal relation began to disappear, to be supplanted eventually by a sharp class differentiation. The well-to-do landowners underwent an *embourgeoisement* that transformed them from traditional peasants into modern farmers. Even earlier than in the cities, they adopted a small-family system by which the relation between the land and the number of landowners was kept almost constant. The farmworkers, converted into a landless proletariat, were released from the institutional and moral inhibitions to procreation implicit in the old system. In the century following 1775, their number in the province of Groningen increased four times.[30]

[29] This relation between soil type and human fertility patterns has been analyzed by E. W. Hofstee in "De landbouw en de migratie," *Economisch-Statistische Berichten*, 35 (December 20, 1950), 1024–1026; "De functie van de internationale migratie," *Tijdschrift voor Economische en Sociale Geografie*, 15 (January–February, 1949), 10–22.

[30] See E. W. Hofstee, *Het Oldambt: Een sociografie* (Groningen: Wolters, 1937), pp. 193–235. Of the several articles in which the theme of this work is analyzed more intensively, the most recent is "De ontwikkeling van de huwelijksvruchtbaarheid in het Oldambt in de periode 1880–1950," in J. Brummelkamp *et al.*, eds., *De wereld der mensen* (Groningen: Wolters, 1955), pp. 295–353. This is a report of the marital fertility of the total sample of first marriages in three townships of the Oldambt, with a detailed analysis of differentiation by social class and religion.

(4) If the fertility of agricultural workers increased when they became a *rural* proletariat, should this not have taken place also when they moved to the towns and were there released from the same checks to procreation? That urban fertility in the Netherlands was higher than that in the countryside until about seventy-five years ago has long been an established fact, but its implications have seldom been explored until a recent paper by Hofstee.[31] In order to supplement the existent compilations of township data, Hofstee compiled from provincial and township archives his own breakdown for 1850–80, and thus obtained a valuable new base for analyzing fertility during this transitional period. Average birth rates for 1851–55 showed a regional patterning almost precisely the opposite of that to be seen today. The highest birth rates at that time—35 per thousand or more—were in the agricultural provinces with a clay soil (Zeeland, Friesland, and Groningen) and the country's urban center (North and South Holland). This differentiation is not due, as one might suspect, to a difference in age structure; it holds also when the fertility is compared by other measures.

Birth rates in specific cities varied somewhat, but in general they were close to the level of the surrounding countryside. At one time something like the three-generation household that was standard in the Dutch countryside seems to have existed also in the towns. So long as apprenticeship entailed

[31] E. W. Hofstee, "Regionale verscheidenheid in de ontwikkeling van het aantal geboorten in Nederland in de 2e helft van de 19e eeuw," Koninklijke Nederlandse Akademie van Wetenschappen, *Akademie-dagen*, 7 (1954), 59–106. A typical instance of a certain blindness usual in earlier analyses can be seen in a paper by the highly competent demographer and former director of the Central Bureau of Statistics, H. W. Methorst. In an article published in 1913 he compared the trend in birth rates in townships with more than and fewer than 20,000 inhabitants—a rough but sufficiently accurate differentiation between "urban" and "rural." According to his data, the urban birth rate was higher until 1890, the two were almost identical at the end of the 1890s, and only in the twentieth century was the urban birth rate lower. Yet his analysis is limited to a discussion of the very latest trend. H. W. Methorst, "Nederlandsche bevolkingsstatistiek," *Economist*, 62 (1913), 126–154, 250–259, 367–400.

living in the master craftsman's home-workshop, which was passed on from father to one son, the similarities with the rural system were clear, though the number of persons affected was of course smaller.[32] In both town and countryside, the principal check to fertility was by the relatively high proportion of the population that remained single.

It is reasonable to suppose that the same forces that prevented the marriage of some tended to postpone that of the others. However, the secular trend in the median age at marriage cannot be realistically discussed in statistical terms, for the following reasons:

(1) Data are completely lacking for the earlier period.[33]

(2) As is well known, in societies where the postponement of marriage constitutes an important method of family limitation, the age generally rises and falls according to economic conditions.[34] Given the poor statistics, it is therefore still

[32] Some of the heterogeneity supposedly typical of urban life can be discerned in Dutch cities, but until well into the modern period the guilds—or at least the style of economic organization that they represented—remained one important factor. They were in decline in the eighteenth century, but toward its end there were still fifty-one trade and craft guilds in Amsterdam, for example. Guilds were formally abolished during the French occupation, but remnants of the system persisted into the nineteenth century. See Cornelius Wiskerke, *De afschaffing der gilden in Nederland* (Amsterdam: Paris, 1938); A. J. M. Brouwer Ancher, *De gilden* (The Hague: Loman & Funke, 1895).

[33] The degree to which this is the case can be illustrated by an article by Van Nierop that, with painstaking effort, has winnowed every bit of information from the marriage records in Amsterdam for the last decades of the sixteenth century. As is generally the case until national compilations of civil records began in the middle of the last century, direct data on age at marriage were scarce and deficient in the Amsterdam records, and a number of complicating factors made it difficult even to estimate the trend. Leonie van Nierop, "De bruidegoms van Amsterdam van 1578 tot 1601," *Tijdschrift voor Geschiedenis*, 48 (1933), 337–359; 49 (1934), 136–160; 52 (1937), 144–162.

[34] This was true of the Netherlands until about 1870, although apparently less so than of some other countries. See J. H. van Zanten and T. van den Brink, *Population Phenomena in Amsterdam in Comparison with Other Big Towns* (Statistical Communication No. 103a; Amsterdam: Municipal Bureau of Statistics, 1939), pp. 4–39.

more difficult to discern a possible long-term trend underlying these fluctuations.

(3) In any case, the trend in the median age at marriage of the whole population, if it were possible to establish it for the early modern period, would not reveal the changes presumably taking place in several of the social classes.

Even so, although the point cannot be statistically documented, it is reasonable to assume that the same institutional changes that permitted a larger number to marry also tended to reduce the age at marriage.[35]

With respect to fertility, a more important consequence of the breakdown of the moral and institutional norms inherent in the joint household was the probable rise in illegitimacy. Like all Germanic countries, the Netherlands has inherited a tradition of "window wooing."[36] By this folk norm, premarital intercourse is usual, and marriage does not take place until the bride is pregnant. According to a government survey made just before World War II, the percentage of forced marriages in the Netherlands ranged from just over 13 in large

[35] In contrast to rural Ireland, there is apparently no impetus to the early marriage of the heir. In Ireland the young man takes over the management of the farm when he gets married, but in the Netherlands one of the frequent sources of friction noted in recent publications is that, on the contrary, even responsible family men are still given no voice in managing the property. In some areas—for example, the bulb-growing region in Holland Province —fathers try to keep all their sons single as long as possible, paying them small wages for long hours of work. See, e.g., I. Gadourek, *A Dutch Community: Social and Cultural Structure and Process in a Bulb-Growing Region in the Netherlands* (Netherlands Institute of Preventive Medicine, Publication 30; Leiden: Stenfert Kroese, 1956), pp. 173–174. The effect of this practice on fertility is ambivalent, however, for while marriage is postponed, each horticulturist has an economic incentive to have many sons, which reinforces his traditional, often Catholic, morality.

[36] This is the literal translation of "venster vrijen," one of the terms by which the custom is designated in Dutch. Most books on the family written in English pass lightly over this important element of the West European cultural tradition. The best general account is by a Swede: K. R. V. Wikman, *Die Einleitung der Ehe: Eine vergleichend ethno-soziologische Untersuchung über die Vorstufe der Ehe in den Sitten des schwedischen Volkstums* (Acta Academiae Aboensis, Humaniora XI. 1; Abo: Abo Akademi, 1937).

towns to 16 in villages.[37] In a number of areas, generally quite fundamentalist in religion, the custom is still more prevalent.[38] It is something of a misnomer, however, to call these "forced marriages," a term that suggests a more or less random liaison. With respect to both the timing and the mate chosen, these are usually planned, or at least half-planned, conceptions; and so long as the village's social control is unbroken, marriage follows them almost inevitably. Yet this is a system that all but invites dalliance once the control is released—and in the nineteenth century the urban illegitimacy rates were ordinarily high.[39]

## Conclusions

It is generally believed that the population of the Western world has increased continuously from 1650 on. The decline in mortality that is used in the model of the demographic transition to explain this growth cannot be documented for anything like so long a period. In the Netherlands, as generally in the Western world, the most dramatic rise in life expectation dates from the last quarter of the nineteenth century, and for the prior several hundred years the presumed fall in mortality can neither be proved from the statistics nor even—for a substantial portion of this period—plausibly related to institutional changes.

[37] Kooy, *Het veranderend gezin*, p. 146.

[38] In the village of Staphorst, for example, of the eighty-seven first births in 1937–38, thirty-four were within seven months of the marriage ceremony. In the 1920s, a number of ministers cooperated in a determined effort to stamp out the practice and fulminated from their pulpits against the young people who spent Saturday night in sin and then came to church on Sunday morning. Finally they succeeded—but only in having the traditional night for "window wooing" changed to Friday. Sjoerd Groenman, *Staphorst: Sociografie van een gesloten gemeenschap* (Meppel: Stenvert, 1948?), pp. 96, 153 ff.

[39] In Amsterdam, for example, almost one out of every five births was illegitimate for the period 1811–24, the earliest for which this information is available, and the percentage remained high until the last quarter of the century. "Statistiek der bevolking van Amsterdam tot 1921," *Mededeelingen van het Bureau van Statistiek der Gemeente Amsterdam,* Vol. 67 (1923).

The unlikelihood of a decline in mortality is increased when we examine more closely the other half of the balance—the assumption that fertility remained more or less constant at a high level until it began to fall with the advent of the modern small-family system. It is strange that this thesis has not been challenged more often. It is not even in accord with the established statistical record of the nineteenth century. Because of the accident that the high point in the British birth rate coincided with the Bradlaugh-Besant trial, most demographers know that in that country there had been an upward trend prior to that date. But something of the same pattern can be seen in the course of the fertility of most other West European countries. The French pattern of a steady decline in natality since the beginning of reliable records, which has often been taken as the model with which to analyze the fertility of the Western world, seems rather to be an exception.[40]

For the early modern period a statistical analysis must be based on data poor enough to make it suspect, but the hypothesis that there was a rise in fertility is strongly reinforced by what we know of the institutional changes that accompanied modernization. The Middle Ages bequeathed to the present-day Western world a social system with built-in guards against excessive procreation. Whatever their form, these were expressions of the principle that a man might not marry and beget offspring until he had established an appropriate place for himself which would enable him to carry out his family responsibilities. Perhaps the most precise form of this type of institutional check was contained in the regulations of the English guilds, which prohibited marriage during a long apprenticeship and made it difficult for a period thereafter.[41] In the Netherlands (as apparently in

[40] See, e.g., Gerhard Mackenroth, *Bevölkerungslehre: Theorie, Soziologie und Statistik der Bevölkerung* (Berlin: Springer, 1953), pp. 122–134. This section is divided into two parts: the first on the general development of fertility in Northwest and Central Europe, the second on the reasons for the exceptional development in France.

[41] "Apprenticeship in its fully grown Elizabethan form required that those learning any trade then practiced in England should serve an apprenticeship for seven years or until he was 24 years of

most other Continental countries), the control by the guilds was less rigid, but there too one function of the apprenticeship system was to prescribe, or at least to facilitate, this norm of responsible parenthood.

At any time prior to the most recent past, however, the vast majority of all populations lived in the country, and for a long-term analysis the rural institutions governing fertility demand the most attention. In the Netherlands this institution was the joint household of the stem family.[42] In principle, in each generation only one person on each farm married and had children. The household also furnished a function and a home, however, for the unmarried. Whether as uncles or aunts to the farm-owner's children, or as more distant relatives, or as servants and farmworkers, these had a place as meaningful parts of an economic and social unit. The limitation to fertility in this type of joint household was efficient, but it was dependent on the maintenance of the institutional forms. As the joint household began to disintegrate, in part because in modern times the nuclear family has been more strongly emphasized, or because the unmarried hangers-on found an opportunity to escape from what they began to perceive as sexual and social frustration, it was inevitable that fertility should rise. And this rise can be demonstrated in a number of particular instances.

---

age, with the possible exception of agriculture, in which it was sufficient that he should attain the age of 21 if the parties had been unable to agree on 24. It is clear that these provisions were looked upon quite as much as a check on the exuberance of youth as essential for the technical education of the country." G. Talbot Griffith, *Population Problems of the Age of Malthus* (Cambridge: Cambridge University Press, 1926), p. 112.

[42] In their excellent analysis of the interrelation among social structure, family type, and fertility, Davis and Blake argue, on the contrary, that a joint household favors high fertility. This is indeed the case in classical China and India, the examples they use to illustrate their thesis. In such a household, marriage and procreation are feasible as soon as they are physiologically possible, for the supervision of household affairs does not depend on the social maturity of each individual couple. Kingsley Davis and Judith Blake, "Social Structure and Fertility: An Analytical Framework," *Economic Development and Cultural Change*, 4 (April, 1956), 211–235.

Generalizing from the Dutch case, we can posit the following hypothesis in place of the present theory concerning fertility trends in a Western country undergoing modernization.[43] In the *traditional family* typical of the preindustrial period, the postponement of marriage, plus the nonmarriage of a portion of the population, constituted an onerous but efficient means of holding fertility in check. In the *proletarian family*, typical of the mass of either rural or urban workers released from the prior institutional and normative restrictions, there was no effective bar either to early marriage or to procreation. Indeed, social control was often barely strong enough to compel marriage once a child had been conceived. In the *rational family*, which arose first among the middle classes during the nineteenth century and then gradually spread to the rest of society, a sense of parental responsibility reappeared and with it a limitation of family size. The average age at marriage rose again, and later the same end was achieved with less privation by the use of contraceptives. Thus, in order to trace the changes in the fertility of any country, we would need statistical data on completed family size *by social class* from the seventeenth century on. By this time the disintegration of institutional checks to fertility, the development of new means of death control, and the resultant increase in population were all under way. These data will never become available. But such statistical records as we do have, at least in the Dutch case, support the thesis that the population growth characteristic of the modern West must be explained as the consequence of both a rise in fertility and a fall in mortality.

[43] The following discussion derives largely from Hofstee, "Regionale verscheidenheid," *op. cit.* Hofstee acknowledges a debt to Mackenroth (*op. cit.*, p. 474), who in turn notes that a germ of the hypothesis is to be found in Malthus.

# PART II

# Migration
# and
# Acculturation

# THE "SCIENTIFIC" BASIS OF
# OUR IMMIGRATION POLICY

According to the arguments of many of its opponents, the McCarran-Walter Immigration Act of 1952 is not merely bad policy but a kind of freakish accident. The late Pat McCarran, the son of a poor Irish immigrant, somehow did not develop into the champion of the people one might have expected from his background. Elected to the Senate by the smallest constituency in the United States, he became a permanent fixture there and chairman of several of its key committees. When he sponsored an immigration bill in conflict with American ideals, two-thirds of the Senate passed it over President Truman's veto out of fear of the retaliation that lay in McCarran's power through his control over appropriations.

So at least one standard liberal argument runs. In another version of this devil theory, the culprit was not a single individual but the small minority of the electorate that espouses racism. Somehow, according to this view, the democratic credo has been frustrated by the activities of certain nativist and proto-fascist groups on the periphery of our society.

But the amorphous prejudice that the mass of native Americans feel, or felt, against immigrants was not sufficient in itself, even in its extremist versions, to effect the basic change in American policy that the national-quota system represented. The responsibility must be sought elsewhere. What social group made racist sentiment respectable, and thus an appropriate basis for American legislation? Who, to use the term of Max Weber, "legitimized" the national-quota system?

The process by which a policy becomes legitimate ordinarily begins with its explicit justification in terms of logic, science, or religion—in terms, that is, of universally accepted values. By its very nature, such a transformation can be undertaken only by those whose intellectual authority the society respects—in this case, America's leading social scientists. Before the immigration laws of the 1920s could be passed, a generation of anthropologists, economists, sociologists, and historians had labored to give the principle of the national-origin quota an underpinning that would square with the dominant American value system. By the writings of these scholars during the half century before 1920, a new, alternative system of values was established in sufficient strength to sway the thinking of the mass and, eventually, to set national policy. But if this analysis is correct, proponents of a more liberal immigration policy will not be able to get their ideas written into law until they recognize that this new, divergent value system has achieved a certain legitimation, which can be shaken only by fundamental opposition.

The xenophobia implicit in the present immigration policy was never previously established as a general norm. The Alien and Sedition Acts were repealed under Jefferson, and in the aftermath were an important reason for the eclipse of the Federalist party that had enacted them. The nativist movement of the 1830s, the Know-Nothing party of the 1850s, the American Protective Association of the early 1890s, the Ku Klux Klan reborn in 1915—all these movements, while indicating the persistence of antiforeigner sentiment in America, also reflect the fact that it was, and is, usually limited to noisy groups of merely local importance.

One of the principles established by the American and French revolutions was that—as the French constitution of 1791 put it—"the liberty of all to move about, to remain, or to leave" is a "natural and civil right." In the United States, this doctrine was reinforced by another: this country was ordained as a haven for "the wretched refuse of your teeming shores"—to quote Emma Lazarus' words inscribed on the base of the Statue of Liberty. In the face of America's dominant value system, as exemplified in such fundamental documents as the Declaration of Independence, even the government's power to deny entry to various categories of people universally agreed to be undesirable—prostitutes, "lunatics," "idiots," "anarchists," criminals, polygamists—was established only gradually, after the Supreme Court had denied the constitutionality of a series of state laws. The first attempts at a broader restriction of immigration were formally an extension of this type of regulation. Thus, a number of states tried to check the influx of the poor by imposing a head tax on immigrants, but these attempts were frustrated by several Supreme Court decisions. Similarly, successive bills in Congress barring the admission of illiterates were vetoed by Presidents Cleveland, Taft, and Wilson. As the last put it, illiteracy was a measure not of a man's small innate ability but of his limited opportunities, and in Wilson's day these were not considered a legitimate reason for denying anyone his "natural" right to immigrate here.

Even the laws barring Chinese immigration were enacted without obliterating the distinction between police *regulation* (e.g., exclusion of criminals) and *restriction* based on a broader criterion (e.g., exclusion of illiterates). The argument of white Californians that the Chinese were unassimilable to American life was valid—because, as Milton Konvitz has put it, they were denied citizenship through naturalization, held ineligible to testify in any case in a court of law for or against a white person, subjected to special heavy taxes, denied the vote, excluded from schools. The Chinese were made "the scapegoat for mining and real estate booms and slumps; for crime waves requiring vigilance committees; for corruption, extravagance, and profligacy in state and city government; and for the land and railway monopoly."[1]

But even though the rest of the country had almost no reliable knowledge on which to judge the question, white California could not get its way immediately. American law and institutions were based on principles that could not be used to sanction the exclusion of any ethnic group. Twice the Supreme Court threw out Chinese-exclusion laws as unconstitutional, and it finally accepted them because one member of that court, Justice Stephen J. Field, was able to persuade his colleagues that as a native of California he knew more of the subject than they. The Chinese were thus the first to be excluded as an ethnic group, rather than as individuals with specifically objectionable personal characteristics. So

[1] Milton R. Konvitz, *The Alien and the Asiatic in American Law* (Ithaca, N.Y.: Cornell University Press, 1946), p. 10.

gross a violation of the national ethos, accepted finally only because it affected what was regarded as a peripheral case, set a precedent, and the interpretation of cultural differences in racial terms eventually became the keystone of American immigration policy.

*Whom We Shall Welcome*, the report of the Perlman Commission that President Truman appointed to review and criticize the McCarran Act, pointed out—correctly—that the national-quota system was based on anthropological theories that no reputable social scientist would now defend. America's immigration policy runs counter to the basic credo of the country, and the policy gets no support from present-day science. How then was it established? Let us retrace the steps by which a man's place of birth became a legitimate criterion for judging his application to enter the United States.

## Population Analysis

At the beginning of the nineteenth century one Elkanah Watson noticed that without immigration—which had been interrupted by the wars in Europe—the population of the United States had increased by about one-third during each of the two decades following the 1790 census. His calculation as to how the population of the country would continue to increase up to 1900 if that same extraordinary rate of growth were maintained was widely accepted as a significant contribution to demography.[2]

In 1873, Francis A. Walker, the Superintendent of the Census, wrote an article gently deriding Watson's thesis and those who took it seriously.[3] In the first place, Walker wrote, "geometrical progression is rarely attained, and never long maintained, in human affairs. Whenever it is found, the most improbable supposition which could be formed respecting it is that it will continue." That is, the fact that the popu-

[2] Cf. Winslow C. Watson, ed., *Men and Times of the Revolution: or, Memoirs of Elkanah Watson* . . . (New York: Dana, 1856), pp. 455–456.

[3] Francis A. Walker, "Our Population in 1900," *Atlantic Monthly*, 32:192 (October, 1873), 487–495.

lation of the United States had twice increased by about a third within ten years warranted no prediction concerning the future. That Watson's forecast had been confirmed for a while was simply a matter of luck: "Mr. Watson simply bet nine times upon the red. Five times the red won—a wonderful run of luck, certainly." The rate of population growth would have declined much earlier had not immigration happened to compensate for the decline in the birth rate:

> The change [in the birth rate] came; came later even than it had been reasonable to expect. It began when the people of the United States began to leave agricultural for manufacturing pursuits; to turn from the country to the town; to live in up-and-down houses, and to follow closely the fashion of foreign life. The first effects of it were covered from the common sight by a flood of immigration unprecedented in history.

All this Walker wrote in 1873, when the number of immigrants from Southern and Eastern Europe totaled only 12,703.

Twenty years later, when the new immigration was approaching its peak of more than half a million a year, Walker wrote three articles in an entirely different vein.[4] Immigration, he now found, "instead of constituting a net reinforcement to the population, simply resulted in a replacement of native by foreign elements." He proved this by using Watson's projection of American population growth, but now in the contrary sense. In 1840 and 1850, he pointed out, in spite of the large immigration during this period, the census count differed from Watson's projection by only a few percentage points. The threefold increase in immigration from one decade to the next, Walker asserted, had merely caused the native birth rate to decline proportionally; for the American "was unwilling himself to engage in the lowest kind of day labor with these new elements of population . . .

[4] "Immigration and Degradation," *Forum*, 11 (August, 1891), 634–644; "Immigration," *Yale Review*, 1:2 (August, 1892), 124–145; "Restriction of Immigration," *Atlantic Monthly*, 77:464 (June, 1896), 822–829.

[and] even more unwilling to bring sons and daughters into the world to enter into that competition."

The typical immigrant, in Walker's view, had changed from "the most enterprising, thrifty, alert, adventurous, and courageous of the community from which he came" to "the least thrifty and prosperous . . . [from] every foul and stagnant pool of population in Europe, which no breath of intellectual or industrial life has stirred for ages." He therefore proposed a new policy—the exclusion not only of criminals, paupers, etc., but also of hundreds of thousands of people "the great majority of whom would be subject to no individual objections" but who came from the wrong sort of country. For Walker, the question was how to protect "the quality of American citizenship from degradation through the tumultuous access of vast throngs of ignorant and brutalized peasantry from the countries of Eastern and Southern Europe."

In spite of Walker's high standing as a social scientist, it is rather easy to show that his later articles were ad hoc concoctions designed to lend scientific flavor to certain ethnocentric prejudices without foundation in empirical data. The most significant fact to be noted about the three articles in which he advanced his vehement objections to immigration is their dates: 1891, 1892, and 1896—the decade after the main source of American immigration had shifted to Southern and Eastern Europe. His emotional reaction to the foreignness of "tumultuous" hordes of "brutalized" peasants led him to conclude that immigration had to be curbed; then, and only then, did he look for a scientific theory that would support this conclusion. Nor did he even attempt to refute his own earlier article; he simply ignored it.

## History

In the meantime, American historians had been fashioning evidence to show that a fundamental affinity existed between the Germanic peoples and the American way of life. Edward Saveth has given us the story of this episode of historiography in a fascinating work.[5] Historians like John Fiske, John W. Burgess, and Henry Cabot Lodge, Sr. (until he became a candidate for political office) held that American institutions were derived from the ancient Teutons, either directly or through the Anglo-Saxons; and they supported this hypothesis by finding analogies, say, between the structure of the Teutonic and the New England village. Accordingly, an infusion of such "alien" and "inferior races" as the Latins or the Slavs would weaken the foundations of American society.

A revolt against this "Teutonic hypothesis" was led by Frederick Jackson Turner, who emphasized the original elements, without European precedent, of America's frontier society. But he, too, considered immigrants from Southern Italy to be "of doubtful value judged from the ethical point of view," and the Jews a "people of exceptionally stunted growth and of deficient lung capacity." He wrote: "Italians, Slovaks, Poles and other immigrants of Eastern Europe, together with the Russian Jews, have struck hard blows since 1880 at the standard of comfort of the American workmen. They have made New York City a great reservoir for the pipe lines that run to the misery pools of Europe." Though the eminent John Bach McMaster, for instance, sounded a contrary note, this was the dominant tone of American historians up to the 1920s, when the national-quota act was passed. And their theories provided a good part of that act's scholarly underpinning.

The only important counterweight to the pro-Nordic tendency of the professional historians was the ancestor veneration (what Saveth calls "filiopietism") of the amateurs with non-Anglo-Saxon names. However, "because their insecurity was greater," he writes, "the jingoism of the historians of recent immigrant ancestry far exceeded the chauvinism of historians derived from the older American stock." The patent exaggerations of the writings sponsored by the Huguenot Society of America, the Scotch-Irish Society of America, the American Irish Historical Society, the American

[5] Edward N. Saveth, *American Historians and European Immigrants, 1875–1925* (New York: Columbia University Press, 1948).

Jewish Historical Society, and the rest probably served only to reinforce by contrast the Teutonic and frontier myths, which were at least offered with the proper professional credentials and the appropriate academic apparatus.

More important, however, in clearing the way for the national-quota act of 1924 than either Walker's or the historians' theories was the *Report* of the Senate Immigration Commission of 1907–11, headed by Senator William P. Dillingham of Vermont. The sheer mass of data contained in this document, much of it based on firsthand investigation, tended to overwhelm opposing views: no one person or organization could stand up against four years of investigation and forty-two volumes of evidence and interpretation. Even the one member of the Commission who disagreed with some of its important recommendations, Congressman William S. Bennet of New York, did no more than say so in a half-page statement: "As the report of the Commission is finally adopted within a half hour of the time when, under the law, it must be filed, there is no time for the preparation of an elaborate dissent." The Commission presented its views in abridged form in two volumes; and a more popular version by Jenks (one of the Commission's members) and Lauck long remained a standard text on immigration.[6]

One of the forty-two volumes prepared by the Senate Immigration Commission was a *Dictionary of Races or Peoples* that classified immigrants to the United States in forty-five ethnic groups in accordance with the practice of the Bureau of Immigration. These groups were defined in different ways—by physical differences (for example, Negroes); by language (Germans, including German-speaking Swiss, Austrians, etc.); by nationality, even when not associated with a state (Ruthenians); by geography (Scandinavians, West Indians). Though the practice of the Bureau of Immigration had included Jews among the Slavs, the more "scientific" *Dictionary* pointed out that the "Hebrews" were in the Chaldaic "group" of the Semitic "stock" of the Caucasian race.

[6] Jeremiah W. Jenks and W. Jett Lauck, *The Immigration Problem: A Study of American Immigration Conditions and Needs* (3rd rev. ed.; New York: Funk and Wagnalls, 1913).

Almost all the data that the Commission collected on the different peoples of the world were broken down according to "race." Sometimes the scarcity of the individuals available from which to draw conclusions about a specific group in a specific situation was disguised by presenting the data as percentages: thus, of the Greeks employed in the packing industry who had been in the United States for over ten years, "60 percent" had visited abroad—or three out of a total of five persons.

The main body of the Commission's *Report* traced in great detail the immigration from Southern and Eastern Europe, and declared it to have a causal connection with the economic dislocations and troubles in the United States over the same period—which was marked by rapid industrialization and urbanization. In the only significant contemporary rejoinder to the *Report*, Hourwich's *Immigration and Labor*,[7] a wealth of data was presented to show that this causal relation was specious. Hourwich pointed out that the correlation between immigration and unemployment was negative, not positive; that the "displacement" of native American girls from the mills was motivated by their own desire for the new office jobs then opening up; and that, similarly, miners and those in other low-status jobs were "displaced" not by unemployment but by the attraction of better-paying, higher-status jobs.

Strangely enough, Hourwich was accused by the other side of having *too much* documentation behind him. "It is a safe assumption," said an important review of the book by Professor Henry Pratt Fairchild of New York University, "that the impressive mass of material—statistical tables, charts, diagrams, and footnotes—will seem to the ordinary reader a sufficient proof of any conclusions which the author wishes to draw from them. It is because this assumption is grounded in human nature that the book is dangerous." This was a peculiar criticism altogether, and especially as applied to a book written in answer to forty-two volumes crammed tight

[7] Isaac A. Hourwich, *Immigration and Labor: The Economic Aspects of European Immigration to the United States* (New York: Putnam, 1912).

with tables, charts, diagrams, and footnotes, and stamped with official authority to boot.

### Eugenicists

The most direct connection between racist doctrine and American immigration policy was established by the influence of Dr. Harry H. Laughlin of the Eugenics Record Office of the Carnegie Institution of Washington. Well known as an advocate of sterilization of inmates of institutions, Laughlin became "expert eugenics agent" to the House Committee on Immigration and Naturalization. A report he submitted to it in 1922, *Expert Analysis of the Metal and the Dross in America's Melting Pot*,[8] so impressed Congress that, according to one authority, "it is often considered the principal basis of the Act of 1924."[9]

Laughlin used a so-called contingency analysis, in order to show that the distribution of social ills was not random. He compared the proportion of persons from each ethnic group in prisons, asylums, and similar institutions with the proportion of the country's total population that this ethnic group constituted. For example: in 1910, persons of Italian birth made up 1.46 percent of the total population and, if proportionally represented in the ninety-three insane asylums that Laughlin surveyed, they would have constituted 1.46 percent of the total number of inmates, or 1,228. Since there were actually 1,938 Italian-born persons in these institutions, the incidence of insanity among Italians was concluded to be more than one and a half times that of the general population. For social inadequacies of all types, Laughlin found that the various groups into which he divided the population were represented as follows in relation to their expected figure of 100:

[8] U. S. House of Representatives, *Hearings before the Committee on Immigration and Naturalization*, November 21, 1922 (67th Congress, 3rd Session, Serial 7-C; Washington: U. S. Government Printing Office, 1923).

[9] Roy L. Garis, *Immigration Restriction: A Study of the Opposition to and Regulation of Immigration into the United States* (New York: Macmillan, 1927), pp. 239–240.

| Total native white | 91.89 |
| Of native parents | 84.33 |
| Of mixed parents | 116.65 |
| Of foreign parents | 109.40 |
| Total foreign-born white | 145.75 |
| Northwest Europe | 130.42 |
| Southern and Eastern Europe | 143.24 |

Laughlin concluded from these statistics that all foreigners were inferior, and especially those from Southern and Eastern Europe. He also asserted that the "first and primary factor" that had caused the different proportions of ethnic representation in institutions was "differences in constitutional susceptibility of specific races and nativity groups to certain definite types of social inadequacy." That is to say, such "degeneracies" as "criminality" were "inherited in the blood." The implications of such an analysis for policy were clear:

There has, thus far, been no suggestion in our laws of any requirement except personal value in our sorting of would-be immigrants. [However] the surest biological principle . . . to direct the future of America along safe and sound racial channels is to control the hereditary quality of the immigration stream.

The flaws in this "expert analysis" were numerous and fundamental. The notion that "criminality" and most other social inadequacies are hereditary was no longer generally accepted even in the 1920s, so unfounded had it been shown to be. Today only crackpots dare repeat it.

Strangely enough, Laughlin's own data on feeble-mindedness (one of the few such inadequacies that *may* be inherited) refute his general conclusion. Only two foreign groups showed a ratio of feeble-mindedness higher than 100—Serbians, with *two* cases, and Australians, with *three* cases. The foreign-born as a group showed a ratio for feeble-mindedness of only 31.6, and those from Southern and Eastern Europe one of 33. In contrast, native whites as a group were above 100, as also the subgroup formed by those with native parents.

Moreover, even if one should grant that "criminality" is

inherited, it does not follow that its heredity can be traced through such vague and ambiguous groups as Laughlin's "races." In general, he used the classification of "races" recommended in the Senate Commission's *Report*, but he went beyond even its grossly unscientific methods—breaking down, for example, native white Americans into four subgroups: "Mountain White," "American Yankee," "American Southerner," and "Middle-West American." That these classifications should have been accepted as "races or nativity groups," rather than as the cultural groups they patently were, indicates an extraordinary will on the part of the Congressmen to accept Laughlin's main point.

His data were in any case incomplete and statistically biased. He had returns from only 445 of the 657 state and federal institutions that were relevant to his analysis, and he made no allowance for the bias that this incomplete sample introduced. He did not correct for the differences in age structure and sex ratio of the several groups, although immigrants tended to be concentrated in the middle male age-group, which in every society has the highest incidence of many social ills.

Finally, Laughlin ignored the differences in the availability of institutional care in the various sections of the country. Institutions were relatively scarce in the immigrant-free South, for instance, while immigrants were concentrated in Northern cities, where social care was much more adequate. As one commentator has demonstrated, by Laughlin's method of analysis Negroes prove to be far less afflicted with "social inadequacies" than white Southerners. Feeble-mindedness is eight times more prevalent among native white Southerners than among Negroes, epilepsy nearly ten times, blindness twenty-four times, tuberculosis two and a half times, insanity one and a half times, deafness one and a half times, physical deformity eight times, dependency four times. In only one social ill, crime, is the quota fulfillment of Negroes higher than that of native whites, for the one institution with which the Southern Negro is adequately supplied is prisons.[10]

[10] Antonio Stella, *Some Aspects of Italian Immigration to the United States* (New York: Putnam, 1924), Appendix.

## From Theory to Law

Laughlin submitted his report in 1922, and two years later the policy he recommended was enacted into permanent law. It is true, as many have pointed out, that the immigration laws of the 1920s were passed during the period of xenophobia and labor unrest following World War I. But it is not true—as this observation is meant to imply—that these laws, like the Palmer raids, were merely another manifestation of temporary hysteria. Their enactment came as the culmination of decades of effort, and on the basis of principles that had thus become legitimized.

Congressman Walter declared time and again that the act of which he was cosponsor has removed the racial discrimination contained in the old law of 1924. This assertion was based principally on the fact that most Asiatic countries, whose emigrants used to be barred altogether, are now given a face-saving annual quota of 100 persons each. In every other respect, however, the McCarran-Walter law has continued and even extended the racism implicit in the 1924 act. Quotas used to be based on the country of birth, and this is still so except for a person who is Asian "by as much as one-half of his ancestry"; such a person, no matter where born, must immigrate under the minuscule quota assigned to the country of his Asian parent. Similarly, by the new law natives of the British West Indies—many of whom are Negroes—may no longer immigrate under the large British quota: they now have one of their own amounting to 100 per year. More fundamentally, the McCarran-Walter act has retained the national-origin system as the basis of American immigration policy, and this system can be justified only by the racist principles Mr. Walter ostensibly disavowed.

Why was it that American social scientists of the pre-1914 period generally supported a national-quota system and the anthropological theories implicit in it? Without attempting a definitive answer to so large a question, one can suggest three probably relevant factors:

1. The main source of immigration to the United States shifted from Northwest Europe to Southern and Eastern

Europe at about the same time that the American economy
underwent a fundamental transformation. The German or
Swedish peasant who immigrated during the years right
after the Civil War took advantage of the Homestead Act
and became an American farmer; but when the Italian or
Polish peasant arrived this frontier was closed, and burgeoning American industry had begun to call for more and more
unskilled labor. The new immigrants, therefore, had simul-
taneously to undergo two processes of adjustment: from
their native cultures to the American one, and from a rural
to an urban way of life; and the second adaptation was much
the more difficult one. The social ills attributed to the innate
inadequacies of the new immigrants were the result basically
of the extremely rapid development of an industrial society,
but it was the new immigrants who became the most con-
spicuous casualties of this process. Not only did city slums
(for example) develop much faster after large numbers of
Poles (for example) began to arrive, but it was the Poles who
lived in the slums and thus developed the characteristics
typical of slum residents. Given the level of their scientific
disciplines at that time, social scientists drew the "obvious"
conclusion that Poles had caused slums.

2. Such a conclusion, moreover, was in line with the
general climate of opinion of the period. The Darwinian
theory, having conquered biology, was advancing into the
social sciences: this was the heyday of social Darwinism and
physical anthropology. Man had finally come to be viewed as
part of nature, and his physical group characteristics—such
as pigmentation and cerebral index—acquired a new significance by analogy with the characteristics differentiating
other animal and plant species and varieties. While a racist
analysis at that time often had the same nastiness that it
has today, as in the writings of Madison Grant and Lothrop
Stoddard, sometimes it also became, by the dispassionate
application of evolutionary theory to human origins, the
expression of a kind of naïve, science-oriented progressivism.
We contemporaries of Adolf Hitler have been taught that
false anthropological theories can have horrible consequences, but it would be anachronistic to expect people
living before 1914 to have either our greater knowledge on

this matter or our far greater sensitivity to the implications.

3. Finally, virtually all the men who legitimized the national-origin system were themselves of Anglo-Saxon background. The new immigrants, just because they had come to this country only recently, had not yet produced their share of professors or statesmen. The men who wrote the important works on immigration and race were named Walker, Fiske, Burgess, Lodge, Turner, Dillingham, Fairchild, Hall, Commons, Ross, Garis, and so on; while the few who answered their arguments were named, for example, Hourwich and Stella—and, as an exception to the rule, Willcox. With respect to any one individual, such a distinction would be invidious, but the predominantly Anglo-Saxon family background and German intellectual tradition of the American scholarly community as a whole in that period certainly had some influence on the theories it evolved.

None of these three points holds today. We now know that the scholarly basis on which the national-origin quota rests was itself compounded out of ignorance and prejudice. Why, then, though aware that racist theory is both false and gravely dangerous to our democratic system, do we retain a law deriving from that theory? In broadest terms, it is because the national-quota system has acquired an independent legitimation: during the thirty years that it has been part of the law of the land it has established a certain tradition, so that the burden of proof now lies with those who advocate a different immigration policy. The opponents of the national-quota system have two enormously powerful weapons—our present knowledge concerning group differences and the continued pertinence of the basic American credo—but very often these weapons have not been used effectively.

What alternative shall we offer in place of the present act? Eliminating racism, and going back to deny entry only to specific persons with *objectionable individual characteristics* would not suffice of itself to define an immigration policy. The standard of living in the United States is high enough to make migration attractive to a sizable proportion of the world's three billion people, and some more or less arbitrary limit must therefore be set to the number of those admitted in any one year. The Perlman Commission recommended that the annual maximum of immigration be set at one-sixth of one percent of the country's current population—which, at the present time, would amount to about 300,000 persons, compared with the 150,000 admissible under the McCarran-Walter Act. But how would these 300,000 be selected?

Certain persons would continue to be excluded (criminals, prostitutes, etc.); and the Commission recommended that preference be given to applicants in four specific categories—those seeking asylum, those seeking to rejoin their families, those who could fill occupational needs in the United States, and those in areas suffering from population pressure that could be relieved by emigration. But there would certainly be enough in the last group alone to fill the full quota of 300,000 many times over—not to mention the hundreds of thousands who would find a way to escape from the Communist countries if they could hope for a final refuge in the United States. In 1953, the year of the riots in East Berlin, exactly 305,737 refugees were registered in West Berlin alone. There are more than a million refugees from Communist China in overcrowded Hong Kong.

Finally, the Perlman Commission recommended a fifth category of "general" immigration:

> The standards to be applied under this category should not be rigid. The agency charged with such a responsibility should have a reasonable latitude in reaching a fair, impartial and workable result, and should safeguard this category so that no one country, group, or area would obtain unfair advantages under its operation.

But in a dispute over values, such words as "reasonable," "impartial," "fair," and "unfair" mean nothing unless they are very explicitly defined. In effect, the Commission has recommended that, within the very broad limits set by the law, actual policy should be determined by an administrative agency. Such a flexible system has been in force for decades in Canada, for example, where our same policy of discrimination against all but Northwest Europeans has been practiced in fact without ever being written into law. As a matter of fact, the Senate Immigration Commission of 1911 itself recommended that serious consideration be given to the convenient and flexible procedure that Canada had developed:

> The Canadian immigration law is admirably adapted to carrying out the immigration policy of the Dominion. Under its terms no immigrants [except Chinese] are specifically denied admission solely because of their race or origin, or because of the purpose for which they have come to Canada, but the discretion conferred upon officials charged with the administration of the law does make much discrimination entirely possible.

The responsibility of finding an adequate basis for policy cannot be evaded by establishing one more Washington bureau.

## Liberal vs. Progressive

Our thinking about the values underlying immigration policy, as about many other social and political issues, can be clarified by distinguishing between the views of two types, which we will term Liberal and Progressive. The Liberal is attached to those values of rationalism, humanitarianism, and individual rights characteristic of the modern Western world at its best. The Progressive, though he often speaks with the same words, got many of his ideas of what is socially desirable from Leftist politics, either directly or indirectly. The Liberal and the Progressive are not real persons; indeed, part of our problem lies in the very fact that these two patterns of thought are not so sharply distinguished in American society as they are drawn here in the effort to define them.

The nativist argument against immigration has been in terms of values: "100-percent Americanism," and in terms of alleged fact: the immigrant never completely loses his alien culture. From the beginning, proponents of a less restrictive immigration policy have tended to ignore the first point and to concentrate on answering the second. Thus, a generation ago the nativist campaign against "hyphenated Americans" was answered with Israel Zangwill's gruesome metaphor of "the melting pot."[11] Everything we have learned since then, however, corroborates the stand of Henry Pratt Fairchild and the others who denied that those put into the pot were melted down into an indistinguishable mass. To cite only one example, but a crucial one: we now know from such studies as those by Paul F. Lazarsfeld and Samuel Lubell that a person's vote is strongly influenced by his religious and ethnic affiliations. "The Jewish vote" or "the Irish vote" is not a reactionary stereotype, but a fact of American politics; it is a fact, however, that the Progressive cannot use and so must suppress.

Since the Progressive cannot make the new empirical data indicating that distinctive ethnic differences persist fit *his* idea of the good society, he is reduced to his own brand of Know-Nothingism. He refuses to use words that designate any group differences other than those of social class. Negroes are "the colored people," Italian-Americans are "the Italian-speaking people," Puerto Ricans are "Spanish-speaking Americans," and so on. Such somatic characteristics as skin color and hair texture must be glossed over, and the facts of cultural difference are equally taboo.

That is to say, the nativist and the Progressive disagree sharply concerning the facts of acculturation; but the nativist, who insists that significant group differences do exist, is closer to the truth as we know it. Concerning the values underlying immigration policy, however, the disagreement between the nativist and the Progressive is less sharp. An answer to xenophobia that consists principally in an attempt to cover over and disguise existent group differences implicitly affirms the "100-percent Americanism" assumption that all such differences are reprehensible. To deny the fact of the Jewish vote, for example, is only superficially a discussion of empirical data; more fundamentally, it is to assert that there may not legitimately be a connection between a man's being Jewish and the way he votes. But this is a moral issue, which can be discussed meaningfully only in terms of values. The immigrant generation of the 1920s was too insecure to

[11] Israel Zangwill, *The Melting-Pot* (Rev. ed.; New York: Macmillan, 1920).

face this issue squarely, and this pattern of evasion set a precedent that is still often followed.

In terms of values, the nativist has a weak case, for his claim to represent the fundamental American credo is fraudulent. In what do the "100-percent American" and the "un-American" differ? Is the distinction ethnic, cultural, or political? It is all three together, and indeed the essence of the dichotomy is that it tends to fuse the three into one. It is of the nature of such invidious distinctions to spread: the Nazi persecution of the Jews eventually extended to "Jews" with one Jewish grandparent and then to "Jew-lovers"; the Soviet persecution of kulaks eventually included that most urbane of city-bred intellectuals Nikolai Bukharin, because of his "kulak soul." The American nativist is not typically a totalitarian, but he does tend to see the world as black or white, and all who differ in any way from his parochial provincialism essentially one. It is therefore entirely in keeping that the McCarran-Walter Act, which continues and reinforces the racism of the immigration laws of the 1920s, should also impose a more rigid bar to "subversives"— a term it defines loosely and broadly.

There is much in the American culture that facilitates such a trend toward the absolute uniformity of the mass society, but the American democratic credo does not. That all men are equal does not mean that all men are the same, for the egalitarian theme is balanced by one of federalism. *Liberté, égalité, fraternité,* later the slogan of the French revolutionaries, gave some of its ideological underpinning to the revolt of the American colonies, but the motto of the United States became *E pluribus unum.* By now, the doctrine of states' rights has too often turned into what Samuel Johnson called patriotism, the last refuge of scoundrels; but the federal framework of values remains, and with it the task of defining in modern terms the legitimate range of group differences within an encompassing national unity.

Unhappily, this is a task in which few are interested. The interrelation among America's diverse ethnic strains, which *is* American history, is still studied principally in terms of pious exhortations to mutual tolerance and of filiopietistic success stories—as though the success of immigrants and

immigrants' sons were still something to be considered remarkable. The brilliant pioneering work of Marcus Lee
Hansen, cut short by his untimely death, has not established
a new school, as had Turner's grosser insight a generation
earlier. Hansen's masterwork was to have been a trilogy on
modern emigration from Europe; but only the first volume,
which took the reader only up to 1860, was ever written.[12]
The four years Hansen had spent on research in the
countries of Northwest Europe gave his volume a unique
authenticity; and the mass of data he accumulated, which
might have overwhelmed a lesser historian, Hansen used to
give his account greater depth. "The" immigrant never merged
into a vague, flat stereotype; immigrants were persons who
wrote letters home (which Hansen quotes), and whose
difficulties and successes were recounted in the local newspapers (which he dug out of dusty files). On the other
hand, the common experience of pulling up roots and
establishing themselves in a new country cut across
individual and cultural differences: immigrants were not
only persons but also the raw material out of which Americans, a new cultural type, were formed.

Hansen's extraordinary ability to combine psychological
insights with historical data is well illustrated by a small essay
on "the third generation."[13] It is well known—and perhaps
even true—that the second generation tends to reject its
parents, whose alien origin it regards as a stigma. The third
generation, on the contrary, is secure enough to take its
Americanism for granted, and is often interested in the
cuisine, history, and folk art of its grandparents in the Old
Country. In this article, Hansen gave some empirical substance to this generalization by showing that the various
filiopietistic historical societies in America had generally been
founded at one generation's remove from the time when the

[12] Marcus Lee Hansen, *The Atlantic Migration 1607–1860: A
History of the Continuing Settlement of the United States* (Cambridge: Harvard University Press, 1951).
[13] Hansen, *The Problem of the Third Generation Immigrant*
(Rock Island, Ill.: Augustana Historical Society, 1938); reprinted
in *Commentary*, November, 1952, pp. 492–500.

respective ethnic group's immigration was at its quantitative peak.

The concept of a multicultural society implicit in Hansen's work has not been developed to the full. It consists of two basic propositions—that Old Country traits do not completely disappear in American society, and that the resultant cultural pluralism does not of itself weaken national unity.

If the theories that were developed in the decades before 1920 were largely rationalizations to justify the primitive dislike that Americans of Anglo-Saxon stock often felt for the new immigrants from Southern and Eastern Europe, the counterarguments offered now will have to be rationalizations of some other, more humanitarian sentiment. In the end, something more than an appeal to scientific evidence or self-interest is needed. For, though the arguments of Walker, the Senate Immigration Commission, and Laughlin are no longer acceptable, this does not mean that a larger immigration would necessarily bring the benefits that the Perlman Commission spells out in its report. Immigration of a politically feasible size will in general have no marked effect, whether detrimental or beneficial, on this country's population structure, economy, or culture. It is easier to suppose that America's foreign relations would be improved if the discriminatory restrictions against certain aliens were removed, but even this point may have been exaggerated. Immigration to the United States will not solve any problems overseas, and it will never make an important contribution to the national interest of this country, if this interest is defined in terms of Realpolitik.

There is really only one reason for a less restrictive immigration policy—human decency.

# ACCULTURATION AND GROUP PREJUDICE

The mass emigration from Europe to the United States during the century up to the First World War was generally analyzed at the time as part of the operation of a vast, international labor market. Migrants left their homes because of economic pressure, and went wherever there were better economic opportunities. Like any other market, this one was deemed to be self-regulating. Just as within each country the best men rose to the top by the "natural" process of competition, so the best among the potential migrants succeeded in establishing themselves in new countries. In both cases, the state had to intercede only to keep antisocial elements under control.

In such a context of ideas, cultural assimilation was more or less taken for granted. According to a representative statement of twenty years ago,

> Assimilation . . . goes on wherever contact and communication exist between groups. Much of it takes place automatically, without formal or official interference. It is as inevitable as it is desirable. The process may be hastened or delayed; it cannot be stopped.[1]

This process of assimilation was not only inevitable but, when completed, total. The immigrant group would be *spurlos versenkt* in the receiving culture, which itself would remain as unchanged as the sea that swallowed up a foundered vessel. In the United States, the nativists' demand that the immigrant become a "100-percent American," and the immigrant's own aspiration to lose himself in the American "melting pot," expressed essentially the same concept despite their different political overtones.

[1] Maurice R. Davie, *World Immigration, with Special Reference to the United States* (New York: Macmillan, 1949), pp. 498–499.

That immigrants in the pre-1914 period were defined primarily in terms of their economic function meant that their broader cultural attributes were, in theory at least, less important; prejudice against aliens, whatever its "real" causes, had to be justified by economic arguments. The bar to Asian immigration, for example, was in both the United States and Australia the consequence principally of the trade unions' demand for what might be termed a tariff on cut-rate foreign labor. In the United States it took two generations of social scientists to shift the emphasis from immigrants as economic men operating in a free market to immigrants as carriers of alien cultures.[2]

The revival of international migration since 1945 has not meant a renewal of the same type of movement from country to country that characterized the pre-1914 period. All governments now take an active part in regulating the migration process. This restriction of international mobility is, of course, only one expression of the over-all transformation of laissez-faire society. The nineteenth-century liberal's faith that the uninhibited, "natural" operation of social institutions like the market would automatically produce the greatest benefit for the greatest number has all but disappeared, to be superseded by the demand that the state itself take all possible measures to further the good society. And today countries that receive immigrants do not merely select good workers or permit their automatic selection by the operation of the market, but favor individuals who belong to social or ethnic groups that are considered easier to assimilate culturally. The difficulty, however, is how to define such assimilability in operational terms.

The shift in emphasis from the immigrant's economic role to his total contribution to his new country has meant also a shift in conceptual framework from economics to anthropology. The very word that social scientists now use, *acculturation,* was taken over from the German and American anthropologists, who coined it about the time of the First World War. First by anthropologists and now more generally, acculturation has been seen as a continuum, with

[2] This process is analyzed in the previous essay.

total assimilation at one extreme, total nonassimilation at the other, and most cases falling somewhere between.

Perhaps the most satisfactory method of analyzing this continuum is in terms of a tripartite typology devised by the American anthropologist Ralph Linton.[3] He divided the social roles in any culture into "universals," "specialties," and "alternatives." If the behavior of immigrant groups is described in these terms, much sharper and more meaningful distinctions can be drawn than simply the answer, yes or no, to the question whether they have been assimilated.

Total conformity is expected of immigrants only with respect to those ideas and behavior patterns to which all natives must likewise conform. These are the "universals" of the society in question. In the United States, at least three things have been demanded of all immigrants—that they support themselves, learn the English language, and pledge political allegiance to their new country. And while the norms of other countries differ to some degree, there, too, conformity to these three universals usually meets the minimum definition of acculturation.

In even the most homogeneous culture, not all values are universal; there is always a legitimate diversity of ideas, attitudes, and tastes. In the United States today, those who prefer popular music to Bach, or hiking to bowling, or bow ties to cravats, have chosen certain "alternatives" over others. In the abstract, immigrants are free to make similar choices; and if they retain Old Country ways, they are often commended for "enriching" the culture of their new homeland. In practice, however, exotic tastes in such things as food are sometimes taken as a sign of unreliability in more fundamental respects. In the 1920s, thus, the head of a ladies' Americanization society asked her audience, with poorly restrained impatience, "What kind of American consciousness can grow in the atmosphere of sauerkraut and Limburger cheese, or in that of garlic?" More recently, the Immigration Service in San Francisco supported its charge that a certain alien advocated world Communism, and thus its petition for a deportation order, by eliciting the informa-

[3] Ralph Linton, *Study of Man* (New York: Appleton-Century, 1935), Chap. 16.

tion that he had once served his guests beef Stroganoff. This same confusion is found in more important matters. The American state is enjoined by its own fundamental laws from trying to enforce religious conformity on its population, but nativist opposition to immigration has been shaped to a large degree by both anti-Catholic and anti-Semitic prejudice.

Linton's third type of social role, "specialties," pertains to the kind of work a man does. Specialties divide any population into subgroups, both at the occupational level (stock brokers, stenographers, automobile workers) and at the more inclusive level of social class (businessmen, employees, wageworkers). That is to say, the division of labor sets people apart not merely according to their economic function but also, to some degree, with respect to their average income, way of life, political attitudes, and so on. Even in democratic America, a lawyer and an automobile mechanic, say, differ in their style of life almost as much as in their occupation.

This fact marks the principal limitation of the old melting-pot view of assimilation, for immigrant groups are typically congregated in only a few places in the receiving country's social structure. The original differentiation by ethnic origin, though reduced by the general acceptance of universal cultural traits, is to some degree maintained by social class and region or neighborhood. It is true that immigrants typically begin at the bottom and that their children, or they themselves, climb to higher positions, but different ethnic groups climb different ladders toward different goals. Despite our high degree of social democracy, ethnic groups have not generally diffused throughout the American social structure. And ethnic differentiations are still more of a factor in most spheres of American life than is commonly thought. In the oldest immigrant group in the United States, the New England Yankees, identification with the home country, even at a distance of a half-dozen generations, is strong enough to be discernible in the voting record when American policy toward Britain becomes a crucial issue.[4]

The interest in the assimilation of immigrants, which was

[4] See Samuel Lubell, *The Future of American Politics* (Rev. ed.; New York: Doubleday-Anchor, 1956), p. 141.

great in the 1920s, has waned in the United States. If we want to see how present-day analysts are studying the process, we would do better to look abroad. In Israel and Australia, for instance, the considerable current importance of immigration in the national life has resulted in two interesting analyses.

## Israel

Acculturation can be described as the interaction between a constant and a variable—that is, between an essentially stable receiving culture and an adapting immigrant group. Something like this relation has obtained in the United States, in spite of the very important influence that particular immigrant groups have had on one or another element of American culture. The other extreme is represented by Israel, where one of the problems is precisely how to define the "native" culture to which immigrants are to adapt.

The movement of Jews to Palestine-Israel has been, in proportion to the population of the receiving country, one of the largest migrations in history. Five out of eight of the Jews in Israel are immigrants, and almost one out of two came in since the founding of the state in 1948. In any other host country, the native-born dominate simply by reason of their numbers; but in Israel the native-born *sabras,* one ethnic minority among others, do not dominate even in a legal sense. Immigrants to all other countries arrive as petitioners, admitted under conditions set down by the receiving country, while Israel's Law of Return proclaims that "every Jew has the right to come to this country as an immigrant." In principle, this is an unconditional right: the state that has declared itself the Jewish homeland can make no legitimate demands on any Jew who wants to come "home."

On the other hand, Israel will not become a nation in a meaningful sense unless her diverse peoples acquire some degree of homogeneity. Her polyglot population has a tremendous cultural range, from Viennese psychoanalysts and Frankfort judges to Yemenite shepherds and Moroccan water-sellers. The strongest bond uniting these various ethnic groups is negative—resentment of the anti-Semitism many Jews had met in the Gentile world. Most of their positive bonds are not universal, and within the confines of a single country can thus be divisive. Not all Israelis, for instance, are Zionists. Nor are all of them religious Jews, and some even object to being called "Jews" altogether.[5] All are, indeed, "Israelis," but what is the cultural content of this designation? The Hebrew language is only beginning to acquire a secular literature, and Israel's society is still in the process of evolving some of its basic institutions.

Under such conditions what does it mean to say that an immigrant is acculturated or, to use the term current in Israel, "absorbed"? According to the ideology of Zionism, the assimilation of Jews to any national culture other than Israel's is either impossible or, when it does take place, reprehensible. Acculturation to Israel, by this view, is not required of the real Jew, because he brings with him his "Jewish" culture, which is also the culture of Israel. But this is too simple a view by far.

What seems to be happening is a struggle on the part of each minority to establish its own norms as the universals to which all other Israelis must conform. Four minorities can be distinguished as the most important in this connection: the pioneer settlers who came to Palestine as Zionists; the native-born, who speak Hebrew as their mother tongue and are the first heirs of the Zionist tradition; the refugees from Nazism, the self-conscious carriers of Western culture, as contrasted with the rough-and-ready *sabra;* and the Middle Eastern immigrants, the latest arrivals, who represent a traditional Judaism relatively untouched by secularist influence. All four of these subcultures have a legitimate status in Israel, and while they share some features, their differences are important.

In view of its complexities, it is not surprising that neither the problem of acculturation nor the broader one of Israel's

[5] This is the small but symptomatic group called the "Canaanites," who publish the periodical *Aleph.* See Robert L. Lindsey, "Israel's Coming Crisis over 'Jewishness,'" *Commentary,* July, 1954; Trude Weiss-Rosmarin, "Defining Jewishness," *Jewish Spectator,* September, 1958.

immigration has yet been adequately analyzed. The work by Dr. S. N. Eisenstadt, chairman of the Sociology Department of the Hebrew University in Jerusalem, is largely a disappointment.[6] Its strong point seems to be the theory of acculturation, which is adapted from Linton's analysis of the three types of roles. The indices ordinarily used to measure this process, Eisenstadt points out, are all inadequate—in large part because they were constructed as indices of full assimilation, which seldom or never takes place. Immigrant groups are not usually dispersed throughout the social structure of the receiving country, but tend to congregate in one part of it, where they maintain some degree of separate identity. There thus arises a "pluralistic" society the various parts of which are different in both ethnic origin and social class. Whether an immigrant is able to adjust satisfactorily depends on what his desires and expectations are, and on

[6] *The Absorption of Immigrants: A Comparative Study Based Mainly on the Jewish Community in Palestine and the State of Israel* (Glencoe, Ill.: Free Press, 1955). The impression that the book was hurriedly written is reinforced by the extremely careless copyediting. M. J. Herskovits appears as "Herskovitz," Bronislaw Malinowski as both "Malinowsky" and "Malinovski." A. I. Hallowell has lost one of the l's in his name, but this reappears in "Millbank," one of the spellings for the Milbank Memorial Fund. C. Wright Mills is listed as "C.S.," "W.," and "W. E. A. Mills," and the co-authors of *The Puerto Rican Journey* (perhaps luckily for them) do not appear at all. If the work by Georges Mauco is "the most complete illustrative casebook on this type of migration" —which it is—then his name should not be given as "G. Manco." E. W. Hofstee was so mangled that I barely recognized him as "E. Hoffstree." On page 28 the number of Jewish migrants to the United States between 1881 and 1930 is given as 2,885,000; on page 30 the "ultimate" number (thus including the subsequent refugee migration) is given as "about 2 million." In the various tables sometimes the percentage columns add up to 100, sometimes they get no closer than, for example, 81.7. The index is so inept as to be laughable. The countries of Jewish emigration, for example, are listed in the following form: "Bulgaria, immigration from, see Immigrants from (to Israel)"; or, as a variant, "Iraq, immigrants from (to Israel), see immigrants from." Under "Immigrants" the reader is then instructed to "see migrations." Under "Migration," finally, there is a list of countries, but Bulgaria and Iraq are not among them.

how well these can be met in his new country. But how
relevant is all this to the particular case of Israel?

Eisenstadt's main argument can be summarized in three
theses: (1) The core of the Israeli nation is the Hebrew-
Zionist tradition. (2) The adaptation of other groups, therefore, can be indicated by measuring the degree to which
they have accepted this tradition. (3) The range of cultural differences among the various sectors of the Israeli
population is less wide than might appear on the surface,
and the prospects of achieving a homogeneous nation are
good.

Let us examine each of these theses briefly.

One of the main points of the Zionist program, the use
of Hebrew, is indeed becoming a universal of Israeli society,
though more as a matter of principle than of fact. According
to a survey by Roberto Bachi to which Eisenstadt refers,
"even after some time in Israel only 10 percent [of the "new"
immigrants] used Hebrew in their family life, and only 25
percent in other social contexts." This is a problem, of course,
that will lessen as the proportion of native-born Israelis
rises.

The complex of ideas and convictions called Zionism,
which is the other constant factor of Israeli culture in
Eisenstadt's view, is in a state of flux. Even without the dilu-
tion by refugee (largely non-Zionist) immigration, much of
the idealism of the early years would have been dissipated
by the successful achievement of the main Zionist aim, the
founding of the state. *Halutziut* (which can be translated
as the mystique of the pioneer) and the glorification of
manual labor no longer retain their former relevance. As the
agricultural collectives, or *kibbutzim*, decline in proportion
to the rest of the economy, their values are being transformed
from a guide to present action into a historical source of
inspiration—somewhat like the "rugged individualism" of the
American pioneer.

My impression is that Eisenstadt consistently overstates
the present strength of the Zionist tradition, and he certainly contributes to the building of its legend by exag-
gerating the heroic aspects of the pioneer settlements. Thus,
in his discussion of the motives for Jewish emigration, he

contrasts the "economic or other satisfactions" sought by those Jews who went from Eastern Europe to America with the "social and cultural aspirations" that motivated those who went to Palestine. Actually, anti-Semitism was the main impetus of *all* Jewish emigration; each *aliyah* (migratory wave to Palestine) followed immediately on a major pogrom. And, on the positive side, migrants to the United States saw this country, too, as one where Jews might fulfill their "social and cultural aspirations." That Zionists (or at least Zionists outside the United States) believe this to be an empty hope is precisely the point I am making—that Eisenstadt's account of the past is colored by present-day polemics.

One index of absorption that he uses is whether or not children go to public school, which for the Middle Eastern immigrants is a new and often disagreeable experience. But if he had also asked whether the children go to *cheder*, the traditional Jewish religious school, then the secularized West Europeans and Zionists would have scored lowest. In contrast to Middle Eastern immigrants, who "adapt" less readily in part because they hold on to their traditional norms, Serbian and Bulgarian Jews are adjudged as fitting into Israeli society without difficulty. This is in part because "their lack of *traditional*, nonformal Jewish identification [has] made this process much easier for them." Thus pious Orthodox Jews, "returning" to Israel after long exile, are welcomed with a request to shed some of their "less assimilable" Jewishness. It is a measure of Eisenstadt's partisanship that he appears to have no inkling of how strange this looks to the outsider.

Not only does Eisenstadt tend throughout to understate the wide range of cultural differences among the peoples making up Israel's population and, consequently, the difficulty of absorbing them; he hardly mentions the intergroup hostility that, according to other sources, exists in Israeli society.[7] Thus, according to his own data, European-Levantine, Ashkenazi-Sephardic, and even German-Yiddish marriages are uncommon, a fact that would seem to indicate that these

[7] For a recent example, see Judith T. Shuval, "Emerging Patterns of Ethnic Strain in Israel," *Social Forces*, 40:4 (May, 1962), 323–330.

subcultures are not only relatively stable but jealous of their particularity. We are told in a one-sentence footnote that "the Oriental groups usually identify European immigrants and the old Yishuv [settlement] as 'Yiddish.'" Such a characterization, I would say, is an important symptom of the Oriental Israelis' attempt to deny the exclusive legitimacy of the Western version of Israeli society by reducing it to the status of one more subculture; and this is a point which might well have been discussed at length.

An undue emphasis on homogeneity likewise characterizes Eisenstadt's cautious discussion of Israel's class structure. His conclusion is that, all in all, "the picture is complex, and differs from place to place." Actually, this complexity is in part the consequence of a rather simple conflict in values. As in the United States, Israel's value system promises the immigrant a full equality that in practice he is seldom able to attain. The process of acculturation takes place in large part by a dynamic interaction between this promissory note and the partial failure to pay it. The situation is much like what Gunnar Myrdal termed, with special reference to Negro-white relations, the "American dilemma."[8] According to the first moral principle of the Jewish homeland, all Jews are equal, but in actuality some Israeli Jews are more equal than others.

Certainly the pressure of the surrounding Arab states has helped enormously to hold the state together; indeed, without this enemy it might not have survived. What will happen to the polyglot population of Israel no one knows, but one can point out three possibilities. It may be that, in line with the book's assumption, the Zionist tradition will predominantly define Israel's culture, and that all other groups will eventually adapt to it. Or it may be that this secular Western element will be swamped by Levantine obscurantism. Or it may be that a stable compromise will be achieved somehow between these essentially incompatible ways of life.

In any case, the main question in Israel is: which subculture will be established as the norm for the country? To

[8] Gunnar Myrdal, *An American Dilemma: The Negro Problem and Modern Democracy* (New York: Harper, 1944).

treat the present struggle between subcultures merely as a process of *adaptation* to an already existent norm is to distort the picture. It is rather as though one were to study British-French relations in eighteenth-century North America, before the struggle for the continent was settled, in terms of French acculturation to the culture of the assumed future British victors.

## Australia

On the face of it, the problem of analyzing immigration to Australia is much simpler. Until World War I, her non-aboriginal population was almost wholly of British stock. A law passed in 1901 effectually barred further Asian immigration, and the Chinese minority already in the country soon dwindled to a few thousands. Continental Europeans were discouraged from coming to Australia by the great distance, a difficulty that was mitigated for British immigrants by subsidizing the cost of their passage. In 1925 this physical isolation was reinforced by a law empowering the Governor General to deny entry to aliens of any nationality, race, class, or occupation that he specified.

During the war, however, the Japanese threat taught Australia what a liability her sparsely inhabited territory was in the face of the overcrowded countries within striking distance, and in 1945 she proceeded to launch the biggest immigration program of her history. Fully half her immigrants since then have been non-British in origin. Several large questions soon arose, which experts have been trying to answer. How would these new nationality groups adapt to "the Australian way of life"? Would the admission of Italians, Poles, Dutchmen, and Yugoslavs add to Australia's national strength, as the sponsors of the program intended? Or would the rapid increase of population and the wide variety of "New Australians" have the contrary effect—which is what its opponents feared?

One way of getting an answer to such questions was to find out what happened to Australia's non-British minorities, such as they were, before 1945. Wilfrid D. Borrie, the author of a number of excellent works on Australia's population, studied the diverse fates of two such immigrant groups, and the resultant work makes a valuable contribution to our knowledge of acculturation.[9] Borrie combined census data with local history in a coherent narrative and supplemented this with a field survey among the Italian immigrants and their second-generation school children. The fact that he studied two minority groups rather than one adds immeasurably to the value of his analysis, for some of his most interesting points concern the contrasts he found.

As in the United States, one of the major differences between the two nationalities was in the period of settlement, with the Germans beginning to immigrate before 1850 and the Italians several decades later. The first Germans were mainly pioneer peasants, and the culture they brought with them was transplanted to an empty land. The Lutheran church—the dominant social force among them—set the pattern of their communities' development, establishing German-language schools and other institutions whose conscious aim was to preserve *Deutschtum.* Although later German immigrants were motivated by secular rather than religious factors, once in Australia they were drawn into the religious life of the original settlements, or else intermarried with British Australians and disappeared from the social historian's view. The fact that the Lutheran church kept splitting —eventually into six different synods—had the paradoxical effect of reinforcing its total influence, for the very emotion generated by these quarrels helped intensify and maintain allegiance to the various churches.

The dominant theme of the Germans in Australia, thus, was isolation—at first physical, then social. The original settlements worked out their own way of life, and it was this way of life rather than the general Australian pattern that most subsequent German immigrants adapted to. Even when they moved to the cities, Germans in Australia retained something of their isolation: being mostly shopkeepers or independent businessmen, they did not enter into competition with other Australians for jobs, or into contact with them in the trade unions.

[9] *Italians and Germans in Australia: A Study of Assimilation* (Melbourne: Cheshire, 1954).

In the early years, the Germans in Australia were universally praised for their sobriety, frugality, honesty—"a community remarkable for probity and respect for our laws." That they preserved their own language and customs, and even a dual political loyalty, was not found disturbing until Britain and Germany began to clash on the international scene around the turn of the century. In the years before 1914, the most important of Australia's German-language newspapers, the *Australische Zeitung,* repeatedly expressed its sorrow at this "estrangement of the Teutonic races." But it took the war itself to make dual loyalty no longer possible. Later, in the 1930s, the intensive Nazi propaganda carried on in Australia found some echo among German-Australians in the cities but, surprisingly enough, almost none in the rural areas, where German was still the domestic language of the third generation.

From the experience of the German-Australians Borrie concludes, perhaps too hastily, that "where there is no conflict on economic grounds, the cultural persistence of a minority which forms only a fraction of the total population is unlikely to be a cause of tension unless that minority's country of origin pursues a political or international policy which is opposed to the interests of the receiving country."

The pattern of Italian acculturation, according to the survey Borrie made among a group of Italian-Australians in six shires of Queensland, was markedly different. The Italian-born in Australia, fewer than 1,000 in 1871, increased slowly to 8,000 in 1921, and then rapidly to 27,000 in 1933. These rather small numbers represent those who stayed; other Italians worked in Australia for a number of years and then returned to Italy, either permanently or to seek wives. Most Italians began in Australia as fieldworkers, but by the time of the survey about two-thirds of them (including 95 percent of the Sicilians) had acquired their own farms. "In the initial stages this was frequently achieved by two or three Italians operating on a share basis and carrying a much heavier load of debt than the individualistic Australian farmer was prepared to risk. Further, the Italians were not deterred by having to pay high prices for their properties, and in this situation there were always Australian farmers who were willing to sell." Thus, in contrast to the Germans, the Italians came into sharp economic competition with other Australians, and the reaction of the latter was "unsympathetic, and at times clearly hostile."

Partly as a consequence of this hostility, Italians tended to establish themselves in insulated groups, some of them very tiny. Children brought up in such communities began school with no more than a rudimentary knowledge of English but, unlike the children of German immigrants a generation or two earlier, they went to the regular Australian schools. The second-generation Italians, like their counterparts in American cities, learned to fit into a bicultural pattern that was Italian at home and Australian away from it. This pattern had no institutional basis, however: there were no special Italian schools or churches. To some degree, there was not even an "Italian" minority, for most of the immigrants were peasants who felt that they were Piedmontese, Venetians, or Sicilians before they were members of the nation-state of Italy. Although many had left Italy after Mussolini's rise to power, most of them had no strong political sympathies, either Fascist or anti-Fascist, and most were also indifferent to religion. Once their vestigial ties to Italy had been definitely broken by the Second World War, no cultural reasons seemed to remain why the differences between them and other Australians should not have begun to vanish rapidly.

That this has not happened is primarily due, in Borrie's estimation, to the competitive and largely successful struggle of the Italians for economic survival:

The opposition to the Southern European which still lingers in Australia, although frequently expressed in terms which may seem to have a racial content, is still basically economic. What the average Australian still fears first is the introduction of a minority who may threaten to undercut his material standard of life.

I wonder, however, whether it would not be equally valid to say, "The opposition to the Southern European, although frequently expressed in economic terms, is still basically related to the fear of any minority that may threaten the higher status associated with British stock." If it is true that several rather ugly anti-Italian riots took place during the 1930s in the areas most affected by the depression, it is also true that even when there was no economic competition social contacts were inhibited by the "suspicion on the part of Australians that Italians were inferior to British or Nordic stock." From this distance, the persistent determination to maintain a "White Australia" does not seem to be merely a rationalization of the desire to preserve a high standard of living.

Borrie still uses the international market as his principal analytic model: in his view, people migrate mainly for economic motives, and the reaction in the host country is based mainly on the effects of their economic behavior. If natives seem to react most strongly to immigrants' cultural traits (say, to the fact that they speak with a "funny" accent), such reactions can, in his opinion, usually still be interpreted as manifestations of underlying, now half-hidden, economic factors. While this theory is quite inadequate, if not in dealing with nineteenth-century immigration then certainly with that of the post-1914 world, Borrie's attempt to analyze antiforeign sentiment in terms of the actual behavior of immigrant groups is a useful corrective to many studies of acculturation. We typically assume that nativist attitudes are wholly irrational, with no necessary relation to the way immigrants act; and in many cases this assumption is certainly well based. Sometimes, however, newcomers are disliked because *they* work for less, because *they* are disloyal. To restrict the analysis a priori to the "authoritarian personality" of the native population, for instance, may be begging the question.

### The Special Case of the United States

The two examples of Israel and Australia hardly support the notion that assimilation is an automatic and inevitable process. In the first case, the government prohibited the publication of Yiddish newspapers in order to foster the general use of Hebrew; and in Australia, as also in Latin America, third-generation German communities were still speaking German as their first language. Anywhere in the world a minority often tries to maintain its language, its religion, or some other specific cultural features; and this effort is often countered by state action designed to enforce assimilation. The reports of the League of Nations or the United Nations commissions on such questions reflect the judgment of these international bodies that this pattern is *the* minority problem. European history is strewn with recurrent examples—Alsace-Lorraine and Trieste, pre-independence Ireland and Memel; and in spite of manifest differences, the minority-dominant relation is similar also in Indonesia's effort to absorb or expel its Chinese and Ambonese, in the Congo's demand that Katanga yield to the central government, and in other acts by new nations.

An American, a native of a country of ethnic minorities, should find such instances reminiscent of his own experience, yet what strikes him is not the similarities with his own country but some difference that, it may be, he cannot quite pin down. The reason, I suggest, is that for an American *the* minority problem is that associated with Negro-white relations. Both numerically and in other respects, Negroes constitute the most significant minority in American society, and in relation to general analyses this importance has been enhanced by the fact that the best study by far of any minority, Myrdal's *An American Dilemma,* is about the Negro.

But Negroes differ fundamentally from the minorities studied by the United Nations commissions. They are set off from the white majority by such racial characteristics as skin color and hair texture; and according to the unanimous judgment of present-day biologists, these features are all superficial, irrelevant to the roles that Negroes could play in American society. Races do not differ genetically in intelligence, diligence, "criminality," or other psychic qualities of comparable significance. The racist doctrine that Negroes are inferior in such respects, however, has led to cultural patterns by which they are *made* inferior. If, for example, Negroes are defined as innately unintelligent, then they need have only second-rate schools—and the inadequate training they get there results, indeed, in an over-all lower level of intelligence. That is to say, the segregation of Negroes from white society depends on only two factors: the superstition of racism, and the social policies that follow from this superstition.

The same point can be made positively rather than negatively: the American Negro is—or was until very recently—wholly assimilationist. It is true that the racism of the Black Muslims, and the Negro intellectuals' sympathetic interest in the new nations of Africa, represent a new trend. But the essential goal is not changed. The ordinary Negro's many demands can be summed up in a single one—that he become invisible in white society. He wants his ghettos to merge into the rest of the cities they now disfigure; he wants the differentials by occupation, by mortality, by illegitimacy, by any other kind of social statistics, to become a thing of the past; he even wants (if this were possible) his color to disappear. No American of European stock, not even a descendant of the first colonists, is so thoroughly embedded in American culture as the typical Negro, so lacking in vestigial emotional ties to the "home country."

The Negroes' moral case, therefore, is tremendously powerful. This minority demands no special privileges but only the civil rights to which they are entitled by the nation's fundamental law. Since 1945 the degrading patterns of Negro segregation have been successfully attacked one after another, and the goal of full civil equality seems to be in sight. This struggle has been constantly in the public eye, and it is perhaps natural that Negro-white relations should constitute the model most American analysts use, sometimes not wholly consciously, in their studies of any minority. In so doing, however, they identify a minority that wants only justice with others that are identified by specific, and perhaps objectionable, characteristics that they wish to retain or even to impose on the majority. This is too important a distinction to be buried in a common term. What precisely should one mean by "minority group"?

The first necessary characteristic of a minority group is that it is truly a group, a coherent body of persons with a specific pattern of interaction and not a more or less random collectivity. It is not appropriate, thus, to exemplify "group prejudice" by "dislike or disgust for the 'dirty Japs,' the 'Red menace,' the not-to-be-trusted Catholics or capitalists or labor unions or foreigners."[10] Although not arranged in an order to suggest this, the list constitutes a continuum from broad, heterogeneous aggregates ("foreigners") to clearly defined organizations with rather definite social or political purposes (the Catholic Church, world Communism). The difference between the two is fundamental. Antipathy to "foreigners," since it cannot be based on knowledge of all of them as a group, *must* be irrational; and it makes good sense to look for the cause of such prejudice in the psyche of the *subject*. Hatred of trade unions or of Catholicism or of Communism may also be and often is a neurotic symptom; but in this case the *object* is clearly enough defined to make possible an unambiguous attitude among the well informed, and given certain values as the premise, this could be sharply negative.

Of course, all groups are heterogeneous to some degree, and one common argument is that it is therefore impermissible to denigrate any of them or even to recognize their separate existence. Thus, according to the liberal cliché there is only one race, the human race. *Race*, in any other sense than a synonym for *species*, is, in Jacques Barzun's phrase, the "modern superstition,"[11] as though there were no empirical basis for classifying Chinese, Bantus, and Englishmen into separate physiological categories. The argument rests on the fact that racial differentiation is not sharp or permanent, that however one classifies races there will be intermediate subgroups, if not immediately then perhaps after the gene pools have been realigned during the next historical period. On the same basis, however, it would be reasonable to deny the reality of larger biological groups, for the differentiation between species or orders or even phyla is often arbitrary in the same way and is sometimes a point of dispute among specialists in systematics. Race is a fact; the superstition, the abomination, is *racism*.

Two kinds of generalizations are made in the social disciplines, statistical and generic. The first, statistical, is of the

[10] Ronald Lippitt and Marian Radke, "New Trends in the Investigation of Prejudice," *Annals of the American Academy of Political and Social Science*, 244 (March, 1946), 167–176.

[11] Jacques Barzun, *Race: A Study in Modern Superstition* (New York: Harcourt, Brace, 1937).

type, "City people have small families," or "Jews vote Democratic"—meaning that the designated group shows proportionately more of a measurable quality than the rest of a defined population. A proscription of such generalizations on
the ground that they do not apply to *all* individuals in the
group would, if generally applied, mean the end of social
disciplines and of much of physical sciences as well. Virtually every statement that we make about human groups,
comparing the middle class with the working class, or urban
dwellers with rural, or even males with females, can be only
a statement of probability. If we demanded universality of
every generalization there would be none; for just as there
are different kinds of Negroes, so there are different kinds of
city-dwellers, and just as there are persons marginal to
"Negroness," so there are suburbanites.

The generic type is an attempt to transcend the totality of
statistical statements and describe the typical rather than the
average. For example, the Chicago anthropologist Robert
Redfield has distinguished two ways of life, "urban" and
"folk" society,[12] and Ruth Benedict, in *The Chrysanthemum
and the Sword,* has characterized the Japanese as a paradoxical combination of delicate artistry and militarism. To delineate the Japanese or any other people as a "type," however,
is to attempt so tenuous an abstraction from the factual base
that the result may be difficult to distinguish from a "stereotype." Indeed, some of the studies of "national character"
have been marked by gross bias, and others have blown up
dubious Freudian hypotheses to preposterous dimensions.[13]
In short, it is seldom easy to delineate precisely a social group
of any kind, and much that has been written on this subject
can be justly criticized. Yet man is a social animal whose
"human nature" is buried in his group life, and if we are to
understand man at all we cannot abandon the study of his
social environment.

Does it make sense to hold, as Louis Wirth did, that "the

[12] "The Folk Society," *American Journal of Sociology,* 52:4
(January, 1947), 293–308.
[13] Richard M. Brickner, *Is Germany Incurable?* (Philadelphia:
Lippincott, 1943); Geoffrey Gorer, *The American People* (New
York: Norton, 1948).

people whom we regard as a minority may actually, from a numerical standpoint, be a majority"?[14] To extend thus the meaning of the word is not only semantically inelegant but also conceptually impermissible, if only because it glosses over the important distinction between democratic and non-democratic societies. The very idea of a minority suffering from discrimination implies a democratic moral judgment. In most of history, as well as in most of the world today, the overwhelming social division has been between a small ruling elite and a vast ruled mass, with the latter not significantly differentiated by the possession of civil rights or their lack. All of the 96 percent of the Soviet population who are not members of the Communist Party, for instance, suffer from what in democratic terms would be considered discrimination, but this is no reason for designating this 96 percent a "minority." The "American dilemma" reflects a conflict between the democratic ideal of equal opportunity for all and the actual inequality. In this sense, there is no Nazi and no Soviet dilemma. It is only in a democratic state that what Tocqueville called "the tyranny of the majority" can exist, and "minority problems" in this American sense are restricted to democratic societies.

Not every coherent statistical minority, however, is a minority group, as this term is properly used in sociological analysis. It makes sense to classify the Negro tenth of the population in one group and the non-Negro nine-tenths in another.[15] For while there are intermediate groups between

[14] Louis Wirth, "The Problem of Minority Groups," in Ralph Linton, ed., *The Science of Man in the World Crisis* (New York: Columbia University Press, 1945), pp. 347–372.

[15] In many of its summary documents, the U. S. Census Bureau divides the population into two racial classes, whites and "nonwhites." Why it persists in this practice is something of a puzzle. No information is added concerning the smaller racial groups, for Negroes constitute more than 95 percent of the "nonwhites." But in analyses of particular areas—for example, the Pacific states with their relatively high proportion of Chinese and Japanese, or the Southwest with its Indians—the delineation of Negroes is blurred. If a dichotomy is insisted on, it would perhaps make better sense to divide the population into Negro and "non-Negro," for at least the Asian minorities are fast moving into the standard middle-class way of life.

Negroes and non-Negroes, both other minorities and whites committed to the fight against discrimination, the dichotomy reflects the most significant features of Negro-white relations. Though Lutherans, for example, comprise a small proportion of the American population, it would not ordinarily be appropriate to designate the rest simply as "non-Lutherans." In this case, the division obviously should not be into two sectors but into the many religious denominations in the United States. Yet if the Lutherans were trying to get the rest of the population to accept a portion of their specific program, to transform their "alternatives" into "universals," they might be tempted to clothe themselves in the great moral authority associated with a true minority group.

Fundamentalist Protestants have attempted to make Prohibition the law of the land, Catholics to regulate all marriages in terms of their dogma on divorce and birth control, Zionists to influence American foreign policy in the Middle East. Such activities are completely legitimate; they are the stuff of which democracy is made. What is not legitimate is to behave like a pressure group and at the same time demand the protection morally due a minority. This kind of opportunism has worked well for ethnic and religious minorities, and now occupational groups have also begun to define themselves as minorities. We are told by an officer of the National Grange that farmers, who then comprised 13 percent of the American population, were therefore a "minority group," and that higher education "must shoulder increasing responsibility for helping minority groups acquaint the vast majority of the population, especially the thought leaders, with the problems and characteristics of their particular segment of the business and professional world."[16] That is, American colleges ought to set themselves up as propaganda agents for the farmers; but if for farmers, then why not also for plumbers, and physicians, and service-station attendants—and professors of sociology?

With the spread of American sociology to other countries,

[16] Roy E. Battles, "Higher Education and Agriculture," in Raymond F. Howes, ed., *Higher Education and the Society It Serves* (Washington, D.C.: American Council on Education, 1957), pp. 44–55.

it was perhaps inevitable that some of this confusion between minority group and pressure group should have gone with it. The distinction is ignored, for example, in a recent book on religious life and "discrimination" in the Netherlands— W. Goddijn's *Catholic Minority and Protestant Dominant.*[17] This study illustrates very well the dangers involved in transporting sociological concepts from one culture to another. Dutch Catholics, who at the time of the last census constituted about 38 percent of the population, are the largest coherent group in the political and social life of the country. The remaining 62 percent, too heterogeneous to be considered a unit, are not "dominant"; and the Dutch Catholics are not a "minority" but a plurality.

By a "minority group" as a sociological term we mean, then, a small sector of a specified larger population, a sector distinguished by a relatively clearly defined subculture and separate pattern of social interaction, and opposed in broad terms by all or most of the rest of society. Whether any particular example falls within the definition may be difficult to decide. Depending on the context, American Catholics, for instance, could legitimately be identified as a minority group, as a pressure group, or as one of a list of religious denominations, parallel to Lutherans.

With respect to its minority groups, to recapitulate, the United States is in part the special case I have called it, for Negroes constitute a special type of minority. But America also has minorities like those standard in the rest of the world, and most fall somewhere between these extremes. Americans of whatever ethnic, religious, or cultural background generally identify with the general American culture in terms of its "universals," but want also to maintain their own "alternative" values. For example, members of the various churches are at one with the rest of the population in upholding the democratic credo, but differ with respect to their several dogmas. In the United States such a differentiation is regarded as not merely permissible but good; but even a society that considers cultural variation to be healthy cannot permit it over an infinite range. The Mormon practice of

[17] W. Goddijn, *Katholieke minderheid en protestantse dominant* (Assen: Van Gorcum, 1957).

polygamy was declared to be illegitimate, even for this very small sect. Whether in the particular case this was a correct decision is not the point, but rather that some general values are felt to be so absolute that no alternative to them can be tolerated; and if the line was not drawn at polygamy then it would have had to be at cannibalism or ritual murder or what have you.

### Prejudice and the Facts

The common confusion concerning the proper definition of minority group implies a confusion also concerning what one's attitude toward such groups should be. If to oppose unreasonably the legitimate aspirations of a minority is to display prejudice, with the indefinite expansion of the meaning of *minority group*, where does prejudice end and sound judgment begin?

Literally, *prejudice* means prejudgment, a judgment before knowledge. By group prejudice, then, we should mean both (1) a judgment, an evaluation, of an ethnic or other group and its individual members, and (2) an incomplete or otherwise inadequate factual base to this evaluation. How far in many cases the concept has departed from this original meaning can be best indicated by citing a few examples. Thus, four experts writing in the authoritative *Handbook of Social Psychology* define the word as follows: "By prejudice we mean an ethnic attitude in which the reaction tendencies are predominantly negative. In other words, for us a prejudice is simply an unfavorable ethnic attitude."[18] According to one of the best and most widely used texts in social psychology, "A prejudice is an unfavorable attitude—a predisposition to perceive, act, think, and feel in ways that are 'against' rather than 'for' another person or group." It is contrasted with a "predisposition toward intimacy and/or helpfulness."[19] Or,

[18] John Harding, Bernard Kutner, Harold Proshansky, and Isidor Chein, "Prejudice and Ethnic Relations," in Gardner Lindzey, ed., *Handbook of Social Psychology* (Cambridge, Mass.: Addison-Wesley, 1954), Vol. 2, pp. 1021–1061.

[19] Theodore M. Newcomb, *Social Psychology* (New York: Dryden Press, 1950), pp. 574–575.

according to a recent sociology text, "Prejudice refers to those negative attitudes that create a predisposition toward unfavorable responses to a racial or minority group."[20]

One element common to these definitions—and more could be cited—is the substitution of "adverse judgment" for "prejudgment," or, in other words, the removal of the concept of prejudice from a factual context. But, one could ask, might not a "negative" or unfavorable attitude be, not a prejudgment, but rather the end product of a conscientious effort to arrive at the truth? Indeed this might be so, we are told by the first of these books, but "common experience would suggest that . . . the objective support for stereotypes is at best a minor aspect of stereotypic thinking." However, it begs the question to identify unfavorable attitudes as stereotypes, which by definition are not based directly or mainly on empirical data. Surely not *all* unfavorable attitudes concerning *all* ethnic groups are prejudices, in the sense of prefactual judgments. For example, the statement that Egyptians are 77 percent illiterate does not reflect a prejudice. On the other hand, many stereotypes are either favorable or, at worst, ambivalent. Is it insulting, per se, to call the Irish witty, or the Jews clever, or the Germans industrious?

There is a considerable number of studies of such stereotypes, but in none of them (so far as I know) is there a thought that it would be relevant to relate individuals' ideas about various peoples to the actual characteristics of those peoples. In one study, for example, Princeton undergraduates were asked to name the traits characteristic of ten different ethnic groups.[21] They designated the Chinese, for instance, as "superstitious, sly, conservative, tradition-loving, loyal to family ties, industrious, meditative, reserved, very religious, ignorant, deceitful, and quiet." It is a commonplace that the Chinese family is an extraordinarily tight and resilient insti-

[20] T. Lynn Smith, *Social Problems* (New York: Crowell, 1955), pp. 423–424.

[21] Daniel Katz and Kenneth W. Braly, "Verbal Stereotypes and Racial Prejudice," in Guy E. Swanson, Theodore M. Newcomb, and Eugene L. Hartley, eds., *Readings in Social Psychology* (Society for the Psychological Study of Social Issues; New York: Holt, 1952).

tution, and sinologists would agree that the Chinese are typically—or were until very recently—"loyal to family ties." Many Chinese are also "ignorant," if by this we mean illiterate; but it would be difficult to determine whether they are "sly." The stereotype thus comprises statements that are true, some that can be interpreted as true, and some that cannot be validated at all. But the authors make no attempt to differentiate in empirical terms among the twelve traits. Like other analysts of stereotypes, they implicitly maintain that a judgment of an ethnic group—*any* judgment—is a prejudgment.

Sometimes the irrelevance of facts to one's judgment of a people is stated explicitly. The moral yardsticks with which we measure the relative worth of cultures, it is maintained, are themselves part of the cultures, and one may not evaluate any society except by the standards that its members use to judge themselves. Some peoples like beef, some pork, and some human flesh; it is all, as Molotov once said of fascism, a matter of taste. This version of "cultural relativism," as it was developed by anthropologists a half century ago, was perhaps a necessary condition to understanding a primitive culture in its own terms; for if the equality of all cultures had not been postulated, a representative of Western civilization living with a tribe of two hundred naked food-gatherers would probably have been able to see nothing but their patent inferiority.

The classic statement of cultural relativism with respect to moral values is Ruth Benedict's *Patterns of Culture*. I have used it as one of the readings in an introductory sociology class, and even the dullest freshman can detect that her pretense not to judge among the three primitive peoples she describes is—a pretense. The brighter ones understand also that this was in part a comment on American culture; the contrast between the warlike Dobu or the highly competitive Kwakiutl on the one side, and the quiet, peaceable Zuñi on the other, was an anthropologist's restatement of the reactionary-progressive, aggressive-peaceloving dichotomy of the mid-1930s. (Today, however, when a different sort of dichotomy is in fashion, the Zuñi seem suspiciously "other-directed," if not downright "conformist.")

It is not usual in discussing Benedict's characterizations of these primitive peoples, or those of the Japanese in *The Chrysanthemum and the Sword*, to suggest that she may be expressing her prejudices. In the *Handbook of Social Psychology* noted above, the chapter preceding the one on prejudice reviews many of the studies on national character, and the reader passing from one to the other may well be puzzled by the sudden change in climate. Identical generalizations—of the type "The Irish are witty"—are discussed in the chapter on national character by referring to the *object*, the Irish, and in the chapter on prejudice by referring to the *subject*, the person making the statement. Brickner and Gorer, for example, have been sharply criticized, but the criticism has always been of their works; no one has suggested that Brickner has an "authoritarian personality" or that Gorer's frustrations have made him aggressive.

That one's attitude toward various groups might reasonably differ according to what these groups stand for would not seem to be a very remarkable statement. In an area less dominated by sentimentality and confusion than the analysis of ethnic relations, it would be no contribution to point out that to fight discrimination against Negroes, to disagree with Catholics about the moral legitimacy of birth control, and to abhor and oppose Communism, are not inconsistent attitudes simply because all three are termed "minority groups." In many recent writings on this subject, however, such a patent distinction has been passed over, either explicitly or by concentrating on the allegedly prejudiced person rather than on the object of his alleged prejudice. Hatred of Negroes is typically irrational, and anti-Catholicism or anti-Communism is often irrational. If we conceive of prejudice as the expression of irrationality of the *subject* and devote our main effort to understanding the mental process that results in such an attitude, it is a matter of relative indifference what the *object* of the prejudice may be. This emphasis, of course, has been in part a reflection of the professional interests of psychologists, but it is remarkable how much it has overlapped with a tolerance of Soviet totalitarianism. From the point of view of Communists and their sympathizers, it has been very convenient to analyze, say, anti-Semitism and anti-Communism—though not usually anti-Catholicism—as analogous expressions of a sick mind.

An early expression of this emphasis on the subjective and psychological was John Dollard's *Frustration and Aggression*, issued by the Institute of Human Relations at Yale University in 1939. The thesis of this work, that the frustration of a desire typically leads to aggressive attitudes and behavior toward those regarded as actual or potential frustrators, was developed so broadly that the author very nearly succeeded in bringing all of human history within its confines. The theme is introduced with a *solo piccolo:* little James wants an ice-cream cone, is denied it, has a temper tantrum. This reaction might have been avoided by putting "the aggressive response into a response-sequence that leads to non-rewards"—or, translating, by punishing James. As he grows up, however, he will find that life is full of frustrations and that in many cases the aggressive behavior allegedly resulting from them is nonrewarded. Thus, with the theme fully orchestrated:

> In Marxian doctrine, the theories of the class struggle and of the nature of the state depend to some extent . . . on the frustration-aggression principle. . . . In his *The State and Revolution*, [Lenin] states plainly: "The State is the product and the manifestation of the *irreconcilability* of class antagonisms. The State arises when, where, and to the extent that the class antagonisms *cannot* be objectively reconciled."

The Leninist theory of the state as the "special repressive force" is thus subsumed under Freud's theory that all culture frustrates the primal libidinous desires of man.

A theory that encompasses everything from ice-cream cones to class struggle would not leave out group prejudice: "The existence of a social prejudice against a group of people is evidence, first, that those who have the prejudice have been frustrated and, secondly, that they are expressing their aggression or part of it in fairly uniform fashion." However, this frustration-aggression theory, even if we accept it as valid, tells us nothing about prejudice. Frustration is a universal component of human existence, and the interesting question is not whether within each psyche this frustration develops into aggression, but why some of the aggression should be expressed in some "fairly uniform fashion." The theory that a minority group is a "scapegoat" implies that the scapegoat might just as well have been anyone else, not only that the victim is innocent of the charges made but that the charge has no relevance to the social context.

One of the striking instances of this mode of analysis was a symposium by a group of distinguished social scientists. Dr. Ralph W. Burhoe, executive officer of the American Academy of Arts and Sciences, posed the question to be discussed: "Is our [hostile] attitude toward Russia based on deliberately falsified information, or on misinterpretation?"[22] As late as 1947, a group of professional students of society were so ignorant of the infamies perpetrated by the Soviet dictatorship that they excluded, even as one possibility among others, that hostility toward the Soviet regime might be based on accurate information correctly interpreted. If the anti-Soviet feeling in the United States is due to psychically generated aggression, then the problem is to find a substitute scapegoat. "If one can find a villain who is opposing cooperative behavior and get the group to attack that villain, then cooperative behavior might emerge" (Professor Erich Lindemann, Harvard University). "Couldn't the scapegoat be the Congressmen who oppose the Marshall Plan? . . . Here is the pos-

[22] *Journal of Social Issues*, 4:1 (Winter, 1948), 21–41. In a criticism of my article, Herbert C. Kelman and Thomas F. Pettigrew objected to my citation of an originally oral discussion, without "the usual caveats and qualifications which one expects to find in written documents." Such a citation had "ominous implications for those who value free inquiry." My reply was as follows: "If the point of view of any of the discussants was seriously misrepresented in the subsequent *published* report, he was certainly able—indeed, as a responsible scholar, he was obliged—to call this fact to the readers' attention in the journal's next issue. No one did so. . . . Nothing that happened ten or even twelve years ago, when many social scientists carefully guarded their ignorance of the less positive aspects of Soviet society, is supposedly pertinent to any discussion today. Even to recall such cases would seem to be almost a breach of civil liberties. Such an attitude recalls one commonly found today in West Germany, where many valiantly try to forget the whole of the Nazi period as an unpleasant interlude, irrelevant to today's tasks." "How to Understand Prejudice," *Commentary* (November, 1959), pp. 441–445.

sibility for an alternative scapegoat" (Professor Bernard T. Feld, Massachusetts Institute of Technology). "Isn't it conceivable that our objective should be to recognize the scapegoating mechanism and the projectivity mechanism? . . . For instance, you expose some of the Red-baiters, and show just what's biting them. Or you analyze a good case of race prejudice" (Professor Gordon W. Allport, Harvard University[23]).

The most influential application of psychological concepts to the analysis of prejudice is *The Authoritarian Personality*, by T. W. Adorno and his associates.[24] The thesis of this work, in brief, is that different patterns of child-rearing in the United States have led to two contrasting types of personality, designated as "authoritarian" and "democratic," and that prejudice or the lack of it is essentially a reflection of these two psyches. "The political, economic, and social convictions of an individual often form a broad and coherent pattern, as if bound together by a 'mentality' or 'spirit,' and that this pattern is an expression of deep-lying trends in his personality." The social context of prejudice is ignored: "historical factors or economic forces operating in our society to promote or to diminish ethnic prejudices are clearly beyond the scope of our investigation."[25] The term *prejudice* is rejected

[23] But see also Gordon W. Allport, *The Nature of Prejudice* (Garden City, N.Y.: Doubleday-Anchor, 1954), which offers a more useful analysis of the subject.

[24] *The Authoritarian Personality* has been subjected to a barrage of criticism and paid the homage of many imitative studies. Eight years after it was published, a bibliography of works discussing it—which is not even a complete one—included 230 items: Richard Christie and Peggy Cook, "A Guide to Published Literature Relating to the Authoritarian Personality through 1956," *Journal of Psychology*, 45 (1958), 171–191.

[25] But before one invoked psychological, even psychoanalytic, theory ("deep-lying trends"), it would seem reasonable to look at the configurations of values and attitudes to be found in social groups. The difference in approach can be illustrated by an article on authoritarianism written by a sociologist. There is a good deal of empirical evidence to show that members of the working class are more disposed than the middle class to support authoritarian political parties or religious sects, and to display ethnic prejudices and antidemocratic attitudes generally. Such behavior, however, is ascribed not to a "personality type" but to "the typical social

as too narrow; for it the authors substitute *ethnocentrism.* Both are defined wholly in psychological terms:

Prejudice is commonly regarded as a feeling of dislike against a specific group; ethnocentrism, on the other hand, refers to a relatively consistent frame of mind concerning "aliens" generally. . . . Ethnocentrism . . . has to do not only with numerous groups toward which the individual has hostile opinions and attitudes but, equally important, with groups toward which he is positively disposed.

The indifference to the factual context of prejudice indicated in these general introductory remarks continues throughout the work. Take, for instance, the important "Anti-Semitism Scale." This consists of a large number of statements about Jews with which the respondent is required to express agreement or disagreement. All are weighted equally in the scoring, even though they vary widely in their content and implications. At one extreme we find paraphrases of the Nazi program: "The Jewish problem is so general and deep that one often doubts that democratic methods can ever solve it." At the other extreme there are statements to the effect that in various senses the Jews are and should remain a separate group, assertions that no rabbi or Zionist would find objectionable: for instance, "It is wrong for Jews and Gentiles to intermarry." In between is a mishmash of more or less dubious, more or less valid, allegations concerning the Jews. Most sociologists would agree, for example, that compared with other components of Western populations the Jews are probably the most "alienated" (as Marx used this word), the most restless, what Arthur Koestler called the most "urban." In such a statement as the following, are we to respond to the iota of this truth that it contains, or to the hostile and obnoxious attitude conveyed by the phrasing: "One big

situation of lower-class persons"—namely, "low education, low participation in political organizations or in voluntary organizations of any type, little reading, isolated occupations, economic insecurity, and authoritarian family patterns." Seymour Martin Lipset, "Democracy and Working-Class Authoritarianism," in William Petersen and David Matza, eds., *Social Controversy* (Belmont, Calif.: Wadsworth, 1963), pp. 242–255.

trouble with Jews is that they are never contented, but always try for the best jobs and the most money"?

The authors of *The Authoritarian Personality* might answer such a criticism by saying that the typical anti-Semite is confused and illogical. True; but my point is that they have imitated this confusion; and they have done so, moreover, partly because they concentrated their analysis on the personality of the anti-Semite, rather than going on and also studying anti-Semitism as a social phenomenon.

The contrast made between "authoritarian" and "democratic" personalities is worth looking at in another context. The "democratic" respondents were chosen in large part from the membership of a Communist-controlled trade union and the student body of a Communist-influenced school, as well as from various national groups that in California had a sizable Communist infiltration. The political views of these respondents, in other words, fitted in with the ideology of the Popular Front: the Soviet Union is a member of the democratic, antifascist camp, and indeed is the most democratic among its components. The study reflects the Soviet myth that fascism is extreme conservatism (rather than the no less radical twin of Communism). Thus, in the words of the study, "conservatives are, on the average, significantly more ethnocentric than liberals are. The more conservative an individual is, the greater the likelihood that he is ethnocentric." The "proof" offered to support this assertion is so dubious that one can explain the general assent it has won only by assuming that many people accept the implicit political framework of the analysis.

## Summary

In the United States, the social scientists' professional interest in immigration and acculturation rose to a peak in the 1920s and then subsided almost to indifference. If we want to see how these phenomena are analyzed today, we can find more examples in countries like Israel and Australia, where immigration policy is a current concern. The two examples suggest, however, that little advance has been made over the best of the earlier American studies. Borrie retains the premise of economic determinism that in the United States was rejected a generation ago, and in spite of his astuteness he does not convince me that it is a more satisfactory framework in the Australian context. Eisenstadt's seeming adeptness in theory is deceptive, for he applies a theory inappropriate to the Israeli case.

The interest in minority-dominant relations has focused in the United States on the Negroes and their struggle for civil equality. The tendency to generalize from the Negro case, while understandable, is most unfortunate.

In the long years of the Negro's discouragingly slow advance against his country's long-entrenched practices of segregation, the historically unique feature of this struggle has been largely unnoted. It is that the Negro, a distinct racial minority, was trying to become more American—not less.[26]

The analysis of "intergroup relations" is no longer restricted to racial or ethnic minorities, but now includes minorities defined by religious, cultural, occupational, or political criteria. Very often basic principles underlying a study of Negro-white patterns in the United States have been applied to the analysis of superficially similar relations to which they are not relevant.

With respect to ethnic minorities, it may be generally true that the problems surrounding group relations derive less from actual differences than from the way these differences are interpreted. But there is a real and significant difference between, for example, Communism and democracy, and to understand why a man is anti-Communist it is necessary first to look not into his mind but at Soviet society. The same kind of tolerance that in a democratic society is morally due ethnic minorities cannot legitimately be extended to totalitarian groups. The difference is a fundamental one, and the way to maintain it is to analyze alleged prejudices in a factual context, abandoning the definition of prejudice as simply a hostile attitude and returning to an understanding of it as an attitude based on incomplete or distorted knowledge.

[26] Ralph McGill, "The South Will Change," in Hoke Norris, ed., *We Dissent* (New York: St. Martin's Press, 1962), pp. 14–24.

# RELIGIOUS STATISTICS IN
# THE UNITED STATES

"Every society," I remarked to a Dutch sociologist, "has its sacred subjects, protected from empirical research and analysis by a high wall of magical taboos." I was commenting on his statement that a Kinsey report would have been impossible in the Netherlands.

"Indeed," he replied; "in Holland the sacred area is sexuality, and in the United States it is religion."

The contrast is apt. In the Netherlands, where the church is recognized as a significant social institution and religion as an important ideological force, the time and effort that sociologists devote to studying them are correspondingly large. In the United States, on the contrary, research in this area engages few sociologists and is generally of indifferent quality, in part because even the most elementary data are faulty or absent.

## What Influence Has Religion?

The weakness is apparent with respect to the most fundamental sociological issue—what are the social effects of religious faith? The usual answers to this question in theoretical works, derived from either Karl Marx or Emile Durkheim, consist in paraphrases of these men's dicta that religion is the opium of the people, or that it functions to unite those who adhere to it into a single moral community. Such characterizations, wholly negative or wholly positive, are no prelude to analysis, which must start with an attempt to distinguish, to differentiate, to compare.

This contrast in social philosophy is matched, moreover, by a parallel one in national mythology. One official doctrine in the United States is that religious faith has no social consequences of any importance. Immigrants urged to acculturate in every other sense were guaranteed the right to religious freedom by the Constitution itself. No religious test may be put to a candidate for public office, even the highest and the most important. The implication of such designations as "the Jewish vote" or "the Catholic vote" is resented, for by this view each voter or legislator is an individual, reflecting only his personal preferences. This point is spelled out, for example, in *Catholicism and American Freedom*, the book that James O'Neill wrote in reply to Paul Blanshard. In his analysis of the voting records of Catholics in Congress, Mr. O'Neill made two points: (1) Most Catholics voted on the liberal side of most issues, as one would expect from the fact that they are concentrated in the liberal Northern wing of the Democratic Party. But (2) this record was not consistent, for Catholic Republicans (Senator McCarthy of Wisconsin) or Catholic Southern Democrats (Senator O'Conor of Maryland, Representative Hébert of Louisiana) voted as one would expect from their party or regional affiliation.[1] Similarly, when Senator Kennedy was asked to comment on the relevance of his religion to the presidential post he was seeking, his reply, given on a number of occasions, was a full and unequivocal assurance that there was no relation between the two. "Whatever one's religion in his private life," he said, "nothing takes precedence over his oath."[2]

On the other hand, it would not be accurate to describe the separation of church and state in the United States as absolute. In most of the recent cases specifying this relation,[3]

[1] James M. O'Neill, *Catholicism and American Freedom* (New York: Harper, 1952), Chap. 9.

[2] The Jesuit journal *America* commented: "Mr. Kennedy doesn't really believe that. No religious man, be he Catholic, Protestant, or Jew, holds such an opinion. A man's conscience has a bearing on his public as well as on his private life." Both statements are quoted in Peter H. Odegard, ed., *Religion and Politics* (New Brunswick, N.J.: Oceana, 1960), p. 156.

[3] For a recent short survey, see Victor S. MacKinnon, "Freedom?—or Toleration? The Problem of Church and State in the United States," *Public Law*, Winter, 1959, pp. 374–395. See also the more detailed analysis in Leo Pfeffer, *Church, State, and Freedom* (Boston: Beacon, 1953).

the courts have applied the constitutional prohibition of religious establishment, or the correlative prescription of religious freedom, with respect to particular practices that allegedly discriminated against one denomination or illegitimately favored another. Thus, members of Jehovah's Witnesses need not salute the flag, children may ride to parochial schools in buses paid for out of general taxes, and so on. But the fact that *all* Americans now pledge allegiance to one nation "under God" has not been successfully challenged.[4] It is taken for granted that churches are partly supported out of public funds: the institutions themselves pay no taxes, and individuals may deduct donations from their taxable income. During the 1960 presidential campaign, both Senator Kennedy and Vice-President Nixon asserted that a member of any church, so long as he was a member of some church, could be a suitable candidate for the nation's highest office. Even in the empty piety of campaign speeches, thus, where phrases like "irrespective of race, color, or creed" are used as fillers, the leaders of both parties ruled atheists out of the national community, and this in the very process of declaring their support of what they took to be the separation of church and state.

It cannot be both that religion generally has no effect on social attitudes and behavior, and that it typically has an effect. Most people apparently hold to both positions, and sociologists have done remarkably little to resolve the contradiction. One could assume, as a hypothesis, that under some circumstances some religions affect certain types of social behavior of some people, and that both this pattern and its contrary have been generalized into the two incongruous myths. If we were to try to specify each of the variables, the first thing we would require is accurate statistics relating religion to other social facts, information such as would be available in a census. But the census in this country has no information on religion. The local data gathered in

[4] Congress added the words "under God" to the Pledge of Allegiance in 1954. In 1960, a unanimous decision of the Appellate Division of the New York State Supreme Court, affirming the ruling by a lower court, refused to order the State Educational Department to delete the phrase. See *New York Times,* December 3, 1960.

community surveys or similar studies, however valuable they may be in other respects, cannot be accepted as an accurate description of religious behavior over the whole nation. And the information from national public-opinion polls on the social correlates of religious faith, contrary to what some persons have alleged, is not an adequate substitute for official statistics.

A timely illustration of this last point is the consensus among all pollsters and commentators that Kennedy's religion was an important factor in the 1960 presidential election.[5] According to Roper's estimate (which is more or less in line with that of the other polling firms), between 75 and 80 percent of the Catholic voters, but only about 35 percent of the Protestant, supported Kennedy. The contrast is striking and one would think decisive. On the basis of such evidence, so responsible a personage as Reinhold Niebuhr has stated that the anti-Catholic bias in the United States, "unmatched in any other nation," reaches "the level of paranoia."[6] Others have condemned the Catholic supporters of Kennedy with comparable epithets.

It is undoubtedly true that proportionately more Catholics voted for Kennedy than non-Catholics, but it does not follow automatically that the two factors can be described as cause and effect. For we know from even our poor statistics that Catholics are concentrated in social groups with a normally high proportion of Democratic voters—in Northern cities, in trade unions, in some ethnic minorities (such as Puerto Ricans and Mexicans), among young voters (who, according to Gallup, supported Kennedy by a 3-to-2 margin). And Protestants, on the contrary, are concentrated in social groups that are normally Republican—businessmen, Midwestern farmers, and so on. Whether religion actually influenced the vote or was merely an accidental characteristic can be determined only by analyzing several factors at once. Among trade-union members, for instance, or among farmers, was the

[5] See, for example, American Institute of Public Opinion release, September 29, 1960; Elmo Roper, "Polling Post-Mortem," *Saturday Review*, November 26, 1960; Cabell Phillips, "About the Election: A Second Look," *New York Times*, November 20, 1960.

[6] "The Religious Issue," *New Leader*, December 12, 1960.

vote for and against Kennedy split along religious lines? This the polling firms do not tell us; nor can they, for their samples are too small to permit the simultaneous analysis of several variables.

My point is not that the voters did *not* decide on the basis of Kennedy's religion, but only that this charge, offered irresponsibly on insufficient evidence, was nevertheless universally accepted.[7] In the 1928 election, Smith's Catholicism was actually only one of a half-dozen important issues.[8] Now, similarly, it has become "history" that in 1960 Nixon was defeated by his Protestantism.

From this example one can reasonably draw three conclusions: (1) Whether or not religious faiths are differentially associated with social attitudes, the national myth denying that this *may* be so really convinces no one. Indeed, the very fact that the relation contradicts the myth makes it "news," so that journalists often seize on it and pass over other, better established, and therefore duller, explanations. (2) We cannot depend on polling firms to correct this tendency. They are business enterprises catering to mass journalism, and this market hardly induces them to analyze a complex social pattern with adequate care. I do not mean to suggest that such commercial firms are illegitimate, but only to comment on the notion that in such an area as religion one can—or, indeed, should—depend on private agencies to furnish the kind of data that the government usually collects. (3) On the other hand, the fact that a question on religion has been asked in several dozen polls during the past decades proves

[7] In 1948, the last election before the inexplicable charisma of Eisenhower reduced all *social* factors to secondary importance, the Democratic candidate, a Protestant, also just barely won. Truman was opposed not only by the Republicans but also by two minority parties, the Dixiecrats and the Progressives, which together reduced sharply the large majority implied by Democratic registrations. A priori, I think this pattern offers a better explanation of the 1960 election than one based on the effect of religion. Kennedy was also opposed—or, at best, weakly or indifferently supported—by recalcitrant Southerners and by progressives who found his foreign policy too militaristic. Texas and California, thus, had the largest votes for splinter groups.

[8] See Seymour Martin Lipset, "Some Statistics on Bigotry in Voting," *Commentary*, October, 1960.

that by and large Americans have no objection to it. Even when the query is put by a private firm and for the specific purpose of linking religious faith with other social facts, the number who refused to reply has always been insignificant.

Census data on religion would not enable us, of course, to analyze the 1960 election precisely, since the vote is secret. Even so, a comparison of religious affiliations and votes by precincts would probably be an improvement over the polls, or at worst a valuable supplement to them. And the limitation does not apply to the analysis of other real or supposed social effects of religion.

Take as another example the relation between religious faith and family size. For decades the higher fertility among Catholics was generally believed to be a direct consequence of their membership in a church that prohibits the use of the most effective contraceptives. But Catholics were also concentrated in nationalities that had immigrated from the 1880s on and were therefore heavily represented in the working class. Until a substantial number of Catholics became established in the middle class, their larger families could be ascribed with almost equal probability to their religion, their class position in American society, and vestiges of old-country peasant cultures. Now that the last two factors have become less relevant, it would seem that middle-class values are often stronger than Catholic ones. According to a sample survey conducted in cooperation with the Census Bureau, Catholic fertility is barely higher than that of the rest of the population.[9] Even so "obvious" a conclusion that a doctrinal ban on contraceptives resulted in the procreation of more children seems to have been true only at the first level of analysis—the only one feasible without adequate religious statistics.

## The Available Statistics

National statistics on religion in the United States are available from three sources: the membership figures of various churches, as reported in the *Yearbook* of the National

[9] See Ronald Freedman, Pascal K. Whelpton, and Arthur A. Campbell, *Family Planning, Sterility, and Population Growth* (New York: McGraw-Hill, 1959), Table 9–1.

DISTRIBUTION OF THE POPULATION
by CLAIMED CHURCH MEMBERSHIP AND STATED RELIGIOUS PREFERENCE,
UNITED STATES, 1956 AND 1957

| | Claimed Church Membership[a] | | U.S. Census Bureau Sample Survey[b] | | Gallup Poll Sample Survey[c] | |
|---|---|---|---|---|---|---|
| | | | | | Total[d] | Actively Religious[e] |
| | Thousands | Percent | Thousands | Percent | | |
| Protestant total | 60,149 | 58.6 | 78,952 | 66.2 | 58.1 | 59.8 |
| Baptist | 19,934 | 19.4 | 23,525 | 19.7 | 11.3 | 12.6 |
| Methodist | 11,946 | 11.6 | 16,676 | 14.0 | 13.1 | 12.7 |
| Lutheran | 7,401 | 7.2 | 8,417 | 7.1 | 8.2 | 9.4 |
| Presbyterian | 3,963 | 3.9 | 6,656 | 5.6 | 5.2 | 5.4 |
| Protestant Episcopal | 2,853 | 2.8 | } 23,678 | } 19.8 | 3.5 | 2.8 |
| United Church of Christ[f] | 2,179 | 2.1 | | | 2.1 | 2.2 |
| Other Protestant | 11,873 | 11.6 | | | 14.7 | 14.7 |
| Roman Catholic | 34,564 | 33.7 | 30,669 | 25.7 | 21.9 | 28.3 |
| Jewish | 5,200 | 5.1 | 3,868 | 3.2 | 2.5 | 0.2 |
| Other religion | 2,791 | 2.7 | 1,545 | 1.3 | } 16.4 | 11.2 |
| No religion | — | — | 3,195 | 2.7 | | |
| Religion not reported | — | — | 1,104 | 0.9 | 1.1 | 0.5 |
| Total | 102,704 | 100.0 | 119,333 | 100.0 | 100.0 | 100.0 |

For footnotes to table, see page 255.

Council of Churches; the one nationwide sample survey made by the Census Bureau, in 1957; and data of public-opinion firms and institutes.[10] Representative breakdowns from each of these three sources are given in the table. Later membership figures and poll data are now available, but these have been chosen because they are most directly comparable with the 1957 survey.

The compilation of membership figures, as shown in the first two columns, is deficient in a number of respects:

1. The data depend on the voluntary cooperation of the denominational leaders. Some sects, in particular Christian Scientists, prohibit the publication of their membership figures. Many others are certainly not equipped to maintain an accurate register, and the *Yearbook* lists annually the latest available figures for each denomination, even though in some cases these are quite out of date.

2. "Membership" is defined differently by the various denominations. Most Protestant groups include only those who have been confirmed and are currently enrolled with a specific congregation. As defined by the Catholic Church, the Protes-

[10] For annotated bibliographies of the statistical sources available, see Dorothy Good, "Questions on Religion in the United States Census," *Population Index*, 25:1 (January, 1959), 3–16; Benson Y. Landis, "A Guide to the Literature on Statistics of Religious Affiliation with References to Related Social Studies," *Journal of the American Statistical Association*, 54:286 (June, 1959), 335–357.

[a] *World Almanac and Book of Facts for* 1958 (New York: New York World-Telegraph, 1958), pp. 711–712; based on National Council of Churches of Christ in the USA, *Yearbook of American Churches*, 1958, supplemented by a private questionnaire.

[b] U. S. Bureau of the Census, *Current Population Reports*, Series P-20, No. 79 (February 2, 1958). Civilian population 14 years and over.

[c] The data from this poll, taken during the 1956 campaign, were furnished to me by Charles Y. Glock.

[d] Sample of the voting population weighted regionally according to the proportion of the electorate that votes. N = 1,484.

[e] That is, all who said they attended church or its equivalent at least once a month. N = 951.

[f] Formed in 1957 by the union of the Congregational Christian Churches and the Evangelical and Reformed Church. The Gallup poll figure pertains only to the Congregationalists.

tant Episcopal Church, and several Lutheran groups, however, "members" are all who have been baptized, and thus include infants and children up to the age of confirmation, as well as some who have drifted away from the church but not specified their alienation. The definition of a "Jew" is particularly difficult, and apparently synagogue officials typically include totally irreligious persons who could be designated as Jewish by their family background and culture.

3. A writer in the *Catholic World* deplored the "ecclesiastical charlatans, paper churches, fictitious hierarchies, and ambitious churchmen," whose membership lists are "closer to a chamber of commerce report than an audited statement." This tendency to inflate membership rolls, he says, does not exist in the Catholic Church, for every priest is "an honest man" and, in any case, must pay a per capita tax to the diocesan apparatus and thus has a monetary interest in maintaining his honesty.[11] It is probably true that the statistics of the older, well established denominations are more accurate than those of the fluid world of the sects. But it does not follow that the latter are in their aggregate overrepresented in the published statistics. A priori one would suppose, on the contrary, that many of the groups meeting in store-front churches, which lack the ecclesiastical apparatus necessary for the collection and transmission of accurate rolls, might be passed over entirely in such a compilation as that by the National Council of Churches.

4. The classification of denominations is inadequate. In the traditional trichotomy into Protestants, Catholics, Jews, "Protestant" is little more than a residual class, which includes groups (like the Unitarians) who are not even Christian as this term is ordinarily used. Most of the major denominations, moreover, cannot be interpreted as altogether meaningful units. In 1959 there were 27 subdenominations among the Baptists, 21 among the Methodists, 18 among the Lutherans, and 19 in the Eastern Orthodox Church. Such divisions are based on differences in doctrine, in language, and in social class or region (particularly the splits between North and

[11] William J. Whalen, "A Closer Look at Religious Statistics," *Catholic World,* January, 1958.

South and between Negro and White). Undoubtedly both theological doctrine and social attitudes differ more between the fundamentalist and modernist wings of any one denomination than among the variegated Protestants (or even Americans, apart from religion) in the same social class and region. The largest single denomination by a considerable margin is the Roman Catholic Church, which also reflects to some degree the ethnic composition of its adherents—Irish, Italian, Polish, and French Canadian in the New England and Middle Atlantic states, French in Louisiana, and Mexican in the Southwest.

5. Membership rolls tell us nothing, of course, of those who are not members of any church. In 1957 these apparently totaled more than 67 million, or not quite 40 percent of the population—a rather substantial proportion in view of the much discussed postwar revival of religion. The estimate includes infants and children, but so do the membership figures of some of the churches. On the other hand, this number, obtained by subtracting the sum of the inexact and noncomparable membership figures from the total population as estimated by the Census Bureau, is obviously not a precise measure of the irreligious.

The next two columns of the table give the results of a sample survey made by the Census Bureau in March, 1957. While this survey was subject to the usual sampling variability, its results were undoubtedly more accurate than the compilation of membership rolls. Enumerators queried only persons aged 14 and over, thus eliminating the infants and children listed as members of some churches. The principal difference between the two sets of data, however, is that the second pertains to the self-identification of respondents rather than to the number of adherents claimed by church officials.

In accordance with the best usage of public-opinion polling, the Census Bureau should have asked the question, "Have you a religion?" and then, if the reply was in the affirmative, followed it with, "What is it?" The question as it was actually put, "What is your religion?," exerted a certain pressure to name some denomination, and it is likely that merely nominal adherents to any faith in general replied by citing it. The sum of these personal preferences for any denomination, then, would certainly be greater than the number of formal members, as indeed it is for the larger Protestant denominations. That the number of persons who reported themselves as Roman Catholics or as Jews was less by a considerable margin than the claimed membership of these churches suggests that the latter figures are very much inflated, even apart from the fact that they include (or may include) children under the age of 14.

The data from the Gallup poll given in the last two columns of the table permit a comparison between the proportion who identify themselves with the various denominations and those designated as "actively religious," who attend church or its equivalent at least once a month.

Let us first compare the total with that from the Census Bureau survey. The Gallup poll question was asked only of voters,[12] and since its main purpose was to forecast the election correctly, major regions were represented according to the estimated proportion of the electorate that had actually voted in the previous election.[13] Thus, the South, which by the usual indices is the most religious region, is underrepresented in the sample; and this bias may be the reason for the finding, certainly erroneous, that the country has fewer Baptists than Methodists. Note that the combined class "Other religion" and "No religion," which made up only 4 percent in the Census Bureau survey, constituted 16.4 percent of the respondents to the Gallup poll.

About two-thirds of those who identified themselves with one or another denomination said that they attended church or its equivalent as often as once a month. This index is not an equally meaningful measure of active participation for all faiths. For example, Catholics are under greater pressure to attend church regularly than Protestants, and indeed a larger

[12] It would have been possible to find a poll not restricted in this sense, but the intent was to select a typical set of data, rather than the best that could be found. In most of the polls that include a query on religion, this was added to a questionnaire designed mainly to investigate another matter.

[13] See, for example, the press release of the American Institute of Public Opinion dated August 27, 1960, in which this procedure is discussed.

proportion do so. Note that by this index Jews almost disappear from the religious population; this finding supports our supposition that many persons of Jewish family background who are more or less secular in their beliefs and behavior are included in membership statistics, and some, though a considerably smaller number, also designate themselves as Jewish in a "religious" census.

As the figures in this table suggest, we have no accurate basis for classifying the American population by religion. The percentage of Baptists, according to the three sources cited, ranged from 11.3 to 19.7, that of Presbyterians from 3.9 to 5.6, that of Catholics from 21.9 to 33.7, that of Jews from 2.5 to 5.1, and so on. These are not the widest ranges to be found. Other estimates of the number of Catholics, for instance, have been as high as 50 million, rather than the 30 to 35 million shown here. And the figures needed for social analysis—the proportion of each denomination living in cities and in the countryside; with large, medium, and small incomes; and so on—are even less precise than these totals, approximate as they are.

Indeed, the question whether membership in churches is growing as fast as the population cannot be answered with any assurance. According to the latest *Yearbook* of the National Council of Churches, the answer is Yes. According to a special survey by the executive secretary of the United Lutheran Church, on the contrary, the number of Americans not affiliated with any church is increasing by about a million persons a year. And a recent survey conducted by the Congregational Christian Churches indicated—certainly not a unique finding—that one-third of its members are only nominally religious.[14] Many analysts can see with Will Herberg a major postwar revival in religion; others join Seymour Lipset in asking "What Religious Revival?"[15] Even so fundamental a question as whether religious affiliation is growing or declining must remain, in twentieth-century America, a matter of speculation. "None of the work done to assess the state of

[14] *New York Times,* April 30, 1960; October 17, 1960; January 8, 1961.
[15] *Protestant-Catholic-Jew* (New York: Doubleday-Anchor, 1960), Chap. 4; *Columbia University Forum,* Winter, 1959.

religion in America currently or historically meets even the minimum standards of scientific inquiry."[16]

## Why No Census Question?

For a time it seemed as though a question on religion would be added to the schedule of the 1960 census, but this tentative plan was abandoned in response to the objection of a small number of persons and a very few organizations. Opposed were the American Civil Liberties Union; various Jewish organizations, including the American Jewish Congress, the American Jewish Committee, and the Anti-Defamation League; the liberal Catholic weekly *Commonweal;* the Protestant magazine *Christian Century;* some Christian Science groups; and James A. Pike, then Dean of the Cathedral of St. John the Divine. Public stands in favor of the question were taken by two professional societies of social scientists, the Population Association of America and the American Sociological Association; a large number of Catholic organizations, including the Jesuit weekly *America,* the editorial staff of the *Catholic Digest,* the Catholic Press Association, the National Catholic Welfare Conference, the National Council of Catholic Men, and the editor of the *Official Catholic Directory;* and Paul Blanshard. Protestant groups were divided, with more for the question (or indifferent) than opposed. The National Council of Churches took no position at this time, presumably continuing the positive stand toward a census question on religion that its executive committee had taken in 1935; its committee concerned with religious statistics continued to be in favor also in the 1950s.

In short, the proposal to ask a question on religion was met with indifference by the vast majority of the population; it was actively supported principally by social scientists and Catholic groups; and it was opposed by one or two liberal organizations and especially by Jewish groups. It is not suggested that the sentiment of the majority is the only criterion

[16] Charles Y. Glock, "The Religious Revival in America," in Jane Zahn, ed., *Religion and the Face of America* (Berkeley: University Extension, University of California, 1958).

to judge such an issue, but it is certainly relevant that so small a minority voiced any objection.

Nevertheless, the Census Bureau announced at the end of 1957 that it would not include the question, primarily because "a considerable number of persons would be reluctant to answer such a question in the Census, where a reply is mandatory. . . . An alternative approach which would avoid the difficulty about the mandatory character of answers would be to rely on the analysis of results obtained on a voluntary basis, such as through the Current Population Survey. Such a survey was taken in March 1957 and the results are now being analyzed and, according to present plans, will be published before very long."[17] "Present plans," however, underwent a change. As we have seen, the breakdown by religious preference was published, and it constitutes the best information we have on the subject. But the additional data collected on the social and economic characteristics associated with the various religions were not. "A decision was reached in the Department of Commerce not to issue any further details."[18] As the dean of American demographers, Walter Willcox, once wrote: "The modern census began in the United States in close association with democratic forms of government, and even at the start the results were immediately made public."[19] I know of no other instance in its long and honorable record when data actually assembled by the Census Bureau were suppressed. This morally disturbing, possibly even illegal, act would be inconceivable with respect to statistics on any other subject.

Why is accurate information concerning religion considered to be reprehensible or dangerous? What were the arguments against including a question on religion in the census sched-

[17] U. S. Bureau of the Census, release, December 12, 1957, and supplementary "Statement of Reasons."

[18] Letter, January 24, 1961, from Howard G. Brunsman, Chief, Population Division, Bureau of the Census. More details are given in Charles R. Foster, *A Question on Religion* (University, Ala.: University of Alabama Press, 1961). The decision was made, according to this source, by Assistant Secretary of Commerce Mueller and concurred in by Secretary Weeks.

[19] "Census," *Encyclopedia of the Social Sciences* (New York, 1930).

ule? They can be reduced to two main points—that religion is so intensely and exclusively a personal affair that no intrusion of society can be permitted, and that in any case this intrusion should not be by the state. In absolute terms, as they often were phrased, these propositions fall by their own weight. Religion is a social institution as well as a private experience, and the separation of church and state in the United States has never been complete. Let us look, then, at the more specific arguments. Do they hold up any better?

1. A question on religion in the census, it was alleged, would be unconstitutional. This point was made, for example, by the American Civil Liberties Union, reversing a prior stand of that organization. According to its revised opinion, "it would be contrary to the First Amendment to ask anyone questions about religion or membership in a religious body," and this would be so even if the response was voluntary. All other arguments are thus nugatory.[20]

*Comment.* The relevant section of the Constitution, the first portion of the first amendment, reads as follows: "Congress shall make no law respecting an establishment of religion, or prohibiting the free exercise thereof." There has never been an occasion for any court to interpret the relevance of this section to the issue, but to a layman it would seem that a question on religion in the census would not establish a religion or inhibit anyone in the free exercise of his faith, at least as these constitutional provisions have been interpreted with respect to other questions. Even the ACLU is not firm in its opinion on constitutionality; its church-state committee intends to review once again the arguments that led the organization to reverse itself some years ago, and the present position may also be rescinded. As a professor of political science at Brandeis University put it: "It seems a pity that the important principle of separation of church and state should be invoked so frequently against such a simple and unthreatening proposal as this one."[21]

2. Sometimes the constitutional issue, though not raised

[20] American Civil Liberties Union, news release, July 29, 1957. See also *New York Times,* July 26 and August 2, 1957.

[21] Letter from Lawrence H. Fuchs, *New York Times,* August 19, 1957.

directly, was implicit in references to legal tradition. In 1957, Leo Pfeffer, director of the Commission on Law and Social Action of the American Jewish Congress, for example, quoted James Madison on why the question should not have been asked in the first census: "As to those who are employed in teaching and inculcating the duties of religion, there may be some indelicacy in singling them out, as the General Government is proscribed from interfering in any manner whatever, in matters respecting religion."[22]

*Comment.* The sentence that Dr. Pfeffer quotes could be used to support either side of the issue. If James Madison believed that including the question might involve no more than "some indelicacy," it is stretching his language considerably to interpret this as relevant to its constitutionality. In any case, Madison's opinion can hardly be taken as decisive in 1960, or 1970. There have been hundreds of extensions of the census from its original narrow purpose as specified in the Constitution, and that such data should be gathered now is never otherwise challenged on the ground that the Founding Fathers did not do so. A law exists expressly permitting the Bureau to take a "census" of religious bodies, based on the existent records, and in the nineteenth century—especially in 1870—this law was interpreted rather broadly. In this century, there were four special "censuses" of religious bodies —in 1906, 1916, 1926, and 1936. In 1946 Congress refused to allocate the funds needed to continue the service, and ten years later no one in Congress was enough interested in the question even to propose that the series be renewed. The compilation is now made by the National Council of Churches, with what results we have seen. In spite of the fact that the government collected statistics on religious affiliation for many decades, Dr. Pfeffer had not thought the issue important enough even to mention it in *Church, State and Freedom* (1953), his excellent and exhaustive analysis of state-church relations in the United States.

3. Asking a question on religion, it was alleged, would constitute an invasion of personal privacy. "Here is the

[22] Leo Pfeffer, "Is It the Government's Business?" *Christian Century*, October 30, 1957.

sort of question which the government has no right to put to
the individual citizen, whose rights of conscience are sacro-
sanct, and this fact is of such paramount importance that it
outweighs all the arguments in favor of including a question
on religious affiliation in the census."[23]

*Comment.* Religious affiliation (rather than religious belief,
which no one proposes should be included in the census) is
a social fact. Whether it is more "personal" than one's occupation, education, income, age, national origin, marital status,
and so on, is a matter of opinion. If we ask, rather, how
many refused to answer questions on these matters, then religion proves to be a somewhat less touchy subject than several
others. In both the 1957 sample survey and an earlier test
(in Milwaukee, November, 1956), the Census Bureau attempted to evaluate opposition to the question. Only 0.5 percent declined to answer it, as compared with 0.6 percent on
the number of their children, 1.3 percent on the respondents'
education, and 7.0 percent on their income. This is a reasonable measure of the alleged invasion of privacy, and in that
case ought these other questions, plus perhaps still more on
matters that were not included in these particular surveys, to
be deleted from the census schedule?

Under the law every adult is required to answer every
legitimate question put by an authorized representative of
the Census Bureau, but as a matter of fact not all questions
are answered by everyone. Many census tables include a residual category of persons of whom the characteristic is unknown. However, according to standard legal compilations,
only two persons have been prosecuted under this law. In
the first case, in 1890, the defendant was a Rhode Island
farmer who "wilfully and maliciously" refused to state the size
of his wife's farm. The obligation to answer concerning one's
family and one's property includes, according to the court's
findings, the obligation to reply also to questions about the
property of family members.[24] The second case, seventy years
later, concerned William F. Rickenbacker, a regular con-
tributor to the Rightist *National Review.* "When the summer

[23] *Commonweal,* August 2, 1957.
[24] U.S. v. Sarle, 45 Fed 191 (1891).

satrap of the Snooper State comes to ask me why I refuse to contribute my share of the statistics to the national numbers games, . . ." he asserted, "I shall not answer [the questionnaire]. Indeed, I have already torn it up." He was subpoenaed to appear before a federal grand jury and, after testifying, was excused "until further notice."[25]

It is not at all accidental that so few prosecutions have been initiated to enforce this law. The Census Bureau is well aware that accurate statistics depend ultimately on the willing cooperation of the population, so that the general reluctance of a democratic state to apply force is in this case strongly reinforced by a particular technical requirement. The director of the Bureau stated that a reply to a question on religion might be made voluntary, so that conscientious objections to it might be respected.[26] A committee of social scientists made the same point in their argument for the question:

> It is important [also] for scientific reasons that the respondent should not be pressed to name a denomination when he displays doubt or resentment. He should be given the option of reporting (a) a general category, for example, Protestant not otherwise specified, (b) no preference, (c) declines to reply.[27]

4. One important reason for opposition to the question on religion was often an intense—though usually also vague—concern about the uses to which the information might be put. Israel Goldstein, then president of the American Jewish Congress, went farther: "If Americans can be compelled to disclose to government officers their religious beliefs, they can equally be compelled to disclose their political, economic, social, and all other beliefs."[28] According to the editor of *Commonweal,* similarly, asking a question on religious affilia-

[25] *New York Times,* December 12 and 20, 1960.
[26] Statement by Robert W. Burgess, then director of the Bureau of the Census, reprinted in its entirety in Foster, *op. cit.,* pp. 18–19.
[27] Population Association of America, "Report of the Work Group on Proposed Census Inquiries on Religion to the Committee on the 1960 Census," mimeographed, 1957.
[28] Letter to the *New York Times,* July 8, 1957.

tion would constitute "a precedent which would allow the government to inquire into the religious beliefs of the individual person."[29] One can suppose that this fear of the government, even when not specified as such, may have been one reason why so many Jewish organizations opposed the question.

*Comment.* Mr. Goldstein's argument is fallacious in both its points. The proposal was that persons shall be asked about their religious affiliation rather than their beliefs; and in any case neither suggestion would be a first step toward the totalitarian regime that he seems to envisage. The very hesitancy of the Census Bureau in this matter, its withdrawal before a miniscule opposition, emphasizes how erroneous it is to think in terms of an inevitable, or even a probable, progression from one fateful precedent.

It must be stressed that census information is completely private, carefully guarded even against other government bureaus, and never published in a form that would make the identification of individuals possible. Under the law, "the Director of the Census is . . . authorized in his discretion to furnish to individuals such data from the population schedules as may be desired for genealogical or other proper purposes, upon payment of the actual cost of searching the records and $1 . . . . Providing, however, That in no case the information furnished under the authority of this act be used to the detriment of the person or persons to whom such information relates." This protection has been upheld in the courts a number of times. On one occasion a life-insurance company claimed that a client had lied about his age and thus forfeited the beneficiary's right to the payment. It petitioned the Census Bureau for information from its records, and the court upheld the Bureau's refusal to give it out, adding the following comment: The legal defense protecting a person against the use of census data to his detriment "is akin to the protection afforded by the prohibitions against the evidential use of communications between attorney and client, priest and penitent, and physician and patient."[30] In 1960 the Supreme

[29] *Commonweal,* September 13, 1957.

[30] Brauner v. Mutual Life Insurance Co. of N. Y., 4 D & C 2d 106 (1929).

Court declined to review a decision by a Circuit Court of Appeals which upheld the Census Bureau in its refusal to release to the U. S. Trade Commission information from the Census of Manufactures about one specified manufacturer.[31]

But suppose these legal protections break down, we may ask; Jewish leaders are not likely to have forgotten the Nazi holocaust that overwhelmed the legal structure of Weimar Germany. This kind of argument is difficult to answer, for logic is overwhelmed by the tragedy of European Jewry. If Jewish leaders practice an exaggerated caution, trusting nothing and no one, can one blame them? Can we be absolutely certain; dare we believe that it can't happen here?

Certainty is not for this world. Let us admit, if only for the sake of the argument, that a Nazi America is possible and ask what has been saved by the lack of a religious census. Most Jews would be known as such through their association with a synagogue or Jewish organizations. Several Jewish agencies, it should be noted, have sponsored local self-surveys of Jewish communities, and these lists of identified individuals are ordinarily available to the public. But there may be a person of Jewish descent, a Jew in "racial" terms, who has no associations with Jewish organizations, has not a Jewish name, does not consider himself a Jew. Would such a person, in all reasonable probability, have designated himself as Jewish to a census enumerator, and thus opened the way to later persecution? Even an exaggerated caution need not include so unlikely a contingency. The lists that the Nazis used to guide their anti-Jewish campaigns, it should be recalled, were usually the rolls of the Jewish community, not the census lists or even the population registers in countries where the latter existed.

On the broader issue of the relation between a religious census and democracy, one should note that the ninety countries where such a question has been put include many of the indisputable bastions of Western democracy. In at least two, Switzerland and the Netherlands, the religious division is closely related to politics and is therefore a sensitive question. In a number of others—for example, Ireland or Norway—one

[31] *New York Times,* November 8, 1960.

faith is dominant in numbers and power, and yet the minorities are carefully measured. Overseas countries of European culture—for example, Australia, New Zealand, and Canada—also classify their populations by religion.[32]

5. The data collected would be of limited usefulness or, in the opinion of some, of none at all. What will we really know with the addition of the religious affiliation question to the census questionnaire? Stated affiliation by itself, Dean Pike suggested, would not be meaningful, and it would be necessary to add questions about church attendance during the past year, the performance or not of Easter duties, and so on. Perhaps the enumerator should also ask, " 'Do you really believe all the tenets of your particular faith' and 'Do you really practice them in your daily life?' " But this, he suggested, would go too far.[33]

On the other hand, a number of persons, including Patrick Murphy Malin of the American Civil Liberties Union, condemned the question in part because it *would* be useful, specifically to the churches. In Mr. Goldstein's words, "It would make out of the Federal government an agent of religious groups and would employ Government instrumentalities for church purposes."

*Comment.* Dean Pike's *reductio ad absurdum* applies almost equally well to every question in the census schedule. For some purposes the information on occupation and income, for instance, is usable as such, but as indices of social class—the typical use to which sociologists put it—it could be usefully supplemented by questions on style of life, on membership in organizations, on social attitudes. Citizens are asked how many years of schooling they have completed; perhaps the enumerator should also ask, "Do you ever read more than the sports page and comic sheet?" and "Do you really appreciate the literary quality of what you read?" In short, since the government cannot base its operations on total knowledge, should it not make do with total ignorance? The issue is whether replies to a question on religious affiliation are a reasonable indication of the religious attitudes and behavior

[32] United Nations, *Demographic Yearbook,* 1956, Table 8: "Population by Religion and Sex: Each Census, 1945–1955."
[33] Letter to the *New York Times,* August 9, 1957.

that Dean Pike designated as really meaningful; in particular, whether they are a better index than any national data that now exist. And are these attitudes and behavior patterns, in the opinion of a church prelate, important enough to be worth studying seriously?

The government furnishes valuable information to corset manufacturers, orange growers, air lines, advertising agencies, schools and colleges, municipal and state bureaus, and so on through the entire body of American commercial and institutional life. It is a strange notion that if a proposed procedure can be shown to be of some benefit to the churches, that fact in itself condemns it.

## Summary

The social concomitants of religion, whatever they may be, cannot be wished out of existence by repeating "separation of church and state" like an incantation. The facts that the data are poor and that the analyses based on them cannot be better do not mean that all interest in social differentiation by religion disappears. They mean only that this interest must operate with misinformation.

Prejudice feeds on ignorance, and those who would combat prejudice should not fight for maintaining ignorance in any area. The know-nothing liberalism of the American Civil Liberties Union and the Jewish agencies is a contradiction of their own basic principles. Whenever liberals have fought discrimination against Jews, against Catholics, against any religious or ethnic minorities, they have been able to make good use of whatever statistics there were, for if discrimination exists, how can it be indicated more effectively than by the correlation between group membership and various social indices? If the designation of race were to be deleted from the census schedule, as various persons have suggested, such a work as Myrdal's *An American Dilemma* would become impossible. One could still write philosophical essays on the virtues of equality, but it would no longer be feasible to show, as he did, that Negroes get less schooling and worse jobs, that their health is poorer and their lives are shorter, that in general the discrimination has social effects.

I do not mean to suggest, however, that their relevance to combatting prejudice is the only reason a social scientist would like statistics on religion. Members of a faith constitute a meaningful subgroup within the broader society, and religious differentiation is thus a part of many research problems. We know from case studies, for example, that relatively few Jews are alcoholics, and that this seems to be so irrespective of their occupation, income, or other social characteristics. But analysts have not yet been able to specify the relation exactly, and better data on religion would probably help. There is also a marked difference by religion in the incidence of cancers and heart diseases, and with better data it would be possible to eliminate extraneous factors (such as that Episcopalians, who are wealthier on the average, therefore see a doctor more often) and establish whether these diseases are actually related to differential patterns of living, as some analysts now believe. As we have already noted, the variation in family size by religion is a complex phenomenon, the analysis of which is seriously hindered by lack of data. Attempts to understand better the relation between ethical values and fertility are not the consequence of idle curiosity; the welfare of the large sector of the world presently undergoing modernization depends on whether national income can be increased faster than the population.

The principal argument for including a question on religion in the census, in short, is the humanist one that knowledge is good, and more complete and accurate knowledge is better. Religion is not only a personal experience and a sacred theology; it is also a social institution. As such, it should not be protected from empirical research and analysis by a high wall of magical taboos.

# A GENERAL TYPOLOGY OF MIGRATION

Most studies of international migration are focused on the movement from or to one particular country, and virtually all of the other, somewhat broader works are concerned with a single historical era. Moreover, the emphasis is usually on description rather than analysis, so that the theoretical framework into which these limited data are fitted is ordinarily rather primitive. In this paper, an attempt is made to bring together into one typology some of the more significant analyses of both internal and international migration, as a step toward a general theory of migration.

The best known model for the analysis of migration is the typology constructed some years ago by Fairchild.[1] He classifies migration into *invasion,* of which the Visigoth sack of Rome is given as the best example; *conquest,* in which

[1] Henry Pratt Fairchild, *Immigration: A World Movement and Its American Significance* (Rev. ed.; New York: Macmillan, 1925), pp. 13 ff. In spite of the fact that it has all the faults of a pioneer effort, this classification has been adopted uncritically in several other works on the subject. See, for example, Maurice R. Davie, *World Immigration with Special Reference to the United States,* (New York: Macmillan, 1949), pp. 2–3; Julius Isaac, *Economics of Migration* (London: Kegan Paul, Trench, Trubner, 1947), p. 1. The most recent and in many respects the best text in the field takes over Fairchild's four types and adds a fifth, compulsory migration; see Donald R. Taft and Richard Robbins, *International Migrations: The Immigrant in the Modern World* (New York: Ronald Press, 1955), pp. 19–20.

Several other discussions are decidedly better than Fairchild's, though not nearly so well known. I found two particularly stimulating—Rudolf Heberle, "Theorie der Wanderungen: Sociologische Betrachtungen," *Schmollers Jahrbuch,* 75:1 (1955); and Ragnar Numelin, *The Wandering Spirit: A Study of Human Migration* (London: Macmillan, 1937). See also Howard Becker, "Forms of Population Movement: Prolegomena to a Study of Mental Mobility," *Social Forces,* 9 (December, 1930), 147–160; 9 (March, 1931), 351–361.

"the people of higher culture take aggressive" action against
one on a lower cultural level; *colonization,* when "a well
established, progressive, and physically vigorous state" settles
"newly discovered or thinly settled countries"; and *immigration,* or the individually motivated, peaceful movement between well established countries "on approximately the same
stage of civilization." That is to say, Fairchild uses, more or
less clearly, two main criteria as his axes—the difference in
level of culture and whether or not the movement was
predominantly peaceful. His four types, thus, can be represented schematically as follows:

| *Migration from* | *Migration to* | *Peaceful Movement* | *Warlike Movement* |
|---|---|---|---|
| Low culture | High culture | | Invasion |
| High culture | Low culture | Colonization | Conquest |
| Cultures on a level | | Immigration | |

Reducing the implicit underlying structure to this schematic
form has the immediate advantage of indicating its in-
completeness. Two types are lacking from the classification,[2]
although they are well represented in history.

Such a paradigm, moreover, suggests even more strongly
than the dozen pages of text it summarizes that the two
axes are not the best that could have been chosen. An
attempt to distinguish between "high" and "low" cultures is
an invitation to ethnocentrism, which Fairchild does not
always avoid. The contrast between "progressive" England
and "newly discovered" India, for example, can hardly be
termed a scientific analysis of *colonization.* Similarly, Rome's
*conquest* of her empire was not merely the migration of a
people of higher culture: much of Rome's culture was adapted
from that of conquered Greece. Nor is the distinction

---

[2] It is patent that this omission was not intentional; this is not an
example of what Lazarsfeld terms "reduction"—that is, the collaps-
ing of a formally complete typology in order to adjust it to
reality. See Paul F. Lazarsfeld, "Some Remarks on the Typological
Procedures in Social Science," mimeographed translation of an
article that appeared originally in *Zeitschrift für Sozialforschung,*
Vol. 6, 1937.

between "peaceful" and "warlike" always an unambiguous one. Colonization is ordinarily neither one nor the other;[3] and the Visigoths' *invasion* of Rome, Fairchild's main example of this type, was predominantly a peaceful interpenetration of the two cultures, accomplished (as Fairchild points out) over more than two centuries.[4]

This criticism of Fairchild's classification illustrates two general points: that it is useful to make explicit the logical structure of a typology, and that the criteria by which types are to be distinguished must be selected with care.

[3] According to Fairchild, "while the resistance of the natives may be so weak as to make the enterprise hardly a military one, yet colonization is carried on without the consent, and against the will, of the original possessors of the land, and is, consequently, to be regarded rightly as a hostile movement. . . . [Moreover,] not infrequently the rivalry of two colonizing powers for some desirable locality may involve them in war with each other" (*op. cit.*, p. 19). In spite of this hedge, classifying *colonization* as "peaceful" is in accord with his main argument, for this is how he distinguishes it from *conquest.*

[4] On the one side, Germans were taken into the Roman army, granted land in the border regions and civil rights in the city; on the other side, after Ulfilas' translation of the Bible into Gothic, Roman culture made deep inroads among the Germans through their conversion to Christianity. The relation between the two cultures, therefore, was expressed not merely in a sharp confrontation on the field of battle, but also in the divided loyalties of marginal types. Alaric, leader of the Visigoths, was a romanized German, a former officer in the Roman army, a Christian; and Stilicho, the de facto emperor after Theodosius' death, was a German-Roman, a German by descent who had reached his high post through a successful army career. Alaric's purpose was not to overthrow Rome but, within the framework of the Empire, to get land and increased pensions (!) for his followers; Stilicho's purpose, similarly, was not to oust the Visigoths, whom he sought as allies against Constantinople, but to keep them under his control. The interpenetration of the two cultures, that is to say, was a complex and subtle process, not too different from the present-day acculturation of immigrant groups. That Alaric put pressure on the Senate by marching his army into Italy was not the characteristic of "a rude people, on a low stage of culture," but the time-honored mode of lobbying used by Roman generals. See J. B. Bury, *The Invasion of Europe by the Barbarians* (London: Macmillan, 1928).

## Psychological Universals

Together with most other analysts of migration, Fairchild implies that man is everywhere sedentary, remaining fixed until he is impelled to move by some force. Like most psychological universals, this one can be matched by its opposite: man migrates because of wanderlust. And like all such universals, these cannot explain differential behavior: if all men are sedentary (or migratory) "by nature," why do some migrate and some not? If a simplistic metaphor is used, it should be at least as complex as its mechanical analogue, which includes not only the concept of forces but also that of inertia.

Thus one might better say that a social group at rest, or a social group in motion (e.g., nomads), tends to remain so unless impelled to change; for with any viable pattern of life a value system is developed to support that pattern. To analyze the migration of Gypsies, for example, in terms of push and pull is entirely inadequate—no better, in fact, than to explain modern Western migration, as Herbert Spencer did, in terms of "the restlessness inherited from ancestral nomads."[5] If this principle of inertia is accepted as valid, then the difference between gathering and nomadic peoples, on the one hand, and agricultural and industrial peoples, on the other hand, is fundamental with respect to migration. For once a people has a permanent place of residence, the relevance of push and pull factors is presumably much greater.

Sometimes the basic problem is not why people migrate but rather why they do not. The vast majority of American Negroes, for example, remained in the South until the First World War, in spite of the Jim Crow pattern and lynch law that developed there from the 1870s on and, as a powerful pull, the many opportunities available in the West and the burgeoning Northern cities.[6]

[5] Herbert Spencer, *The Principles of Sociology* (3rd ed.; New York: Appleton, 1892), Vol. 1, p. 566.
[6] See Gunnar Myrdal, *An American Dilemma: The Negro Problem and Modern Democracy* (New York: Harper, 1944),

If wanderlust and what might be termed sitzlust are not useful as psychological universals, they do suggest a criterion for a significant distinction. Some persons migrate as a means of achieving the new. Let us term such migration *innovating*. Others migrate in response to a change in conditions, in order to retain what they have had; they move geographically in order to remain where they are in all other respects. Let us term such migration *conservative*. When the migrants themselves play a passive role, as in the case of African slaves being transported to the New World, the migration is termed innovating or conservative depending on how it is defined by the activating agent, in this case the slave traders.

The fact that the familiar push-pull polarity implies a universal sedentary quality, however, is only one of its faults. The push factors alleged to "cause" emigration ordinarily comprise a heterogeneous array, ranging from an agricultural crisis to the spirit of adventure, from the development of shipping to overpopulation. Few attempts are made to distinguish among underlying causes, facilitative environment, precipitants, and motives.[7] In particular, if we fail to distinguish between emigrants' motives and the social causes of emigration—that is, if we do not take the emigrants' level of aspiration into account—our analysis lacks logical clarity. Economic hardship, for example, can appropriately be termed a "cause" of emigration only if there is a positive correlation between hardship, however defined, and the propensity to migrate.[8]

---

Chap. 8, for an extended discussion of this point. For an international example, see William Petersen, *Planned Migration*, (Berkeley: University of California Press, 1955), Chap. 3, which discusses the several factors in prewar Holland that seemingly should have induced a large emigration, but did not.

[7] Cf. R. M. MacIver, *Social Causation* (Boston: Ginn, 1942).

[8] Similarly, no principled difference is usually made between what is sometimes termed "absolute overpopulation," which results in hunger and starvation, and milder degrees of "overpopulation," which reflect not physiological but cultural standards. In the first case the aspiration of emigrants can be ignored, for it is a bare physiological minimum that can be taken as universal; but in the second case it is the level of aspiration itself that defines the "overpopulation" and sets an impetus to emigrate.

Often the relation has been an inverse one; for example, the mass emigration from Europe in modern times developed together with a marked *rise* in European welfare. As has been shown by several studies, the correlation was rather with the business cycle in the receiving country,[9] and even this relation explains fluctuations in the emigration rate more than its absolute level. Nor can the class differential in the rate of emigration be ascribed simply to economic differences. The middle class lived in more comfortable circumstances, but for many a move to America would have meant also a definite material improvement. During the period of mass emigration, however, this was stereotyped as lower-class behavior, as more than a bit unpatriotic for the well-to-do. For a middle-class person to emigrate meant a break with the established social pattern; therefore in the middle class, it was marginal types like idealists or black sheep that typically left the country, and these for relevant *personal* reasons. Once a migration has reached the stage of a social movement, however, such personal motivations are generally of little interest.

This kind of confusion is not limited to economic factors. Religious oppression or the infringement of political liberty was often a *motive* for emigration from Europe, but before the rise of modern totalitarianism emigrants were predominantly from the European countries least disfigured by such stigmata. An increasing propensity to emigrate spread east and south from Northwest Europe, together with democratic institutions and religious tolerance. Again, we are faced with the anomaly that those who emigrated "because" of persecution tended to come from countries where there was less than elsewhere.

When the push-pull polarity has been refined in these two senses, by distinguishing innovating from conservative migration and by including in the analysis the migrants' level of

[9] Harry Jerome, *Migration and Business Cycles* (New York: National Bureau of Economic Research, 1926); Dorothy Swaine Thomas, *Social and Economic Aspects of Swedish Population Movements, 1750–1933* (New York: Macmillan, 1941), Chap. 9.

aspiration, it can form the basis of an improved typology of migration. Five broad classes of migration, designated as primitive, forced, impelled, free, and mass, are discussed in turn.

## Primitive Migration

The first class of migration to be defined is that resulting from an ecological push, and we shall term this *primitive* migration. Here, then, primitive migration does not denote the wandering of primitive peoples as such, but rather a movement related to man's inability to cope with natural forces. Since the reaction to a deterioration in the physical environment can be either remedial action or emigration, depending on the technology available to the people concerned, there is, however, a tendency for primitive migration in this narrower sense to be associated with primitive peoples.

Many of the treks of preindustrial folk seem, moreover, to have been conservative in the sense defined above. "There is often a tendency for [such] a migrating group to hold conservatively to the same type of environment; pastoral people, for example, attempt to remain on grasslands, where their accustomed life may be continued."[10] Such conservative migrations are set not by push and pull, but by the interplay of push and control. The route is shaped by both natural and man-made barriers: mountains, rivers, or rainfall or the lack of it; and the Great Wall of China or other, less monumental, evidences of hostility toward aliens. If they are indifferent about where they are going, men migrate as liquids flow, along the lines of least resistance. Conservative migrants seek only a place where they can resume their old way of life, and when this is possible they are content. Sometimes it is not possible, and any migration, therefore, may be associated with a fundamental change in culture.

The frequent designation for migrations of prehistoric primitives used to be "wandering of peoples," a translation

[10] Roland B. Dixon, "Migrations, Primitive," *Encyclopedia of the Social Sciences* (New York: Macmillan, 1934), Vol. 10, pp. 420–425.

from the German that, however inelegant, is nevertheless appropriate, for it denotes two of the characteristics that define it. For usually peoples as a whole migrate, not merely certain families or groups, and they leave without a definite destination, as "wander" implies in English. Let us, then, term migrations induced by ecological pressure as the *wandering of peoples.* Unintended movements over the ocean—an analogous type of primitive migration, which can be termed *marine wanderings*—have occurred more frequently than was once supposed.

> There are countless examples . . . [of] more or less accidental wanderings from island to island over oceanic expanses of water, brought about by winds and currents. The space of time and extent of these voyages seem to play a subordinate part. Journeys covering 3,000 miles are not unusual. They may last six weeks or several months. Even without provisions the natives can get along, as they fish for their food and collect rainwater to drink.[11]

Primitives often move about in another way directly related to the low level of their material culture. A food-gathering or hunting people cannot ordinarily subsist from what is available in one vicinity; it must range over a wider area, moving either haphazardly or back and forth over its traditional territory. Such movements can be called *gathering.* The analogous type of migratory movements of cattle-owning peoples is called *nomadism,* from the Greek word for *graze.* Gatherers and nomads together are termed *rangers.*

The way of life of rangers is to be on the move, and their culture is adapted to this state. Their home is temporary or portable; some Australian peoples have no word for "home" in their language. Their value system adjudges the specific hardships of their life to be good; the contempt that the desert Arab feels for the more comfortable city Arab is traditional. Although their ordinary movement is usually over a restricted area, bounded by either physical barriers

[11] Numelin, *op. cit.,* pp. 180–181.

or peoples able to defend their territories, rangers are presumably more likely to migrate over longer distances (apart from differences in the means of transportation) simply because they are already in motion. Whether any particular nomad people settles down and becomes agricultural does not depend merely on geography. Geography determines only whether such a shift in their way of life is possible—it is barely feasible on the steppe, for example; but even when physical circumstances permit a change, the social pattern of ranging may be too strong to be broken down. The Soviet program of settling the Kirghiz and other nomadic peoples on collective farms, for example, succeeded because it was implemented by sufficient terror to overcome their opposition.[12] That is to say, ranging, like wandering, is typically conservative.

A primitive migration of an agrarian population takes place when there is a sharp disparity between the produce of the land and the number of people subsisting from it. This can come about either suddenly, as by drought or an attack of locusts, or by the steady Malthusian pressure of a growing population on land of limited area and fertility. Persons induced to migrate by such population pressure can seek another agricultural site, but in the modern era the more usual destination has been a town: the migration has ordinarily been innovating rather than conservative. The Irish immigrants to the United States in the decades following the Great Famine, for example, resolutely ignored the Homestead Act and other inducements to settle on the land; in overwhelming proportion, they moved to the cities and stayed there. Let us term such an innovating movement *flight from the land* (again, an inelegant but useful translation from the German).

To recapitulate, primitive migration may be divided as follows:

[12] For a documentation from two sources of divergent political views, see Rudolf Schlesinger, *The Nationalities Problem and Soviet Administration* (London: Routledge & Kegan Paul, 1956); Walter Kolarz, *The Peoples of the Soviet Far East* (New York: Praeger, 1954).

| Primitive | Wandering | Wandering of peoples |
|-----------|-----------|----------------------|
|           |           | Marine wandering     |
|           | Ranging   | Gathering            |
|           |           | Nomadism             |
|           | Flight from the land |           |

These are the types of migration set by ecological push and controls, usually geographical but sometimes social.

## Forced and Impelled Migrations

If in primitive migrations the activating agent is ecological pressure, in forced migrations it is the state or some functionally equivalent social institution. It is useful to divide this class into *impelled* migration, when the migrants retain some power to decide whether or not to leave, and *forced* migration, when they do not have this power. Often the boundary between the two, the point at which the choice becomes nominal, may be difficult to set. Analytically, however, the distinction is clear-cut, and historically it is often so. The difference is real, for example, between the Nazis' policy (roughly 1933–38) of encouraging Jewish emigration by various anti-Semitic acts and laws, and the later policy (roughly 1938–45) of herding Jews into cattle-trains and transporting them to camps.

A second criterion by which we can delineate types of forced or impelled migration is its function, defined not by the migrant but by the activating agent. Persons may be induced to move simply to rid their homeland of them; such a migration, since it does not ordinarily bring about a change in the migrants' way of life, is analogous to conservative migration and can be subsumed under it. Others are induced to move in order that their labor power can be used elsewhere; and such a migration, which constitutes a shift in behavior patterns as well as in locale, is designated as innovating.

Four types are thus defined, as follows:

|                                          | Impelled    | Forced        |
| ---------------------------------------- | ----------- | ------------- |
| To be rid of migrants (conservative)     | Flight      | Displacement  |
| To use migrants' labor (innovating)      | Coolie trade | Slave trade   |

In all human history, *flight* has been an important form of migration. Whenever a stronger people moves into a new territory, it may drive before it the weaker former occupants. The invasion of Europe during the early centuries of the Christian era thus was induced not only by the power vacuum resulting from the disintegration of the Roman Empire, but also by a series of successive pushes, originating from either the desiccation of the Central Asian steppes (Huntington) or the expansion of the Chinese empire still farther east (Teggart).[13]

Many more recent migrations have also been primarily a flight before invading armies.[14] In modern times, however, those induced to flee have often been specific groups among the population, rather than everyone occupying a particular territory. Political dissidents, of course, always were ousted when they became a danger to state security; but with the growth of nationalism ethnic as well as political homogeneity has been sought. The right of national self-determination proclaimed by the Treaty of Versailles included no provision for the minorities scattered through Central Europe; and in the interwar period the League of Nations negotiated a series of population transfers designed to eliminate national minorities from adjacent countries or, more usually, to legitimate expulsions already effected.[15] The separation of

[13] Ellsworth Huntington, *Civilization and Climate* (New Haven: Yale University Press, 1951); Frederick Teggart, *Rome and China: A Study of Correlations in Historical Events* (Berkeley: University of California Press, 1939).

[14] See, for example, Eugene M. Kulischer, *Europe on the Move* (New York: Columbia University Press, 1948).

[15] Cf. Stephen P. Ladas, *The Exchange of Minorities: Bulgaria, Greece and Turkey* (New York: Macmillan, 1932), p. 721: "Both conventions [of Neuilly and Lausanne], and especially that of Lausanne, proved to be agreements confirming accomplished facts," and the Greek-Turkish exchange, while "voluntary in theory, became in fact to a great extent compulsory."

Pakistan from India, another example, was accompanied by one of the largest migrations in human history, in part induced by terrorist groups on both sides and in part arranged under official auspices.

It is useful to distinguish between two classes of those who have fled their homeland—*émigrés,* who regard their exile as temporary and live abroad for the day when they may return, and *refugees,* who intend to settle permanently in the new country. Under otherwise similar circumstances, the acculturation of the latter would presumably be much more rapid than that of persons still living spiritually in another country.

Frequently, even the pretense that the movement is voluntary has been lacking. As part of its European population policy, Nazi Germany exported Jews to camps and imported forced laborers from all occupied countries. The latter movement was a modern variant of the earlier slave trade, but the largely successful attempt to kill off some millions of persons because of their supposed racial inferiority was something new in history. In the jargon of official bureaus, those that survived such forced migration have been termed "displaced persons," a designation that clearly implies their passive role. The forced movement itself is here called *displacement.*

The forced migrations under Soviet auspices have typically served two purposes, to remove a dissident or potentially dissident group from its home[16] and to furnish an unskilled

---

[16] For example, after Poland was divided between Nazi Germany and Communist Russia in 1939, the more than a million Poles deported to Asiatic Russia were chosen not merely on the basis of actual or alleged opposition to their country's invasion but more often as members of a large variety of occupational groups, which were defined as potentially oppositionist. "Regarded as 'anti-Soviet elements,' and so treated, were administrative officials, police, judges, lawyers, members of Parliament, prominent members of political parties, non-Communist non-political societies, clubs, and the Red Cross; civil servants not included above, retired military officers, officers in the reserve, priests, tradesmen, landowners, hotel and restaurant owners, clerks of the local Chambers of Commerce, and any class of persons engaged in trade or correspondence with foreign countries —the latter definition extending even to stamp collectors and

labor force in an inhospitable area. During the first two five-year plans, several million "kulaks" were removed en masse to the sites of cities-to-be, and the inhabitants of the five national units of the USSR abolished during the war were deported wholesale to forced-labor camps.[17] Such movements combine displacement with *slave trade,* or the forcible migration of laborers. While the overseas shipment of Africans during the mercantile age differed in some respects from the use of forced labor in an industrial economy, the two criteria that define the type are the same—the use of force and the supply of labor power.

The analogous form of impelled migration is termed *coolie trade.* This includes not only the movement of Asians to plantations, the most typical form, but also, for example, the migration of white indentured servants to the British colonies in the eighteenth century. Such migrants, while formally bound only for the period of a definite contract, very often are forced into indebtedness and have to extend their period of service indefinitely.[18] But as in other cases of impelled and forced migration, even when the difference

---

Esperantists—were also deported. Many artisans, peasants, and laborers (both agricultural and industrial), were banished too, so that, in effect, no Polish element was spared." Edward J. Rozek, *Allied Wartime Diplomacy: A Pattern in Poland* (New York: Wiley, 1958), p. 39.

[17] The Volga-German ASSR, the Kalmyk ASSR, the Chechen-Ingush ASSR, the Crimean ASSR, and the Karachayev Region were designated as "disloyal nationalities," and the major portion of the 2.8 million inhabitants were removed from their immemorial homeland. The million or so Tatars brought into Crimea to replace the deportees also proved to be unreliable, and in 1945 most of these were also deported to forced labor. See David J. Dallin and Boris ʼ. Nicolaevsky, *Forced Labor in Soviet Russia* (New Haven: Yale University Press, 1947), pp. 274–277. According to a decree dated January 9, 1957, the survivors among five of the uprooted peoples were to be shipped back to their homes over the next several years. Even under this new policy, however, the Volga Germans and the Tatars were presumably to be left in their Siberian exile (*New York Times,* February 12, 1957). A full account is given in Robert Conquest, *The Soviet Deportation of Nationalities* (London: Macmillan, 1960).

[18] See, for example, Victor Purcell, *The Chinese in Southeast Asia* (London: Oxford University Press, 1951), p. 345.

between historical instances becomes blurred, the analytical distinction is clear. Another important difference between slave and coolie migration is that many coolies eventually return to their homeland. The total emigration from India from 1834 to 1937, for example, has been estimated at slightly more than 30 million, but of these almost 24 million returned, leaving a net emigration over the century of only six million.[19]

## Free Migration

In the types of migration discussed so far, the will of the migrants has been a relatively unimportant factor. A primitive migration results from the lack of means to satisfy basic physiological needs, and in forced (or impelled) migration the migrants are largely passive. We now consider the types in which the will of the migrants is the decisive element, that is, *free* migrations.[20]

Overseas movements from Europe during the nineteenth century afford important illustrations of this class of migration. Because of the excellence of its formal analysis, Lindberg's monograph on emigration from Sweden[21] has been chosen as an example. Lindberg distinguishes three periods, each with a characteristic type of emigrant. During the first stage, beginning around 1840, emigrants came principally from the two university towns of Upsala and Lund; they were "men with a good cultural and social background, mostly young and of a romantic disposition" (p. 3). Since the risks in emigration were great and difficult to calculate, those

[19] Kingsley Davis, *The Population of India and Pakistan* (Princeton: Princeton University Press, 1951), p. 99.

[20] As in general throughout this essay, the words used to designate the classes or types of migration are terms in common usage rather than neologisms. Since they are here more precisely defined than in most contexts, however, they denote a narrower range of meaning; thus free migration is not all unforced migration, for it is one of five rather than two classes.

[21] John S. Lindberg, *The Background of Swedish Emigration to the United States: An Economic and Sociological Study in the Dynamics of Migration* (Minneapolis: University of Minnesota Press, 1930).

who left tended to be adventurers or intellectuals motivated by their ideals, especially by their alienation from European society during a period of political reaction. The significance of this *pioneer* movement was not in its size, which was never large, but in the example it set: "It was this emigration that helped to break the ice and clear the way for the later emigration, which included quite different classes" (p. 7). These pioneers wrote letters home; their adventures in the new world were recounted in Swedish newspapers. Once settled in the new country, they helped finance the passage of their families or friends.

Imperceptibly, this first stage developed into the second, the period of *group migration*—the emigration, for example, of Pietist communities under the leadership of their pastor or another person of recognized authority. Even when not associated through their adherence to a dissident sect, emigrants banded together for mutual protection during the hazardous journey and against the wilderness and the often hostile Indians at its end. Again, the significance of this group migration lay not in its size but in the further impulse it gave. During the decade beginning in 1841, an average of only 400 persons left Sweden annually, and during the following decade, this average was still only 1,500.

## Mass Migration

Free migration is always rather small, for individuals strongly motivated to seek novelty or improvement are not commonplace. The most significant attribute of pioneers, as in other areas of life, is that they blaze trails that others follow, and sometimes the number who do so grows into a broad stream. Migration becomes a style, an established pattern, an example of collective behavior. Once it is well begun, the growth of such a movement is semi-automatic: so long as there are people to emigrate, the principal cause of emigration is prior emigration. Other circumstances operate as deterrents or incentives, but within this kind of attitudinal framework; all factors except population growth are important principally in terms of the established behavior. As we have already noted, when emigration has been set as a *social* pattern, it is no longer relevant to inquire concerning the *individual* motivations. For the individual is, in Lindberg's phrase, in an "unstable state of equilibrium," in which only a small impulse in either direction decides his course; hence the motives he ascribes to his emigration are either trivial or, more likely, the generalities that he thinks are expected.[22]

The development of migration as collective behavior is aptly illustrated by the Swedish case. During the decade 1861–70, when the average number of emigrants jumped to 9,300 per year, the transition to the third stage of *mass* emigration began. Transportation facilities improved: railroads connected the interior with the port cities, and the sailing ship began to be replaced by the much faster and safer steamer. While its relation to mass migration was important, this improvement in transportation facilities was not a cause; rather, it is "possible and even probable that emigration and the development of transportation were largely caused by the same forces" (p. 15, n. 17). Not only was the geographical distance cut down but also what Lindberg terms the social distance: as communities in the new country grew in size and importance, the shift from Sweden to America required less and less of a personal adjustment. Before the migrant left his homeland, he began his acculturation in an American-

---

[22] Hansen has pointed out that the migrant's motivation was likely to be pruned to suit the person asking for it. The official in the home country was told of material difficulties, but to cite these in America would confirm the natives' belief that the foreigner was a dangerous economic competitor. The village clergyman, should he attempt to dissuade a prospective migrant, was told that his sons were growing up without a future and becoming lazy and shiftless; but in America these moral motives would give point to the argument that immigrants were depraved. Hence, "the newcomer said, 'I came to the United States to enjoy the blessings of your marvelous government and laws,' [and] the native warmed to him and was likely to inquire whether there was not something he could do to assist him. Immigrants soon learned the magic charm of this confession of faith. They seized every opportunity to contrast the liberty of the New World with the despotism of the Old." Marcus Lee Hansen, *The Immigrant in American History* (Cambridge: Harvard University Press, 1940), pp. 77–78.

Swedish milieu, made up of New World letters, photographs, mementos, knickknacks. There developed what the peasants called "America fever": in some districts, there was not a farm without some relatives in America, and from many all the children had emigrated. According to a government report that Lindberg quotes, children were "educated to emigrate," and he continues—

> When they finally arrived at a decision, they merely followed a tradition which made emigration the natural thing in a certain situation. In fact, after the imagination and fantasy had, so to speak, become "charged with America," a positive decision *not* to emigrate may have been necessary if difficulties arose [pp. 56–57].

The Swedes who migrated to Minnesota became farmers or small-town craftsmen or merchants. In a more general analysis, it is useful to distinguish two types of mass movement according to the nature of the destination—*settlement,* such as Lindberg described, and *urbanization,* or mass migration to a larger town or city. No distinction in principle is made here between internal and international migration, for the fundamentals of the rural-urban shift so characteristic of the modern era are generally the same whether or not the new city-dwellers cross a national border.

## Conclusions

The typology developed in this paper is summarized in the last table. Such a typology is a tool, and it is worth constructing only if it is useful. What is its utility?

This question may be answered against a perspective of the present undeveloped status of migration theory. Classifications of modern migrations tend to derive from the statistics that are collected, whether or not these have any relevance to theoretical questions. It is as if those interested in the *causes* of divorce studied this matter exclusively with data classified according to the *grounds* on which divorces are granted. Even the principal statistical differentiation, that between internal and international migration, is not necessarily of theoretical significance.[23] Similarly, when the species *migrant* is set off from the genus *traveler* by arbitrarily defining removal for a year or more as "permanent" migration, such a distinction clearly has little or no theoretical basis, and it is not even certain that it is the most convenient one that could be made.[24] The preferable procedure in any discipline is to establish our concepts and the logical relation among them, and to collect our statistics in terms of this conceptual framework. The principal purpose of the typology, then, is to offer, by such an ordering of conceptual types, a basis for the possible development of theory.

| Relation | Migratory Force | Class of Migration | Type of Migration | |
|---|---|---|---|---|
| | | | Conservative | Innovating |
| Nature and man | Ecological push | Primitive | Wandering | Flight from the land |
| | | | Ranging | |
| State and man | Migration policy | Forced | Displacement | Slave trade |
| | | Impelled | Flight | Coolie trade |
| Man and his norms | Higher aspirations | Free | Group | Pioneer |
| Collective behavior | Social Momentum | Mass | Settlement | Urbanization |

Migration differs from fertility and mortality in that it cannot be analyzed, even at the outset, in terms of noncultural, physiological factors, but must be differentiated with respect to relevant social conditions. This means that the most general statement that one makes concerning migration should be in the form of a typology, rather than a law.[25] While few today would follow Ravenstein's example by denoting their statements "laws,"[26] most treatments of migratory

[23] Cf. below, pp. 293–294.

[24] Thus in his study of British migration, Isaac found it useful to distinguish between those who intend to settle elsewhere permanently and what he termed "quasi-permanent" migrants or those who leave for a year or more but intend to return. Julius Isaac, *British Post-War Migration* (National Institute of Economic and Social Research, Occasional Paper 17; Cambridge University Press, 1954), p. 2.

[25] This point is very effectively argued by Heberle, *op. cit.*

[26] E. G. Ravenstein, "The Laws of Migration," *Journal of the Royal Statistical Society*, 48 (June, 1885), 167–235; 52 (June, 1889), 241–305.

selection still imply a comparable degree of generality. Even the best discussions[27] typically neglect to point out that selection ranges along a continuum, from total migration to total nonmigration, or that the predominance of females in rural-urban migration that Ravenstein noted must be contrasted with male predominance in, for example, India's urbanization. As we have seen, the familiar push-pull polarity implies a universal sedentary tendency, which has little empirical basis in either history or psychology. Analogously, the distinction between conservative and innovating migration challenges the usual notion that persons universally migrate in order to change their way of life.

Sometimes an analytical problem can be clarified by defining more precisely the two more or less synonymous terms that denote a confusion in concepts. For example, the question of whether the secular decline in the Western birth rate was due to a physiological deterioration or to new cultural standards was often not put clearly until *fecundity* was precisely distinguished from *fertility*. Several such pairs of terms are differentiated here. Whether a movement from the countryside to towns is *urbanization* or *flight from the land* can be a very important distinction; the discussion of Canada's immigration policy, for example, has largely centered on this point.[28] While the distinction between *urbanization* and *settlement* would seem to be so obvious that it can hardly be missed, one can say that the national-quota system of American immigration law is based in part at least on neglect of the implications of this differentiation.[29] The most useful distinction in the typology, perhaps, is that between *mass* migration and all other types, for it emphasizes the fact that the movement of Europeans to the New World during the nineteenth century, the migration with which we are most familiar, does not constitute the whole of the phenomenon. When this type of migration declined after the

[27] See, for example, Dorothy Swaine Thomas, ed., *Research Memorandum of Migration Differentials* (New York: Social Science Research Council, Bulletin 43, 1938); E. W. Hofstee, *Some Remarks on Selective Migration* (The Hague: Nijhoff, 1952).

[28] See Petersen, *op. cit.*, pp. 202 ff.

[29] See above, p. 208.

First World War, largely because of new political limitations imposed by both emigration and immigration countries, this was very often interpreted, not as a change to a different type, but as the end of significant human migration altogether.

# INTERNAL MIGRATION AND
# ECONOMIC DEVELOPMENT

One of the questions asked in the 1960 census was where people had been living five years earlier. Of the 159 million persons aged five years or over, only half were living in the same house as in 1955. Three out of ten had moved to a different house in the same county, one out of twelve had moved to a different state.[1] As these figures indicate, internal migration is highly significant. During the five-year period 1955–60 the United States population grew from both natural increase and net international migration by not quite 15 million. This figure constitutes less than a third of the intracounty movement and only slightly more than the interstate migration. In many parts of the country, internal migration is the most important determinant of population size and composition.

It is still, however, the demographic factor we know least about. In contrast to the fairly reliable and complete data on births, deaths, and immigration, our estimates of internal migration rest mainly on the Census Bureau's annual survey of a sample of about 25,000 dwelling units and on the data available from each decennial census. This information is insufficient for some of the most routine demographic purposes. In 1955–56 (and other years are much the same) interstate migrants included 2.3 percent of the male population and 3.0 percent of the female, 3.2 percent of the white population and 2.2 percent of the nonwhite;[2] but such overall figures reveal almost nothing about the migratory selection operative with respect even to such basic traits as sex and race, to say nothing of more subtle factors.

[1] U. S. *Census of Population, 1960, U. S. Summary: General Social and Economic Characteristics,* Report PC (1)-1C, U.S.

[2] U. S. Bureau of the Census, *Current Population Report,* Series P-20, No. 73 (March 12, 1957).

It is usually assumed that economic motives predominate in determining patterns of internal migration. Indeed, migration, economic development, and social mobility, though ordinarily analyzed separately, are so closely inter-related as to be really facets of the same phenomenon. For example, the rise of manufacturing and services and the relative decline of agriculture, the shift of population from the countryside to the towns, and improvement in income and status of a substantial portion of the American people, are all the same basic transformation of this country's society. The stupendous task of combining these three facets into a single analytical framework and applying this to historical data has not yet been accomplished.[3]

Economic motives, in any case, are not the only ones that stimulate internal migration. There is a considerable move-ment, for example, among retired persons, who by definition have lost the prime economic reason for migrating. The fact that they move primarily to states like Florida and California suggests that they may be seeking a pleasant climate; and this attraction is certainly not limited to the aged. The population of North Dakota, for example, whose recorded temperatures range from a high of 124° to a low of −60°, declined from 681,000 in 1930 to 620,000 in 1950, ris-ing thereafter to 632,000 in 1960.[4] The northward move-

[3] See, however, the study presently in process by a team at the University of Pennsylvania, *Population Redistribution and Economic Growth, 1870–1950*. Two volumes have been pub-lished: Everett S. Lee *et al.*, *Methodological Considerations and Reference Tables;* Simon Kuznets *et al.*, *Analyses of Economic Change* (Philadelphia: American Philosophical Society, *Memoirs,* Vols. 45 and 51, 1957 and 1960). Simon Kuznets and Dorothy Swaine Thomas, who directed this pioneer study, are justly proud of having combined the available data concerning economic development and internal migration into a unified analysis; but they have skimped on the third element, movement between social classes. For a work that attempts to relate economic develop-ment, social mobility, and *international* migration, see Brinley Thomas, *Migration and Economic Growth: A Study of Great Britain and the Atlantic Economy* (Cambridge: Cambridge Uni-versity Press, 1954).

[4] Local boosters have played with the idea of changing the state's name to just "Dakota" or "South Manitoba" or even

ment of Negroes, as another example, is to areas of better schools and homes as well as better jobs. Short-distance moves seem to be motivated less by economic interests than by family matters—the search for a better neighborhood, or a better school, or a larger home.[5] It is plausible that at least a portion of long-distance migrants have similar motives, at the very least in combination with an economic stimulus.

## A Nation of Nomads

The most significant feature of internal migration is its prevalence—the fact that an American who dies in the house he was born in is atypical. This restlessness has much to do with the country's progressive economy and its dynamic culture. The national labor market operates with discernible frictions, but that it should work at all across three thousand miles with a complete absence of forced moves is the anomaly to be explained. The weakness of tradition in American society derives not only from the immigrant background and the frontier tradition, but also from the continuing nomadic tendency.

Free migration exists not only over the large expanse of the United States but also, in practical terms, over the whole of English-speaking North America. The boundary between Canada and the United States does not constitute a barrier to migration in either direction, and the virtual identity of language and other fundamental culture traits mean that, apart from French Canadians, cultural impediments are also minimal. The parallel streams of migration within each of the two countries often merge to become parts of the same movement. The trek westward across the United States at

---

"Miami" or "Dixie"—or "anything, in fact, that would make North Dakota sound gay, cheerful as a bottle of champagne" (*Time,* January 28, 1957). In 1950, even without this fundamental reform, there were 1,940 persons living in the state who had been born in California; no generalization concerning internal migration lacks its inexplicable exception.

[5] Peter H. Rossi, *Why Families Move: A Study of the Social Psychology of Urban Residential Mobility* (Glencoe, Ill.: Free Press, 1955).

the turn of the century, for instance, included a swing across the border into the developing wheatfields of the Canadian West; and twenty-five years later the metropolitan centers of the United States exerted a strong pull on the smaller cities of both countries. The 17 million Canadians (only as many people as in New York State) are stretched in a narrow band along the international border; and even if other circumstances had been less favorable to migration, many Canadians would have sought some of their life goals to the south.

The state-of-birth statistics recorded in each United States census provoke more questions than they answer. That many persons move to California, for instance, is a commonplace, but few would guess that of the native-born Americans living there in 1960 only 43.7 percent had been born in the state. The in-migrants came from all over the United States, and natives of California settled throughout the Union. Even for this single state, these statements denote something of a simplification of the facts, for the various routes and intermediate places of residence are ignored, as well as intrastate movements. In *each* of the forty-eight continental states of the country, there reside persons who were born in all of the other forty-seven. The congeries of accidents and personal motives that results in such utter dispersion has never been studied.

Such data can be summarized as in Figure 1, which shows for each state the percentage of the native-born population that was born outside the present state of residence.[6] For the four states in the southwest corner of the nation (plus Wyoming and Florida), this proportion was half or more; and for every state west of the Mississippi it was at least 20 percent.

[6] The figure given earlier in the text for California and that shown on the map are correct, even though they do not add up to 100 percent. The precise figures were as follows: born in California, 43.7 percent; born in another state, 52.3 percent; born in outlying areas, at sea, etc., 0.6 percent; not reported, 3.4 percent. *U. S. Census of Population, 1960, California: General Social and Economic Characteristics,* Report PC (1)-6C, Table 39.

## The Westward Movement

The more detailed analysis of internal migration has in effect been limited to those several broad streams that can be associated, at least hypothetically, with significant social trends. The most important of such historic patterns of population redistribution is the migration to the West. The point marking the center of the United States population has moved steadily westward at the rate of four or five miles per year, from northeastern Maryland in 1790 to south-central Illinois in 1960. The movement of population that this shift denotes was more erratic, markedly affected by land grants, gold

FIGURE 1. PERCENTAGE OF NATIVE POPULATION BORN OUTSIDE THE STATE OF PRESENT RESIDENCE, UNITED STATES, 1960.

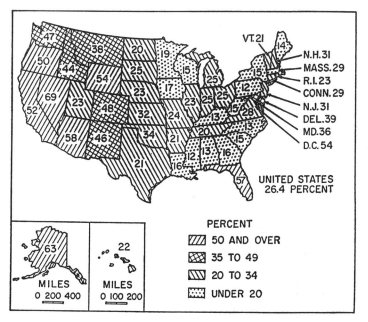

SOURCE: *U. S. Census of Population, 1960. United States Summary: General Social and Economic Characteristics,* Report PC (1)-1C, U.S., p. xiii.

rushes, and transportation facilities, as well as by the several major geographical barriers on the way to the Pacific.[7]

In the most recent period, after the lull in internal migration during the depression decade, the westward movement was greatly stimulated by the government's policy of establishing war plants on the Pacific Coast. The boom thus started has continued without serious interruption and has been an important concomitant of the extremely rapid population growth. During the intercensal decade 1950–60, the population of the three Pacific states increased by 40.2 percent, as compared with a national average of only 18.5 percent. As is obvious from the size of this difference, it was due primarily to migration. In 1957, the Census Bureau expected that this trend would continue at least up until 1970, when it was believed that about 12 percent of the United States population would live in the three Pacific Coast states (compared with the actual 11.8 percent in 1960).[8] In terms of percentages, although not of course in absolute numbers, the growth of some of the Mountain states has been even more spectacular.[9]

The interrelation between the population growth of the West and its economic development is a complex matter. Until World War II, the West imported a substantial portion of the goods it consumed; and the cost of the long haul from the centers of manufacturing, aggravated by discriminatory freight rates, created the equivalent of the protective tariff wall behind which even marginal manufacturing plants

[7] Of these, one of the most important was an invisible line running roughly from Minnesota south to central Texas, delineating an area to the east with twenty to forty inches of rain per year and one to the west with only ten to twenty inches. An amazing feature of the postwar development is that this prior dependence of population growth on the natural water supply has been markedly reduced.

[8] U. S. Bureau of the Census, *Current Population Report,* Series P-25, No. 160 (August 9, 1957).

[9] Morris E. Garnsey, *America's New Frontier: The Mountain West* (New York: Knopf, 1950). See also Carl F. Kraenzel, *The Great Plains in Transition* (Norman: University of Oklahoma Press, 1955); William Petersen and Lionel S. Lewis, *The Changing Population of Nevada* (Research Report No. 2, Bureau of Business and Economic Research; Reno: University of Nevada, 1964).

could be set up. With the growth of population, the consumer market is no longer too small to attract industries; and once new enterprises are established, those who come into the area to work in one factory or office form an attractive market for other new business. By such an interaction, the growth of manufacturing and of population can become cumulative, and under favorable conditions it is appropriate to posit an analogy to the multiplier effect.

The West now has an industrial structure ranging from the several large steel plants established during the war, through such major industries as the space and aircraft firms, to the literally hundreds of smaller factories established every year. California is not only the nation's leading agricultural state—with more than 200 commercial farm products—but the first state in construction and in the generation of electric power, and the third state in the value of its mineral products. In manufacturing, California stands first in the value of processed foods, second in transportation equipment and in wood products, third in petroleum, fourth in fabricated textiles, fifth in printing and publishing.[10] This list comprises both a more impressive and a more diversified economy than that of the West as a whole, but the same forces that have engendered California's remarkable growth are apparent throughout the region.

## The Negro Exodus

One great historical migration, the movement of Negroes out of the South, is significant less because of the number of persons involved than because of its important effect on race relations, and thus on the economy and culture of the area. In 1860, 94.9 percent of the Negroes in the United States lived in the South (including Missouri); and the puzzling

[10] For more detailed discussions, see Warren S. Thompson, *Growth and Changes in California's Population* (Los Angeles: Haynes Foundation, 1955); Margaret S. Gordon, *Employment Expansion and Population Growth: The California Experience, 1900–1950* (Berkeley: University of California Press, 1954); Robert K. Arnold *et al., The California Economy, 1947–1980* (Menlo Park, Calif.: Stanford Research Institute, 1960).

question, as Myrdal pointed out, is not why they have moved north but rather why the migration took so long to start and why so many remained behind.[11] The migration got under way only during World War I, when manufacturers, faced with an acute labor shortage, sent recruiting agents into the South, but since then it has continued without interruption. Even the depression of the 1930s merely cut down the volume of the movement: in the South whites were taking over low-status jobs, and in the North unemployment relief was distributed with less discrimination.

Along with the sizable Negro urbanization within the South, virtually all of the interregional movement of Negroes has been to the cities, and particularly to the largest cities of the North and West.[12] The war of 1941–45 accelerated this trend: though still predominantly rural as late as 1940, Negroes were more than 60 percent urban by 1950 and 73 percent in 1960 (compared with slightly less than 70 percent for the whole population). The largest Negro populations are in New York City, Chicago, Philadelphia, and Detroit, and the most rapid increase has been in California cities.

The internal migration of Negroes has been analogous to the pre-1914 immigration of Southern and Eastern Europeans. In both cases, the shift was from a frequently rural background to low-income jobs in manufacturing and domestic service in the metropolitan centers. Particularly in some of the cities, Negro in-migration to the urban centers was matched by white out-migration to the suburbs; but this widely noted shift may be only transitional. In 1960 the 50 largest cities had 24 suburbs in which nonwhites constituted 20 percent or more of the population.[13] If the fair-housing laws that liberals are pushing for are enacted during the next years, racially mixed suburbs may be less of a rarity in 1970.

[11] Gunnar Myrdal, *An American Dilemma: The Negro Problem and Modern Democracy* (New York: Harper, 1944), Chap. 8.
[12] Harry Sharp and Leo F. Schnore, "The Changing Color Composition of Metropolitan Areas," *Land Economics*, 38 (May, 1962), 169–185; "Racial Changes in Metropolitan Areas, 1950–1960," *Social Forces*, 41 (March, 1963), 247–253.
[13] *Ibid.*

This shift of Negroes into the centers of American civilization will be the basis for a stupendous change in their status
over the next generation. Even their slum houses are markedly
better than those available to Negroes in the South, and with
respect to other conditions of life—schools, employment opportunities and wages, politics—the contrast is much sharper.
In a chapter of its 1963 report headed "Breakthrough to
Equality," the U. S. Commission on Civil Rights lists gains
since 1948 in the armed forces, employment, education, housing, public accommodations, justice, and political participation.[14] Of course, the disparity between the races is still great,
and in a full analysis of the reasons for the progress to date
one would include many other factors. But the basis for the
new trend was laid by the migration of a sufficient number
of Negroes to areas of the country that at least permitted
the rise of pressure groups.

This development of a Northern Negro of a new type will
continue to affect the race relations in the South as well, in
part because of the effect of Negro migration on the ratio
of the two races in the South. By 1940 no Southern state
any longer had a majority of Negroes in its population
(though the District of Columbia, as a consequence of the
sizable in-migration of Negroes, in 1960 was almost 55
percent Negro). In 1960, Negroes constituted more than 40
percent in only one state, Mississippi, and between 30 and 40
percent in three others—South Carolina, Louisiana, and
Alabama. If race relations were governed by reason, this
large reduction in the proportion of Negroes should have
eased the Southern whites' fear of being dominated by their
one-time slaves; and one can hope that it will still do so.

## Conclusions

The examples given here of internal movements in the
United States are obviously not the only ones that could
have been chosen. One thinks of the considerable out-
migration of Southern whites, balanced—at least potentially

[14] U. S. Commission on Civil Rights, *Report, 1963:* "Freedom
to the Free" (Washington, D.C.: U. S. Government Printing
Office, 1963), pp. 121–200.

—by a movement into those Southern states where the long-awaited industrial renaissance is most in evidence; or of the secular decline in New England's economy, culture, and—at least in part—population. An even more intriguing problem is posed by the large number of counties, and even a few whole states, that have experienced a decline in population. This phenomenon of rural depopulation, or "flight from the land" as it was termed, was the focus of nineteenth-century European analysts' attention; and if the moral flavor of their admonitions is well lost, their curiosity in the matter might usefully be revived.

According to the usual theory, a person moves from one place to another in order to satisfy a goal that was unrealized at his first residence. Migration is thus seen as a response to regional differences, and over a sufficient period the migration reduces the difference in wage rates, cultural amenities, or whatever (though not, of course, in climate or other natural features). American society, though increasing in complexity, is thus in some respects becoming more homogeneous. The differences between town and country, or between one region and another, or between the United States and Canada, are probably smaller than they once were. One could extrapolate this trend to hypothesize a future in which few or none would be stimulated to move. This has been done, not once but many times. For example, Frederick Jackson Turner, developing a theme in the 1890 census, marked finis to the Western frontier. The theory he propounded, however, is too simple. There are in American civilization both a recurrent dynamism—a search for new elements—and a constant effort to incorporate these elements into the whole—a search for equilibrium. Nothing in the present scene suggests that this interaction between change and stability is about to be resolved in favor of either.

# PLANNED MIGRATION[1]

Recently "migration" has come to be defined not as the relatively permanent movement of persons or groups over relatively large distances, or in similarly general terms, but as such a movement under conditions specific to the trans-Atlantic migration of the nineteenth century. Large-scale migration, so defined, is then declared to be a phenomenon of the past. During the interwar period, and especially during the depression decade, analysts wrote in terms of the "limits of land settlement"; and the well known book of this title that Isaiah Bowman edited began with the flat prognosis that "the population of the world has become sedentary permanently, . . . [for] most of its inhabitants are where they belong."[2] This thesis was excellently summarized in Forsyth's aptly titled book, *The Myth of Open Spaces.*[3] He analyzed the migratory potential in terms of conditions in part specific to the 1930s—the "incipient decline" of the West European population, the contrast between Europe's social security and the lack of it overseas, the glut of consumer goods, the end of colonialism. From such premises he concluded that the era of large-scale migration has come to an end.

Of all the points that Forsyth made, the one that has re-

[1] The present tense as used in this paper refers to the year of original publication, 1955. No attempt has been made to bring the study up-to-date, for this would have been both difficult and superfluous. Nothing fundamental has changed, but to recount the new details would have entailed a major new study.

[2] Carl O. Sauer, "The Prospect for Redistribution of Population," in Isaiah Bowman, ed., *Limits of Land Settlement: A Report on Present-Day Possibilities* (New York: Council on Foreign Relations, 1937), pp. 7–24.

[3] W. D. Forsyth, *The Myth of Open Spaces: Australian, British and World Trends of Population and Migration* (Melbourne: Melbourne University Press, 1942).

tained the greatest validity is that the state's increasingly important role in controlling international migration has meant principally its inhibition. In his view, migration had developed from individual freedom, which "has proved short-lived." "Everywhere the hand of the community is again lying more heavily upon the individual, and his range of choice is narrowing."

> The more the state became the guardian of national economic life, the more it asserted the right to decide who should and who should not be admitted from abroad to share in that life. . . . Political opposition to immigration sometimes, and perhaps increasingly, stands on purely political grounds. Exaggerated nationalism makes immigrant countries hostile to "alien" elements.[4]

Thus, emigration from Eastern Europe and immigration to the United States—that is, migration between the two most important areas before 1914—have been much decreased or virtually eliminated by political restrictions.

But Forsyth's assumption that increased state control over migration is equivalent to a reduced movement of people—that governments always, under all conditions, regard migration as being against the national interest—has proved to be unwarranted. The increased role of the state has meant a sharp curtailment or cessation of migration in some cases, but in others it has led rather to a change in its character; and when governments now sponsor migration, this also means that purely economic limitations have become less important. It is no longer decisive if a potential migrant cannot finance his passage, for subsidies are now available to a much wider group than British migrants within the Commonwealth. Nor need the capital ventures that accompany migration now yield a profit, as they had to when private investment was the rule. There has been no lack of the "frontier development" that Forsyth saw merely as a remnant from a past age—the American Point Four program, the British Colombo Plan, the heavy private and governmental investment in Israel, and so on. In today's aid programs or

[4] *Ibid.,* pp. 49 ff.

foreign investment, political-social considerations override economic ones, particularly if these are interpreted in terms of short-term profits to individual entrepreneurs. The fact that in countries still usually classed as capitalist the state has been playing an increasing role in economic affairs has meant often that grandiose schemes on a national scale have been carried out. Ordinarily, these projects have demanded more manpower than was available in, for example, the thinly populated British dominions; and in that case, the manpower is being supplied in part through state-facilitated immigration. Even when migration involves a financial loss at both ends, it may be furthered by the two governments because of the dictates of broader national policy.

That 1914 marked a watershed between two eras of international migration is evident, but once the economic and demographic effects of the depression are seen in perspective, the political control of migration becomes more significant than most analysts in the 1930s believed. The principal change since 1914 has not been a decrease in the propensity to migrate, but rather an increased control by the state over migration. The state has sometimes erected barriers that inhibit the free movement typical of the nineteenth century, and sometimes it has induced or forced masses of people to move. In either case, the change in the character of migration is more significant than the change in its size.

## Neo-Mercantilist Migration

Europe's mass emigration of the nineteenth century, based fundamentally on that continent's prodigious population growth and the existence of nonmythical open spaces, was also related to the shift from mercantilist to liberal political theory—from the belief that a nation must hoard its population as it does other forms of wealth, to the concept, in the words—already noted—of France's constitution of 1791, that "the liberty of all to move about, to remain, or to leave" is a "natural and civil right." Mercantilist impediments to migration were first supplanted by state programs to subsidize the emigration of paupers and other socially undesirable types; but this kind of movement, though receiving countries initially raised no bar to it, never gathered momentum. The mass migration from, roughly, the 1840s to 1914 developed by a shift from personal to social motivation—the departure of a few political or religious dissidents or other atypical persons or deviant small groups was gradually transformed into emigration as a normal behavior of broad classes. This geometric growth typically took place outside the range of state control; once started, it developed apart from either the efforts to foster emigration, as in Britain, or to inhibit it, as in Austria-Hungary or tsarist Russia.

The free migration of individuals, which thus developed in size without a change in its laissez-faire framework, has now become in large part the forced or controlled or induced migration of certain sectors of society. Though a very sharp distinction must be made between forced population transfers by totalitarian states and the control of migration by democratic states,[5] they have this in common: that the welfare of the national state has become, to one degree or another, the main criterion for judging whether migration is "good" or "bad." The "natural" right of the passportless person to move about has been supplanted by the "natural" right of the state to control that movement. The new principle, though well established in practice, is not yet axiomatic, so that the absolute sovereignty of the nation-state in setting migration policy has been repeatedly challenged by proponents of two alternative modes of dealing with international migration:

1. Mankind must "return to that only solution of the prob-

[5] A link between the two can be seen in the International Refugee Organization, which was both an expression of Western humanitarian idealism and, when for a time it assisted in forcing the repatriation of East European nationals from Germany and Austria, an instrument of totalitarian government policy. Among the more than two million refugees returned to the Soviet authorities by Western military officials and, later, by UNRRA and IRO, there were many thousands who were repatriated against their will, as indicated, for example, by the high suicide rate among them. This policy continued until mid-1948, when the wartime alliance, already past its prime, was ended by the coup in Czechoslovakia and the blockade of Berlin. For an estimate of the figures, see Eugene M. Kulischer, "Displaced Persons in the Modern World," *Annals of the American Academy of Political and Social Science*, 262 (March, 1949), 166–177.

lem which exists: the liberal solution of a genuine world economy with its necessarily multilateral character and all its other features," namely, free international trade, the gold standard, and a high degree of freedom of the movement of capital and labor.[6]

2. Mankind must work toward some sort of "supreme migration tribunal" to adjudicate differences among nations "in a spirit of most complete impartiality," following the "particularly successful" example of the Empire Settlement Act.[7]

This confrontation of two utopias offers nothing to those living in the real world. If the impossible were to happen and the West did turn back toward the laissez-faire nineteenth century, it would certainly not begin by removing regulations on migration. And however right in principle the pious declarations in favor of international organizations may be, their role in the future, as in the past, will be limited to the compilation of statistics (the ILO) and the execution of technical details (the IRO and its successor, the ICEM).

If the right of the nation-state to control migration is admitted to be inviolable, then the principal problem is the conflict of interest between emigration and immigration coun-

[6] William Röpke, "Barriers to Immigration," in Glenn Hoover, ed., *Twentieth Century Economic Thought* (New York: Philosophical Library, 1950), pp. 607–645.

[7] Albert Thomas (then director of the International Labor Office), "International Migration and Its Control," in Margaret Sanger, ed., *Proceedings of the World Population Conference Held at the Salle Centrale, Geneva, August 29th to September 3rd, 1927* (London: Arnold, 1927), pp. 256–265. Many epithets have been used to characterize the Empire Settlement Act, but seldom "successful." If we take as one example the British migration to Canada during one favorable decade, according to the best estimate, "while over 146,000 Britishers gave the agricultural West as their intended destination during the decade 1919–29, the actual British-born population of the Prairie Provinces increased in the same period by only 3,000." Lloyd G. Reynolds, *The British Immigrant: His Social and Economic Adjustment in Canada* (Toronto: Oxford University Press, 1935), p. 59. This ratio—3,000 in 146,000, or about 2 percent—measures the success of the Empire Settlement Act in this case, for its purpose was not merely to foster migration but to settle migrants on the land as agriculturists.

tries—the conflict that has set the tone of international conferences and bodies during the past several decades. In 1921, the usefulness of the International Migration Conference in Geneva was "greatly restricted" by this difference. Largely because of it, Australia and Argentina sent no delegates, the Polish representative did not attend the sessions, the United States representative attended but took no part in them, the South African delegate resigned on the ground that the conference was considering problems too much from the point of view of emigration countries.[8] Thirty years later, at the Brussels conference in 1951, some of the delegates from emigration countries hoped to set up a system by which international teams would screen prospective migrants and direct them to the most suitable country; but no single immigration country, even if represented on such teams, was willing to compromise its authority in this matter. The ICEM, or Intergovernmental Committee for European Migration, which was founded in the same year of 1951, has been plagued by the same kind of problems.[9]

Much of migration theory has been a continuation of this debate on another level. For example, Carr-Saunders believed that the rate of past population growth that he had calculated could be used as a normative criterion of current immigration rates. If the population of "new countries" is increasing by 2 percent per year, "there will be no substance in the charge that the owners occupy territory that they do not use; for they will be making all due speed toward full exploitation. But, if it [is] not, the charge will lie."[10] Forsyth's

[8] J. W. Gregory, *Human Migration & the Future: A Study of the Causes, Effects & Control of Emigration* (London: Seeley, Service, 1928), p. 165.

[9] In the words even of a propaganda booklet, although the Netherlands, a "classic case of overpopulation," strongly supports ICEM, "it runs its emigration program independently, except for occasional 'supplementary shipping' supplied by the Committee. . . . The Netherlands emigration program is considered by international experts to be the most efficiently organized in the world." Josephine Ripley, *Peoples on the Move* (Geneva: ICEM, 1955), pp. 15–17.

[10] A. W. Carr-Saunders, *World Population: Past Growth and Present Trends* (Oxford: Clarendon Press, 1936), pp. 174–176.

book, on the other hand, was in large part an overseas defense against this "common fallacy that space means opportunity."[11]

In 1945, when the Permanent Migration Committee of the ILO met in Montreal, it pronounced bilateral migration agreements, like the one that had just been made between the United States and Mexico, as "one of the most promising lines of further development." With such limited arrangements, the movement of persons did not depend on the prior growth of international accord but could reach the maximum number consistent with the policies of the two countries concerned. "One of [the Committee's] principal recommendations was that the International Labor Conference should be asked to draw up a 'model agreement' which would guide governments in negotiating bilateral agreements."[12]

## The Dutch-Canadian Case

The postwar migration from Holland to Canada is an example of such a bilateral arrangement. The movement between these two particular countries, moreover, illustrates current trends and practices better than would movements between various alternative pairs of countries:

First, the Dutch are generally regarded as among the most desirable of immigrants; and though the pressure to emigrate was greater in postwar Italy or Germany, for example, this larger potential has been partly negated by the greater reluctance of immigration countries to receive their nationals. On the other side, of all presently important immigration countries, Canada seems to have the best long-term chance of realizing its ambitious postwar developmental program, and thus of continuing its current rapid rate of population growth without serious disequilibrium. In the migration from the Netherlands to Canada, then, the limits of various types

[11] Forsyth, op. cit., p. 3.
[12] Carter Goodrich, "Possibilities and Limits of International Control of Migration," in Milbank Memorial Fund, Postwar Problems of Migration: Papers Presented at the Round Table on Population Problems, October 29–30, 1946 (New York, 1947), pp. 74–81.

are likely to be close to the minimum now attainable anywhere.

Second, the contention that government controls have
become decisive in migration can be tested best not in postwar emigration from Germany, for example, where government intervention might be ascribed in part to vestigial
Nazism; nor in migration within the British Empire, a hybrid
between international and internal migration that has always
been an object of official interest, but in unambiguously international migration between two countries free of any taint
of totalitarianism. Such is the Dutch-Canadian case.

The migration from the Netherlands to Canada, that is to
say, can be taken as an example of planned migration under
almost optimum conditions. This has been no case of cor-
ralling world opinion to bludgeon nations into admitting
their meager quota of refugees, nor one of freeing aspirant
emigrants from the mercantilist grasp of their native states.
The groups whose emigration Holland subsidizes are precisely
those that Canada is seeking as immigrants. Two friendly
countries, sharing a Western culture and a democratic tradition, could cooperate to solve together certain important but
limited problems, and then the flow of migrants would
develop of itself.

Or so it might have seemed. Actually, the elaborate migration programs of the two countries have together succeeded in moving a smaller number than Holland's situation
demands and, probably, than Canada's economy could profitably absorb. The reasons for this are to be found in the nature
of planned migration.

When the government regulation of migration has become
a decisive factor, a migratory movement can develop only
when there is a conjuncture of the interests of the two states
involved. The phrase "conjuncture of interests" denotes,
however, a condition less simple than it would appear. The
migration policy of each of the two countries may be viewed
as primarily either a means of furthering the national interest, selected in place of alternative means by some reasonably reliable criterion, or the resultant of divergent group
pressures exerted within the framework of a democracy.
The policies are ostensibly the first; actually they tend to be

the second. For the economic, demographic, and social effects of migration on each of the two countries concerned are exceedingly complex, and we know really very little about the whole process. The recurrent broad generalizations in migration theory have always had to be emended by a series of inelegant hedge clauses. The works of such men as Willcox, Hansen, and Isaac—a demographer, a historian, and an economist—have not been principally synthesis, but recourse to basic data,[13] cleansed of the bias with which most of the earlier works had presented them.

Migration, especially immigration, is a subject charged with emotion. Ideally, an administrator responsible for selecting those citizens to be encouraged to depart, or those aliens to be admitted into the national community, ought to refer to a set of coordinated facts, so that he could choose those persons best suited to the country's needs. Since such a body of migration theory hardly exists, policy decisions tend rather to be made in accordance with the irrational sentiments impinging on the administrator. Under such circumstances, however, he particularly needs the legitimation that social science can give whatever decision he does make; and there is thus a strong tendency to cloak the irrational sentiments in scientific phrases.

Immediately after the war, restrictive regulations were in force in both the Netherlands and Canada. Following more than six months of negotiations, a flexible system was worked out by which Canada agreed to accept progressively larger groups, first single agricultural workers only and, after two years of pressure from the Dutch, also families and "small businessmen," meaning principally craftsmen. The Canadian Immigration Office in The Hague gives their first Canadian interview to aspirant Dutch migrants, most of whom are

[13] Walter F. Willcox and Imre Ferenczi, eds., *International Migrations*, Vol. 1: *Statistics;* Vol. 2: *Interpretations* (New York: National Bureau of Economic Research, 1929 and 1931). Marcus Lee Hansen, *The Atlantic Migration, 1607–1860: A History of the Continuing Settlement of the United States* (Cambridge: Harvard University Press, 1940); *The Immigrant in American History* (Cambridge: Harvard University Press, 1940). Julius Isaac, *Economics of Migration* (London: Kegan Paul, Trench, Trubner, 1947).

referred to the office by the Dutch authorities. In view of the large number of applicants, it is not necessary to paint a settler's life in Canada as more attractive than it really is. On the contrary, the immigration officer sees it as his function to present a rounded picture, including especially all the difficulties and lacks, because immigrants who arrive with realistic expectations are much better able to adjust. Those who pass the first interview are given a 130-page book in Dutch, describing Canada and its social institutions, as well as I. A. Richards' *Basic English.* These applicants are processed by a staff of five Canadians plus varying numbers of Dutch assistants.

While such details of how the two bureaucracies process the migrants have a certain topical interest, it is of greater moment to ask why the whole machinery was set up. What is to be achieved by this doubly sponsored movement? What national purposes of the Netherlands and Canada are to be served, and how effectively?

### The Effect of Emigration on Holland's Population

From the point of view of the Netherlands, the purpose of the subsidized emigration is to give relief from the country's population pressure. This is the consequence fundamentally of Holland's highly efficient death control combined with a much less efficient birth control. The effect of the growing numbers was aggravated, moreover, by the economic effects of World War II—the loss of the Netherlands East Indies, now independent Indonesia; the devastation wreaked on Holland during the Nazi occupation and the subsequent liberation—and the rising demands on the straitened economy occasioned by the higher aspirations of the working class.

In a population projection by the Central Bureau of Statistics, it was assumed that emigration over the next three decades would be at the rate of 50,000 a year.[14] The choice of the figure 50,000 per year was based on the hopes of the Netherlands Emigration Foundation rather than on its

[14] Netherlands, Central Bureau of Statistics, *Berekeningen omtrent de toekomstige loop der Nederlandse bevolking* (The Hague, 1951), p. 56.

achievement to date: over the postwar period up to the time
the forecast was made, there had been a considerable net
*immigration.*[15] Nevertheless, since any such figure is more or
less arbitrary, 50,000 per year is perhaps as good a guess as
another. But the emigrants, had they remained, would have
had their children in the Netherlands; and thus, according
to this forecast, their departure would decrease the population each year by 50,000 plus a percentage of this figure
based on the probable future fertility. With emigration at this
rate, therefore, the total decline in the population over a
thirty-year period will not amount to $30 \times 50,000 = 1,500-000$,
but, based on hypotheses of minimum and maximum
fertility, between 1,842,700 and 2,000,500.

The notion that under all conditions agrarian population
pressure can be relieved through emigration is based on the
assumption that the whole relation between land and the
number of people who can live on it can be expressed in
the population-resources ratio. If the "optimum" population
density is so many persons per square mile and actual density
is greater than this, one need only effect the removal of the
indicated number of people. In terms of this formula, the
same adjustment could be achieved by increasing the amount
of land available to the people. But twice in Holland's recent
history such a change has, on the contrary, aggravated the
disequilibrium. When artificial fertilizers were introduced
at the end of the nineteenth century, the arable land was
much extended; and the significant increase in natality that
resulted began to build up to the current, much heavier
population pressure. Similarly, the new land created by
draining the Zuider Zee was divided up among landless
peasants who otherwise would have postponed their marriages, and thus also stimulated a rise in the birth rate.[16]

There is indeed an important difference between these

[15] This net immigration was based, it is true, on such specific
and temporary circumstances as the virtually forced emigration of
the Dutch who had remained in Indonesia, and the drastic cut in
emigrants admitted to Australia following a downward turn in the
business cycle. Yet with today's economic and political uncer-
tainties, these adverse conditions might have been expected to
give way to others.

[16] See above, pp. 184–185.

cases and emigration—the settlers on the new land add their progeny to Holland's population, whereas emigrants do not. With respect to emigration, the point is whether the departure of some persons from a densely populated area changes the rate of increase of the remaining population. Since emigration tends both to decrease and to increase natality, its net effect is difficult to determine. Emigrants from the Netherlands, though they include a somewhat larger than typical proportion of married couples and thus of children, are mostly young adults, like international migrants generally. In this respect, therefore, emigration tends to effect a more rapid aging of the population, with a consequent rise in the death rate and decline in the birth rate. On the other hand, since almost the whole of *social* pressure in the countryside is concentrated on maintaining its high fertility, if the opposed *economic* pressure is lessened, fertility may increase, or at least remain constant rather than continue its long-term decline. So far as the emigration program is successful in alleviating population pressure, the economic circumstances of those remaining in the Netherlands will be relatively better, and among some sectors of the population this relative improvement may well be accompanied by earlier marriages and larger families.

Where a traditionalist view toward childbearing prevails, as in much of rural Holland, the decisive element in fertility is the proportion married. The control of population growth through continence can be institutionalized: in nineteenth-century Holland, young men unable to buy or rent a farm of their own often never married but lived with their elder brothers as uncles to their children; and the postponement of marriage is still a very important means of birth control, particularly in the Catholic South. Such a social pattern, however, is never very stable, for it runs counter to the natural desires of every young person. Thus, whenever an improvement in the economic situation, like the extension of arable land, affords the opportunity for earlier marriage, some of the large potential natality is quickly realized and economic conditions soon deteriorate again. With Holland's improved welfare over the past century, of women aged 20 to 60 years, the percentage married rose steadily from almost

54 in 1849 to 70 in 1950. If the emigration program succeeds in reducing population pressure, it may lower the median age at marriage, and thus continue this trend.

How far the emigration to date has been from relieving Holland's population growth is shown in Figure 2, where migration per thousand population is compared with the natural increase. As can be seen, the high fertility and the low mortality have been basic; total population growth has fluctuated only slightly around the natural increase. On the assumption—which has no basis in the record to date—that the industrialization program will be able to absorb the existent rural surplus (even when this is augmented by the very large numbers born immediately after the war), net emigration will have to grow to four times its average over recent years to equal the natural increase and keep the population static.

FIGURE 2. RATES OF NET IMMIGRATION, NATURAL INCREASE, AND TOTAL POPULATION GROWTH, THE NETHERLANDS, 1929–54.

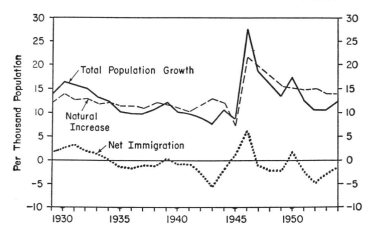

In any case, no one knows what portion of the subsidized emigration has been the consequence of the government's program and how many of these emigrants, on the contrary, were paid for doing something that they would otherwise have managed by themselves. An almost tangible migration sentiment has developed—in part, it is true, by the official encouragement given it, but in greater part out of the contrast between restricted opportunities and greater aspirations.

Holland's subsidized emigration is ineffective in its prime purpose of reducing the pressure of the rural population in the land. Indeed, one might well argue that the main reason the nation supports this program is that it seems to be a substitute for what is really needed—a publicly sponsored project to reduce fertility. Since, however, the emigration is being accompanied by measures designed to maintain Holland's family-building habits, it may be self-defeating. Present-day emigration, indeed the "slight palliative" that Malthus termed it, can be compared with a narcotic in medicine: its proper function is to relieve the social pain so that a more fundamental cure can be effected. If this basic alignment between population and resources is not made, however, emigration can aggravate the problem it is designed to solve. For when the narcotic wears off—when the uncertain and desultory migration opportunities in the present world peter out—the inevitable adjustment will be more difficult.

## Dutch Immigrants in Canadian Perspective

From its side, Canada subsidizes immigration in order to increase its population. In the debates over the immigration policy, its opponents have argued that the country cannot really support more people, or that those paid to enter will be lost to the United States through Canada's leaky southern border. In these fundamental respects, I believe the policy to be correct: as a concomitant of its postwar industrialization, Canada does require a larger population, and if the ambitious developmental program succeeds, Canada will be able to compete with the attractions of the United States economy. But combined with this over-all rationality is a screening process that is less well based. Like the United States, though by a different legal device, Canada excludes —either relatively or absolutely—most of the world's population from settling in the country. That at the same time it subsidizes Dutch immigrants is due, presumably, to a judgment that newcomers from this country would fit into the economy better than the average, and thus would assimilate more readily to the Canadian culture. What are the reasons for this judgment?

After those applicants who are unacceptable for such reasons as physical, mental, or moral health have been weeded out, Canada's main criterion for accepting immigrants is their occupation; and the occupational basis of Dutch migration to Canada is the primacy given to agriculturists. This policy, rather surprising in its present context, has been carried over from the railroad boom of a half-century ago, which is the closest analogue to Canada's present developmental program.

In 1896, the same year that a long depression ended, the Liberals were returned to national office. Clifford Sifton, the new minister of the interior, believed that the way to bring the country out of the doldrums was to populate the Prairie Provinces; and he undertook this task with great administrative verve, ably supplementing the efforts of the railroads to the same end. While the consequent rapid growth was accompanied by a good deal of waste, in over-all terms the program was a success. From 1901 to 1911, the land under wheat increased from 4 million to 11 million acres, the value of wheat exports from $6 million to $45 million. Over the same decade, the gross value of manufactured products jumped from $481 million to $1,165 million. The population of Canada increased by more than a third, and the Prairie Provinces changed overnight from an empty wilderness to thinly settled farmland.

A large part of Canada's economy, however, was based on its major crop, and during the 1930s every circumstance associated with prairie agriculture got steadily worse.[17] The dependence on a foreign market was calamitous: the price of wheat fell to a low of less than 40 cents a bushel (compared with the average during 1921–29 of 92 cents); and the yield was cut by drought, grasshoppers, frost, hail, rust, and weeds. The standard of living of the area, whether measured by family expenditures for food and clothing or by provincial or municipal budgets for social services, fell drastically during these years; and even after the rains came and the prices

[17] See G. E. Britnell, *The Wheat Economy* (Toronto: University of Toronto Press, 1939).

rose from their record lows, much of the damage of the depression decade remained. The very dry soil was particularly susceptible to wind erosion, and much good land had been reduced to marginal quality. A generation had had its physical and moral strength sapped by ten years of recurrent disaster.

In one respect, this catastrophic deterioration of prairie agriculture merely accelerated the long-term development of the Canadian economy. The trend toward its diversification, and thus toward urbanization, had been under way even during the height of Sifton's program to settle the Prairie Provinces. From that time the proportion of persons engaged in agriculture declined steadily, and since 1931 this decline has also been absolute. Not only will this trend not be reversed, but in rational terms it has not gone far enough.[18] For raising wheat in an area with a short growing season demands extensive rather than intensive agriculture. Most settlers began with farms smaller and less mechanized than the optimum; and if they were able to weather the first difficult years, they increased their holdings and bought more farm machinery. Every technical improvement, whether of transportation or of machinery, reinforced this trend; within limits, it continued apart from economic conditions, because a good price for wheat made it more possible to buy additional land, while a poor price made it more necessary to cut unit costs.

In Sifton's day, when the purpose of immigration was to develop the West, his emphasis on agriculturists was to the point. The policy set during this period was maintained, however, even after the economic conditions on which it had been based changed radically. The reason for this is not that a pattern set in the past has been followed blindly; it is followed in response to the pressures in present-day Canada.

[18] "The average size of prairie farms still [in 1949] needs to be boosted before the fullest possible advantage can be taken of the economies of industrialized farming techniques. Consequently the population absorptive capacity of the cereal-growing lands of the Dominion is unlikely to be sizable in the near future." George H. T. Kimble, "The Geographical Context," in McMaster University, "Abstracts of Papers Discussed at an Invitation Symposium on Population Growth and Immigration into Canada," Hamilton, 1949, pp. 6–7, mimeographed.

Farm organizations are powerful enough to get price subsidies and other important concessions from the Dominion government; but unlike urban trade unions and professional societies, they do not ordinarily feel that their special interests are threatened by an increase in the number of persons in their particular sector of the economy. The trade unions and other urban groups, on the other hand, exert a negative pressure that encourages agricultural immigration, and this is reinforced by the positive influence of the railroads, which still want to increase the density of settlement along their transcontinental lines.

In the early 1930s, all immigration was cut off except that of close relatives of Canadian residents, and British subjects or American citizens with enough capital to establish themselves—on farms. The restriction was unnecessary in any case, for no one immigrates during a severe depression;[19] but the specific limitation is nevertheless a significant indication of official attitudes. And except for war brides, who constituted a large majority of Dutch immigrants in 1946 and an appreciable percentage in 1947, between two-thirds and four-fifths of the postwar Dutch migrants have been agriculturists and their families.

Most of these immigrant farmers have been remarkably successful, but their success is not the anomaly it might seem to be in view of agriculture's relative decline in the Canadian economy. Even though "the so-called era of agricultural expansion has virtually come to an end . . . [and] Canada's future population expansion will be primarily a phase of urban development,"[20] one specific type of expansion in agriculture is still possible—small, intensively farmed units adjacent to the growing cities. Dutch agriculturists, skilled in dairying and truck farming, are hardly better than urban

[19] Immigration fell to a few thousand a year, and net immigration to virtually nil—lower than at any time for a century. Net inmigration to the Prairie Provinces, which had amounted to 41,000 during 1921–31, changed during the following decade to a net out-migration of some 250,000 persons, or almost four-fifths of the natural increase.

[20] W. M. Drummond, "The Canadian Agricultural Economy," *Journal of Farm Economics,* 33:4, Part 2 (November, 1951), 636–648.

dwellers at growing wheat; but the painstaking care of the typical Dutch farmer, which is an actual handicap in extensive agriculture with a short growing season, pays dividends on a vegetable plot.

So long as the link between agriculture and immigration was held to be axiomatic, the long-term decline in agriculture was used—and, within this framework, correctly—as an argument against admitting more persons to the country. Now the link is broken, yet immigrants are still selected for their skill in agriculture. The economic success of Dutch immigration, it must be emphasized, has nothing to do with the rationale on which it was based: the best laid plans of governments and men sometimes go right. The Dutch work on the land but they are not traditional Canadian farmers: they have settled principally in Ontario, rather than in the "empty spaces" of the Prairie Provinces; they are growing not grain but vegetables; they are a part not of the rural development but, in a special sense, of the urbanization of the country. And if the policy was "successful" by accident, it was nevertheless irrelevant; for if the Dutch had been admitted without the special screening program, they would have chosen the occupation that came closest both to their background in Holland and to Canada's need—they would have become dairymen and truck farmers.

The second reason that immigration of the Dutch is fostered is that they are Nordic rather than Latin or Slav. To attempt to demonstrate that this criterion is irrational is like beating a dead unicorn; for in scientific circles racism no longer has any standing even as a myth. In order to avoid this thankless task, it must be assumed that the rationalization is the reason —that the preference given Nordics is based on their readier acculturation into Canadian society. If the data were available, it would be interesting to test this assumption with respect to the small group of Dutch-Canadians during the past several generations. However, the fact that most statistics are broken down by "racial origin" makes this impossible; for this mode of classification, somewhat dubious at best, is utterly useless with respect to the Dutch in particular.

Before 1945, most persons classified as of Dutch "racial origin" in Canadian statistics were Mennonites. This religious

sect is named after Menno Simons, a sixteenth-century itiner-
ant preacher who left his native Holland with a price on his
head and led a group of his followers to Prussia. Two centuries later, when their pacifist tenets displeased Frederick
the Great, they trekked to southern Russia, where they lived
as a coherent group for another century. In the 1870s, after
the government had attempted to nationalize the various
German-speaking groups in Russia, the more orthodox wing
of the Mennonites migrated to the United States; and of
these, the most rigid went on to western Canada. The core
of the Mennonites in Canada, therefore, constituted the
twice-filtered orthodox wing of a narrow sect.[21] During the
interwar period, aided by a subsidy from the steamship and
railroad companies, about 20,000 more Mennonites from
Russia settled on Canadian Pacific Railway land in the Prairie
Provinces.

Mennonites conduct their church services in German, and
in everyday discourse they use Plattdeutsch. Their culture,
to the extent that it is nationally determined rather than
specific to the group, is German, with an admixture of
Russian borrowings but hardly a hint of Dutch remnants.
Through the 1911 census, most Mennonites in Canada were
listed as of German "racial origin." During World War I,
however, anti-German feeling ran high: a law prohibited the
teaching of the German language in either public or private
schools, and at one time a half-dozen Mennonite preachers
were in the Winnipeg jail for ignoring it. As a result of this
persecution, a large number of Mennonites reported themselves in the 1921 census as of Dutch "racial origin." From
1911 to 1921, thus, though the total Dutch immigration
amounted to only 6,134, the number of "Dutch" in the
country increased by more than ten times this figure.[22] The
rest of the "Germans" who disappeared became "Russians,"
or actually emigrated to Mexico. This shift in "racial origin"
did not, of course, go unnoticed, but the same kind of data on

[21] C. A. Dawson, *Group Settlement: Ethnic Communities in
Western Canada* (Canadian Frontiers of Settlement, Vol. 7;
Toronto: Macmillan, 1936), pp. 95–171.
[22] Canada, Dominion Bureau of Statistics, *Sixth Census of
Canada, 1921*, Vol. 1 (Ottawa, 1924), p. 354.

the Canadians of Dutch and German "racial origin" continued to be collated and analyzed.[23]

If the presumed readier assimilability of Dutch immigrants cannot be proved from prewar data, the actual characteristics of postwar migrants make the thesis unlikely. A large percentage are members of narrow sects that abjure unnecessary contacts with profane society, whether Dutch or Canadian; and most institutions ostensibly designed to assist specifically the Dutch to acculturate, since they are church-connected, also attempt to maintain the rigid differentiation. It would seem that Canada's desire to facilitate the immigration of assimilable persons has been frustrated, because it is implemented in terms of past economic conditions and invalid anthropological theories.

## Summary

The administrative controls set up in both countries ostensibly to facilitate Dutch-Canadian migration have been established more in response to irrational pressures than as a rational means of solving a social problem. In Holland, the need to reduce the rate of population growth could be met most efficiently by instituting a system of birth control as effective as the excellent death control. Since such a solution is ruled out as impermissible, an emigration program has been set up as a supposed partial substitute, and very often the past success and future potential of this program have been exaggerated in an effort to avoid facing the full problem. In Canada, the immigration program is related to the need for more people, but it would be difficult to justify on a rational basis the size of the movement or some of the criteria of selection. The migration between the two countries, the

[23] For example, the Dominion Bureau of Statistics volume on the *Origin, Birthplace, Nationality and Language of the Canadian People*, published in 1929, included a breakdown based on these data; see pp. 36–37, 105–106. A later volume continued to use the same statistics showing, for example, a map of those of "Dutch racial origin" concentrated in the Mennonite settlements: William Burton Hurd and T. W. Grindley, *Agriculture, Climate and Population of the Prairie Provinces of Canada* (Canada, Dominion Bureau of Statistics, Ottawa, 1931), p. 92.

consequence of two ponderous and expensive systems of control, would be larger and otherwise more efficient if some of these controls were removed. If this is so, however, it is less because of any specific conditions in Holland and Canada than because we know little of the whole process of migration.

The effects of migration on the two countries are extraordinarily complex. Migrants have economic roles as workers and consumers (and sometimes as investors), as well as demographic roles as actual or potential parents; and present economic theory cannot deal with the range of possible combinations. One cannot set in advance the economically optimum emigration from or immigration to a real country; and it is questionable even whether this optimum can be approached by adjusting immigration periodically to the unemployment rate or some other reliable index. But in any case migration is set largely by noneconomic factors. It needs no special emphasis that Canada's immigration policy derives in part from racist sentiments, for the virtual exclusion of Asians and the preference given to Nordics is avowedly based on the nation-state's right to express its prejudices in such distinctions. The point is rather that the immigration policy as a whole has little or no valid science to guide it, and that that little is often ignored. During the depression, when in terms of Keynesian theory immigration might possibly have benefited the country, the bars were raised against— no one. Today, when immigrants would come in increasing numbers of their own accord, an expensive program elaborately selects out agriculturists for a country undergoing rapid industrialization—agriculturists who would have come anyhow if given the right. And whenever this system runs into snags, a more comprehensive plan along the same lines is called for.

Every age has its "heavenly city." That of the eighteenth century was Reason; that of the nineteenth, Science; that of the twentieth, Planning. For planning to be rational and scientific, however, the social process being planned must be sufficiently well understood so that the probable effects of changes in policy can be gauged—planning must be the nexus between rational ends and rational means. That is, if "planning" is to be more than a general fetish to answer all specific difficulties, then it must mean the intelligent and systematic control of human action in accordance with the known consequences of such action. Planned migration, on the contrary, has ordinarily meant the institutionalization of irrational sentiments behind a façade of scientific terminology.

# ON THE CONCEPT OF
# URBANIZATION PLANNING

One need have only a casual acquaintance with the twentieth-century world to know that more and more of its social processes are, in one sense or another, planned. Five-year plans, once restricted to the Soviet Union, have now spread not only to other Communist states but to such diverse countries as, for example, India and Brazil. In the United States, which is featured in Communist propaganda as the last capitalist redoubt, the whole social-economic structure was altered by the government's response to the depression of the 1930s and to World War II. As part of this trend policymakers have become increasingly concerned with a congeries of social problems concerning cities. This effort, as yet so indefinite it does not even have a name, is here called "urbanization planning."

Urbanization planning constitutes all over-all schemes of whatever sort relating to the urban sector of a nation's population, especially policies of national governments but also those of regional bodies or international agencies. Cities have been built as part of industrialization programs, as grandiose capitals, as sites of this or that government function. Urban populations have been moved to areas less subject to military attack. Some of those living in metropolitan areas have been dispersed to satellite towns. Efforts have been made to inhibit urban growth—for example, by fostering rural industry. While such measures have varied, of course, between democratic and totalitarian states and between developed and underdeveloped economies, policies of these types have been proposed or put into effect all over the world.

Urbanization planning is both different from city planning and in some ways derivative from it. Until recently city planners have typically tried to cope with each urban aggregate as an isolated unit. To the degree that they can, they control the physical environment of a particular city, both by eliminating such hazards to health and happiness as slums or traffic congestion and by adjusting future growth to a master plan. This control is established and maintained, moreover, mainly through the city's own legal system—through zoning laws, ordinances regulating transportation facilities, laws to "renew" blighted areas or to create parks and civic centers. However, since the city is in fact an integral part of a larger unit, these aims generally cannot be wholly realized within the municipal framework. It is often not possible, thus, to plan facilities effectively if no account is taken of in-migrants and commuters, or to lay out a suitable street plan without considering how it is to be connected with the intercity roads, or to provide even such basic needs as water except by relating the city to its region, or to find the tax money for improvements without establishing a minimum cooperation among the dozen independent municipalities that may be affected. In many cases, what is called regional planning is no more than old-style city planning with some attention given to such programs of integration. But attempts to deal with them have induced some of the men in the profession to look over the city wall and think more about their relation to the larger society.

In this extension of their traditional function, city planners have sometimes encountered planners of the national economy, who until recently also often neglected the intermediate area of urbanization. Of the three main factors in production —capital, labor, and land—the first two are invariably included in national plans. The focus of the planners' work is always on how scarce capital shall be allocated among alternative investment possibilities; and a good deal of attention is given, at the very least in propaganda, to improving the people's homes, health, education, and welfare generally. But the third factor is often neglected. "In the economic development plans of such countries as Indonesia, the Philippines, India, Mexico, and Puerto Rico, almost no consideration is given to where development should occur."[1] This omission

[1] Charles Haar, Benjamin Higgins, and Lloyd Rodwin, "Economic and Physical Planning: Coordination in Developing Areas,"

is related, obviously, to the background of the planners. Location theory is not a highly developed field in economics, and undoubtedly most practicing economists know little more than its elements. The other professionals involved in national planning—administrators, agronomists, social-welfare workers, and so on—by and large know even less of the determinants of urbanization and the criteria by which good policy might be judged. But they are becoming more aware that the neglect of such factors can greatly affect the attainment of other social and economic goals.

From two sides, thus, the attention of policy-makers has been converging on urbanization planning. Sometimes, as in efforts of a national government to alleviate urban housing shortages, the same objectives are sought as in city planning, but in such cases much more is usually changed than the sponsoring agency. And national governments have also set urban policies that transgress entirely the prior scope of either economic or city planning. Implicit in urbanization planning, though not necessarily consciously thought out or precisely stated, are norms about what proportion of the population should live in towns, the ideal size of cities, the optimum ratio of primate to other cities, how industrialization and urbanization should be related, and so on. Sometimes, however, the only value specified is the approbation of "planning" itself. Indeed, the seeming omnipresence of this kind of social regulation is to some extent spurious, the consequence of the fact that quite different processes and philosophies have been identified with an omnibus term.

## On the Meaning of Planning

Before continuing to expound the concept of urbanization planning, thus, it would be well to clarify the broader term. Planning is of at least three types, which can conveniently be identified as "ideological," "deductive," and "inductive." As planning of any type is ordinarily understood, it connotes the injection of rationality into a particular area of human

*News Sheet of the International Federation for Housing and Planning*, 52 (June, 1959), 15–19.

life, and in this sense it may be said to be scientific. A scientific proposition is one, first of all, that can be proved fallacious by comparing it with the empirical world, and a scientist constantly shuttles between his hypothesis and his data, between the model he constructs and the pattern he observes. The analogous process, evaluation, is usually a less routine characteristic of social planning, and it differs somewhat among the three types.

With respect to utopian or *ideological* plans, first of all, evaluation has little or no meaning. If the purpose of the plan is one or another paraphrase of David Riesman's "substantial gains in human happiness,"[2] or Erich Fromm's "self-realization for the masses of the people,"[3] it will never be possible to determine in any precise sense whether this has been achieved. A utopian goal keeps receding as we approach it, and it cannot be used to measure progress along the road toward it. Sometimes it is asserted that a consciously unrealistic social purpose is useful as a goal. Only "overbold" plans, in Lewis Mumford's words, will "awaken the popular imagination: such success as totalitarian states have shown in their collective planning has perhaps been due to their willingness to cleave at a blow the Gordian knot of historic resistances."[4] This supposed proximate value of a utopia has never been more than supposed; how could anyone test the proposition that a visionary purpose is an aid in achieving realistic goals? Frequently, perhaps even usually, the utopia is less an incentive than an alternative to social reform. For in the eyes of the true utopian, anything that can be achieved is not worth attempting; every revolutionary party, for instance, has always devoted much effort to fighting reformists.

The evaluation of ideological plans, then, is ruled out as impossible or meaningless, and one must remember that many nonideological plans contain a utopian element.

Most persons, perhaps, are likely to understand planning

[2] David Riesman, *Individualism Reconsidered, and Other Essays* (Glencoe, Ill.: Free Press, 1954), p. 73.

[3] Erich Fromm, *Escape from Freedom* (New York: Rinehart, 1941), p. 272.

[4] Lewis Mumford, *The Culture of Cities* (New York: Harcourt, Brace, 1938), p. 380.

in the *deductive* sense, following what is still the only dictionary definition. The planner draws up a blueprint on a flat surface (or, in Latin, *planum*); and the design is completed before the first steps are taken toward its realization. In this case, one might think, evaluation is easy, almost automatic. But consider a specific example—say, the deconcentration of Britain's metropolitan population. The assignment of the Barlow Commission was—

> . . . to inquire into the causes which have influenced the present geographical distribution of the industrial population of Great Britain and the probable direction of any change in that distribution in the future; to consider what social, economic or strategical disadvantages arise from the concentration of industries or the industrial population in large towns or in particular areas of the country; and to report what remedial measures, if any, should be taken in the national interest.[5]

The Commission inquired, considered, and recommended; and the policy was a success in the minimal sense that the New Towns exist. But have "the social, economic, or strategical disadvantages" of industrial concentration been mitigated? In particular, has London stopped growing, or has it even grown less than it would have without the plan? To answer such a question fully would require another analysis on the same scale as the one the Commission used to support its recommendations. But "all available evidence suggests that the drawbacks to the indefinite growth of the conurbations, and particularly of London, are in fact much greater" than before the Commission made its study.[6]

Or take another example: Several years ago the Venezuelan government housing agency supervised the construction of apartments in Caracas to accommodate an estimated 180,000 persons. In mechanical terms the project was successfully completed: almost a hundred 15-story buildings were erected

---

[5] Quoted in Lloyd Rodwin, *The British New Towns Policy: Problems and Implications* (Cambridge: Harvard University Press, 1956), p. 17.

[6] Peter Self, *Cities in Flood: The Problems of Urban Growth* (London: Faber and Faber, 1957), p. 27.

at a total cost of some $200 million. But 4,000 families invaded the apartments and lived there illegally, while others squatted in the community facilities or in shacks they built on the project site; unpaid rents totaled $5 million; losses in damage to property amounted to $500,000 monthly; delinquency and crime rose appreciably; tenant associations, headed by agitators, impeded control measures and built up a potentially explosive atmosphere. An international interprofessional team, called in to study the situation, recommended that "the government should suspend all construction of superblocks until there exists a defined housing policy related to the economic and social development of the country and within a process of national planning and coordination. It was found that the massive construction programs in Caracas had served to attract heavy migration to the city from rural areas and, therefore, severely intensified the housing problem in the capital."[7]

The two examples illustrate a recurrent type of unsuccessful social reform. A vigorous, concentrated attack on the most visible of social ills may cope only with symptoms and in some cases actually aggravates the disease. When an architect's blueprints are transformed into a building, one can say with full justice that his plan has been realized. But to transfer this kind of simplistic evaluation to more complex matters, as architects who have become city planners typically do, is less warranted. If the master plan of a city has been realized in the physical sense, the most important questions are still to be answered: have slums disappeared; have neighborhoods been reinforced, or shattered; has traffic congestion been mitigated, or made worse? And in the still more complex world of national urban policies, it is still more difficult to state precisely what one means by evaluation.

The third type, *inductive planning,* is defined as the continual coordination of public policies in several overlapping economic and social areas. "Coordination leads to planning or, rather, it *is* planning as this term has come to be understood in the Western world." Planning in this sense is "prag-

[7] Eric Carlson, "High-Rise Management," *Journal of Housing,* 16:9 (October, 1959), 311–314.

matic and piecemeal and never comprehensive and complete"; plans usually constitute "compromise solutions of pressing political issues."[8] What is here identified as "planning," in short, is very close to "muddling through," or the opposite of traditional planning. Evaluation of inductive plans is obviously extremely difficult, since the measuring stick and the entity to be measured constantly interact. Yet apart from the simplest cases virtually all real (that is, more than ideological) plans are at least partly inductive, for in the complex social world one cannot foresee every important contingency. If the "plan" is less a blueprint than a guideline, "success" has to be redefined each time it is measured.

Inductive urbanization planning can be exemplified by the complex of federal housing legislation in the United States. In some cases, it is true, whatever effect these laws had on the nation's cities was twice removed from their main purpose: the first New Deal housing acts were intended first of all to prime the pump of the lagging economy, only secondarily to alleviate housing shortages, and hardly at all to restructure metropolitan areas. The vast, complicated, in part contradictory, totality of housing legislation, established over several changes of administration, nevertheless shows a certain consistency. Its two main goals were to help heads of families purchase a new home of their own, and to raze city slums and replace them with more healthful public housing. While these two types of programs were obviously applied to different social classes, they both helped reinforce the trend already under way toward a particular type of decentralization. Low-rent public apartments have generally been available only to families with incomes no greater than a stipulated maximum, so that not only the projects themselves but the whole neighborhoods that they dominate have in fact become restricted to lower-class residents. At the same time, families

[8] Gunnar Myrdal, *Beyond the Welfare State* (New Haven: Yale University Press, 1960), pp. 23, 63. For similar statements, see Robert A. Dahl and Charles E. Lindblom, *Politics, Economics, and Welfare* (New York: Harper, 1953), pp. 38–39; Melvin M. Webber, "The Prospects for Policies Planning," in Leonard J. Duhl, ed., *The Urban Condition: People and Policy in the Metropolis* (New York: Basic Books, 1963), pp. 319–330.

of the middle and lower-middle classes were helped to buy a one-family house, and this low-density construction, which had to be on the periphery of the city, contributed greatly to what has since come to be called "scatteration" or "urban sprawl."

> A generation ago most experts saw great crowded cities as a destructive anachronism, to be drastically altered by some form of decentralization. But suburban sprawl is clearly no solution, and the big centers have survived despite decay and mounting congestion. Now the new generation of experts and critics tends to glorify the economic and cultural virtues of the Great City, scorning decentralization in any form.[9]

It would be an exaggeration, but one with more than a germ of truth, to say that the plan of one generation has become the social problem of the next. To evaluate this inductive "plan," one must determine whether the federal government's participation in this shift contributed more to the plan or to the subsequent problem.

### "Cities Are Abnormal"

The industrial, urban, democratic institutions of modern Western society have brought about a general welfare exceeding the dreams of previous ages. Today's average American lives not only better than the average contemporary of Louis XIV but in many respects better than the Sun King's own courtiers. His life is about twice as long, for his food is more varied and healthful and his doctors have much better control over diseases. Although much less ornate and expensive, the middle-class American's home is more comfortable, more livable, than the Versailles palace, whose living quarters were built after the manner of railroad flats. Universal literacy, the utopian panacea of the eighteenth century and after that the prime demand of every radical democrat, is a commonplace throughout the West.

[9] Catherine Bauer Wurster, "Framework for an Urban Society," in American Assembly, *Goals for Americans* (New York: Prentice-Hall, 1960).

During the nineteenth century, while the benefits of urban industrialism were still a novelty, those enjoying them—apart from a small minority of highly vocal intellectuals—approved the system that produced them. Today, the usual attitude toward modern Western civilization is curiously ambivalent. Its industrial productivity has stimulated every nonindustrial country to emulate it or even—as the Communists put it—to overtake and surpass Europe and its overseas extensions. The progress that inhabitants of an earlier age saw as miraculous, almost as supernatural in the literal sense, has thus gained greatly in momentum, but at the same time it has lost its power to awe. One now takes this miracle as given (in the West), or one demands that it be repeated in double-quick time (elsewhere in the world), while at the same time often maintaining that the urban-industrial civilization that produced it is essentially evil.

One cannot meaningfully analyze urbanization plans without full attention to the anti-urban bias often embedded in them. For the effect of plans, as we have already suggested, is never limited to the goals specified in them. A decision on the site of a government-subsidized industrial town, for example, might be made ostensibly in terms of the relative availability of labor, raw materials, markets, and the like—in short, in terms of relative costs. No one can be absolutely sure, however, which combination of such rational alternatives will result in maximizing productivity; and if certainty were possible, nonrational factors would nevertheless be relevant. The choice among alternative policies, that is to say, is typically made in part on the basis of criteria never included in the formal statement of purposes, and perhaps not even consciously formulated in the policy-makers' minds. Similarly, the coordination of social reforms, what we have termed inductive planning, is not (as it is often made to sound) merely neutral administration. In fact, the schedule of priorities set among alternative procedures pushes the society in a certain direction. The mood or frame of mind or ideology—call it what you will—that underlies specific planning objectives is no less important a determinant of the outcome because it is difficult to specify and analyze.

In the view of many of those involved in urbanization

planning, human virtues flourish in the countryside and die off in cities, especially large ones. "Cities are abnormal."[10] The metropolis "subordinates life to organized destruction, and it must therefore regiment, limit, and constrict every exhibition of real life and culture."[11] While these two quotations were chosen for their dramatic irresponsibility, the point of view expressed in them is not confined to a few mavericks. On the contrary, much of city planning has in fact been anti-city planning. Much of the planning of urbanization has consisted of efforts to reduce or eliminate the society's urban characteristics. A few influential figures, such as Gandhi, dislike cities so much that they prefer to forgo the admitted benefits of urban civilization. A very few others see positive virtues in the city's heterogeneity, its bustle and congestion, its excitation of the senses. But the usual stance, the usual over-all goal of urbanization planning, is to secure urban benefits with the minimum urbanization.

The importance of such sentiments can be indicated in many ways—by quoting such influential pioneers of city planning as Ebenezer Howard or such spokesmen for the profession as Lewis Mumford, by noting the pro-rural bias in American farm legislation, in the Indian five-year plans, in postwar Dutch industrialization, and so on. But how did these values arise? What is common in these various types of anti-urban sentiment other than the characteristic that defines them? To answer these questions adequately would take a whole book, and no more than a few suggestions of its possible content can be given here.

One theme in such a volume might be the changes in the meaning of key words used to sum up the social effects of urbanization. At one time, when intellectual and artistic development was typically perceived as a product of the cities in which it flourished, this association was reflected in the connotations of *urban* and *urbane, civil* and *civic, rustic* and

[10] Elmer T. Peterson, ed., *Cities Are Abnormal* (Norman: University of Oklahoma Press, 1946). While this volume of essays was intended as popular polemics, it also included serious contributions by such persons as Paul B. Sears and Warren S. Thompson.

[11] Mumford, *op. cit.,* p. 278.

*boorish*, and so on. The word *civilization* was a new addition to this list; as late as the 1760s Dr. Johnson refused to include it in his dictionary, preferring the older word *civility* for their common meaning.[12] In all languages in which it occurred, the meaning of *culture* was then restricted primarily to "the tending of natural growth," the meaning it still retains in such English words as *agriculture* or *horticulture*. Under the guidance of Samuel Taylor Coleridge, Matthew Arnold, and other English and German Romantics, *culture* not only came to designate "a whole way of life—material, intellectual, and spiritual," but was reified as an abstraction, an absolute.[13] For the Romantics, *civilization* and *culture* were not only separate but antithetic—*civilization*, the rational, technical, soul-destroying, urban; versus *culture*, the artistic, poetic, organic, natural, rural. Thus, William Morris, for instance: "Civilization is passing like a blight, daily growing heavier and more poisonous, over the face of the country."[14] This antithesis between *civilization* and *culture* is still a recurrent prop to literary criticism, sometimes with the two terms as defined by the Romantics, or more often in recent decades with the roles maintained but the terms reversed, and the heroine Civilization being ravished by Mass Culture. When they wrote their poems and novels and even more their "lay sermons," as Coleridge termed his heuristic essays, literary intellectuals were acting as conscious social critics; their argumentation is at the surface, visible to every reader. But after they helped fashion new meanings for such words as *culture* and *civilization* (as well as *organic* and *natural*),[15] their point of view passed into the language, which in others' mouths then expressed it with seeming neutrality.

This criticism-by-redefinition is also a common practice in

[12] E. de Dampierre, "Note sur 'culture' et 'civilisation,' " *Comparative Studies in Society and History*, 3:3 (April, 1961), 328–340.
[13] Raymond Williams, *Culture and Society, 1780–1950* (Garden City, N.Y.: Doubleday-Anchor, 1960), pp. xiv–xvi.
[14] Quoted in Bernard N. Schilling, *Human Dignity and the Great Victorians* (New York: Columbia University Press, 1946), p. 176.
[15] For a fascinating and learned discussion, see C. S. Lewis, *Studies in Words* (Cambridge: University Press, 1960), Chap. 2.

social disciplines, whose professional canons generally inhibit direct value judgments. Indeed, changes in the meanings of some of these same words accompanied the development of the social theory of urbanization. To the extent that this exists, it consists largely of variations on the conceptual opposition between Gemeinschaft and Gesellschaft, which is essentially an elaboration of that between culture and civilization. In Tönnies' view, "The entire culture has been transformed into a civilization of state and Gesellschaft, and this transformation means the doom of culture itself if none of its scattered seeds remain alive and bring forth the essence and idea of Gemeinschaft, thus secretly fostering a new culture amidst the decaying one."[16] In human ecology, the city is seen as an "organism," whose self-corrective tendencies correct all social ills;[17] and urban society is analyzed by dividing it into "natural" areas. But if in theory the ecologists of the Chicago school deprecated social policy, they nevertheless concentrated on the "social problems" that, to others, call for corrective measures. The subjects of the principal works—slums, crime and delinquency, prostitution and family disorganization, the hobo and the taxi-dancer, mental illness, and so on—all exemplified "social disorganization"; and the analytical framework has been continued in the usual course on Social Problems, which on American campuses is perhaps the most popular introduction to social studies.

A "problem" is defined as something currently troubling American society—thus, not famine but agricultural surpluses and overeating, not infant mortality but aging, not rural isolation but traffic problems, not frontier lawlessness but maladministration of the law, not illiteracy but "mass culture." The student, who ordinarily is given no basis for comparison, is likely to conclude from such an ahistoric concern with current problems that there must have been a general deterioration accompanying urbanization. Elderly persons

[16] Ferdinand Tönnies, *Fundamental Concepts of Sociology* (New York: American Book Co., 1940), p. 270.

[17] For a trenchant criticism of this theory of homeostasis, see H. Warren Dunham, "The City: A Problem in Equilibrium and Control," in Dunham, ed., *The City in Mid-Century* (Detroit: Wayne State University Press, 1957).

who have themselves lived through the transformation may reinforce this notion by reminiscing about the "good old days" of their youth. Even such a man as Henry Ford, who profited greatly from the world he helped create with the mass production of the first cheap automobile, used some of the millions he amassed to set up museums of folk art, monuments to the pre-Ford age. "The ultimate solution," he asserted, "will be the abolition of the City, its abandonment as a blunder."[18]

When a comparison *is* made between rural and urban societies, it is often forgotten that with urbanization nothing changes so fast as the various types of measuring rods by which its effects are gauged. Statistics on social deficiencies of all types are generally better in cities than in rural areas, so that the figures taken at face value usually substantiate the contrast indicated in the Gemeinschaft-Gesellschaft typology. But contrary to what the statistics say, "there is probably less crime in the United States than existed a hundred or fifty, or even twenty-five years ago."[19] Or, as another example, it is often stated that the hectic life of an increasingly urban population has resulted in a sharp rise in mental illness, and many data can be cited to support this impression. But if members of a Gemeinschaft like the Hutterite community are specially examined, one finds a high incidence of undiagnosed, unrecorded, and of course untreated mental illness of various kinds.[20] And according to the only analysis of data over a period long enough really to measure the effects of urbanization, for ages under 50 the rate of age-specific first admissions to mental institutions in the United States is the same today as it was a century ago.[21] That is to say, the only rise in mental disorders resulting from the almost complete dissemination of urban influences through American society is that due to the greater average length of life and the higher proportion of old people.

[18] Cited in Arthur B. Gallion, *The Urban Pattern: City Planning and Design* (New York: Van Nostrand, 1950), p. 185.

[19] Daniel Bell, *The End of Ideology* (Glencoe, Ill.: Free Press, 1960), Chap. 8.

[20] Joseph W. Eaton and Robert J. Weil, *Culture and Mental Disorders* (Glencoe, Ill.: Free Press, 1955).

[21] Herbert Goldhamer and Andrew W. Marshall, *Psychosis and Civilization* (Glencoe, Ill.: Free Press, 1953).

There is an analogue to this recurrent statistical paradox even when no numerical data exist, for the mere congregation of social deficiencies in the city may be enough to convince the usual analyst that they are characteristic of the urban setting. The Negro slums in Chicago, the squatter settlements around Baghdad, the people sleeping on the streets of Calcutta, are often described as specifically urban problems. The fact that the urban poor are all in a few places, where they are overwhelmingly apparent to every casual observer, suggests a contrast with a relatively well-to-do countryside. However, the fact that in-migration continues from rural areas should be enough to suggest that this contrast is false, that life in the village is at a still lower level. To appreciate this requires an effort of the imagination, however, for in any single village the amount of destitution obviously is small. But one must remember that in India, for instance, there are half a million such small pockets of human misery, so that the total number of rural poor is half a million times the hundred or so one observes in any one village.

In the transformation of society that urbanization connotes, some social classes lose some of their power and wealth, and the most vehement opponents of the city, consequently, have generally been the rural upper class and those who benefited from their rule. In their eyes the city is mainly a generator of dangerous mobs. In the classic case of the French Revolution, the opposition between Paris and the Vendée is well known, and many subsequent examples seem to validate the generalization that revolutions are made by urban intellectuals leading the urban proletariat. But this conservative fear of the city, while it fits some of the facts, is far too simple. It is certainly true that the city generates social change, and that "pre-urban" and "urban" are apt designations of different types of society. But it is also increasingly true that urban influences do not stop at the city wall and that in the village, by reason of the very contrast with the still continuing pre-urban life, they can be explosive. These urban influences can be of various kinds. The recent extraordinarily effective measures of death control, when combined with village family-building patterns, result in a growth of population that bursts the traditional society. Such rationalist institutions as the plantation disrupt old-style village life no less than a factory. Widely disseminated mass media excite high levels of aspirations that only an urban-industrial society can satisfy.

## Summary

Urbanization planning is defined as attempts by national states or similar entities to control the urban-rural ratio; the location, size, function, and other characteristics of cities; the relation of the large cities to others; and similar broad features of a nation's urban population. Many attempts have been made all over the world to control such variables, for the goals of both local city planning and national economic plans have led into this intermediate area.

The meaning of "planning," which varies with almost every writer on the subject, can be clarified by distinguishing three types. In ideological planning the emphasis is on some utopian goal—one or another version of the good society, or sometimes planning itself. In a deductive plan, a broad over-all scheme is worked out completely before any attempt is made to realize it. Inductive planning, on the contrary, constitutes the coordination of variegated efforts at social reform in a number of overlapping areas. Many plans combine all three types, though in different proportions; in particular, the ideological element is seldom completely absent.

Evaluation, or the systematic comparison of planned and actual changes in order to improve the efficacy of planning, should be a very important part of any attempt to establish rational control over social processes. In fact, few plans are followed by a reasonably adequate evaluation. Several reasons for this lack can be suggested: (1) Movement toward the utopian goals of ideological plans cannot, or can hardly, be measured. (2) Evaluation means possible criticism, and planners of all types tend to close ranks against critics. (3) A planned change often disturbs the existent relation of interdependent factors and thus effects wholly unanticipated consequences. Under such circumstances, "success" must be redefined before it can be measured.

Urbanization means change, and change is opposed by many. It is disliked, first of all, by those at the top of the prior social hierarchy; and many planners, in spite of their professional predilections, have assimilated some of these conservative norms. Urbanization may mean, moreover, a more or less complete transformation of the pre-urban society, and in such a process attempts to maintain order may be overwhelmed in urban "chaos." In the eyes of urban analysts social problems increase alarmingly; they take for granted the substantial improvement brought about by the urban-industrial society and measure deviations from this new base. The choices that urbanization planners make between alternative programs are dictated partly by the rational goals sought, but partly also by unexpressed values and purposes. In particular, the dislike of cities and the hope of keeping urbanization to a minimum are so widespread that one can hardly understand many policies without taking these norms into account.

# INDEX